THAT I
MAY
SEE HIM

THAT I MAY SEE HIM

SEEKING TO BECOME A HERO OF THE FAITH IN THE TWENTY-FIRST CENTURY

RALPH WINGATE, JR.

WinePressPublishing
Great Books, Defined.

WinePress Publishing (PO Box 428, Enumclaw, WA 98022) functions only as book publisher. As such, the ultimate design, content, editorial accuracy, and views expressed or implied in this work are those of the author.

ISBN 13: 978-1-4141-1798-0
ISBN 10: 1-4141-1798-1
Library of Congress Catalog Card Number: 2010905556

DEDICATED TO THE HEROES IN MY LIFE

My mom and dad, who taught me the values of life.

My brother and sister, who have remained faithful to the Lord.

My boys, who have both married godly partners.

My wife, Sydney, who is the real hero in my life. She has taught me not only what love is, but what love does. She has been a godly example of what a hero really is.

—Ralph Wingate, Jr.

Also dedicated to: My mother, Florence Corlas, who always believed I could be a writer.

—Cammie Quinn

CONTENTS

ACKNOWLEDGMENTS

Wanda Slappey, who transcribed all the sermons from audiotapes.

Pat Walsh, who critiqued and edited this book.

The anonymous donors who made this book possible.

Cammie Quinn, who had the vision to develop my series of Hebrews 11 sermons into this book, into which she contributed many of her own ideas. Her struggle with cancer presented unique opportunities which God continues to use for His glory.

INTRODUCTION

ON THE EVENING of Sunday, May 16, 2004, I suffered a heart attack while preaching to several hundred people in my home church. At age fifty-seven, I thought I was in good physical condition, having never experienced a major health problem. I continued preaching, thinking the pain in my chest was either a deep cold or walking pneumonia. When the pain intensified later that night, my wife, Sydney, drove me to the hospital. By early the next morning, my condition had deteriorated so rapidly that doctors performed bypass surgery. They told me that if I had not checked into the hospital the previous night, I would have never seen the light of another day.

My brush with death reawakened my desire to know the Lord. I wanted to *really* know Him—deeply, intimately, and desperately. This was not a mere desire to turn over a new leaf. Rather, during my trial I got a glimpse of God that ignited a passion within me to see Him again and again.

Not long before my heart attack, I preached a series of messages on Hebrews, Chapter 11. This series focused on the heroes and heroines of the faith—Enoch, Noah, Abraham, Sarah, Moses, and others less familiar. The series embodied much of what I had been preaching throughout my ministry. I wanted to know God better by searching the hearts of these heroes and heroines. I wanted to know what touched the heart of God enough to record them in the Hebrews 11 Hall of Fame of Faith. After my heart attack, I plunged more deeply into the lives of these heroes and heroines, expanding my study into a book, because I, too, desire to touch the heart of God.

Hebrews 11:6 is, I believe, key—"But without faith it is impossible to please Him, for he who comes to God must believe that He is, and that He is a rewarder of those who diligently seek Him." The key truth here is so blatant that it is often overlooked. What exactly is the reward?

Very simply, the reward is to see God. God rewards the faithful with visions of Himself. I use the word *visions* loosely here, in the sense of knowing beyond any doubt that His presence has visited you. I believe that this experience is a common denominator in the lives of the heroes and heroines of the faith. They dared to seek the Invisible as if He were visible, and God rewarded them with glimpses of Himself—sometimes through direct sight or sound or touch, sometimes through dreams, sometimes through the pre-incarnate Christ, sometimes through other believers, and sometimes through answered prayer.

Today we see evidence of God all around us. God is present in nature and creation. He is present at the miracle of birth. His hand is evident in the harmonious order of the universe, the perfect symmetry of the hurricane, and the unique intricacy of the snowflake.

But can we go even deeper inside His character, even beyond the fringes of His creation? I believe it is possible to delve deep enough within the lives of the Old Testament heroes and heroines to uncover a greater understanding of God that is awesome to the point of dangerous. This depth of understanding is the embodiment of what made saints tremble and fall suddenly upon their faces. This understanding of God is too brilliant for human eyes, too perfect for the human mind, too loving for the human embrace. It is impossible to convey in human language, yet the earthbound person in love with God longs to try.

As I began to study Hebrews 11, I realized that in the minds of most Christians, these flesh-and-bones heroes and heroines have become larger-than-life statues. Within the pages of this book, I hope to take each of these icons off the pedestal and examine them as fallible human beings. The heroes of the faith were not superhuman; rather, they were humans who learned to trust God fully—some for years at a time, some at intervals, and some for a few unforgettable moments. They were intoxicated with God just as fever-crazed prospectors were intoxicated with gold during the California Gold Rush. They sought treasure without any guarantee and they risked everything to pursue the prize. These individuals, either continually or at crucial points in their lives, took faith overboard.

The Hebrews 11 heroes and heroines discovered something that modern day Christians have misplaced in the midst of our busy, cluttered world. They acquired a taste for the Holy Ground—for those special times and places they could glimpse God. Once they glimpsed Him, they followed Him with breathless awe, often to their own personal detriment. They raised sacrificial knives over their own children; they wandered as outcasts in barren places; they confronted powerful rulers and giants; they ascended fiery mountains; they faced overwhelming armies; and they brought buildings down upon their own heads. They were stoned, imprisoned, sawn asunder, slain with the sword, thrown to the lions, and tortured.

These heroes wanted one thing, and one thing only—they ached to return to the Holy Ground to get one more glimpse of God. They realized that seeing God far outweighed any suffering they encountered while sojourning there. They understood that the joy that comes from encountering Him is far more priceless than the cheap happiness that is found in the comfortable Christian life. To them, this joy was like a pure-running mountain stream, untainted and perfect. They tasted it, and it made them thirsty. Their thirst could not be quenched by anything except more water from this pure stream. They discovered the greatest joy known to man.

But is this possible for modern day Christians, especially those of us who reside within the boundaries of a wealthy nation? After all, what can we conquer? Where are the giants, the pharaohs, the worldwide floods, the formidable foes? Have we advanced into a tamer age that relegates Christianity to the plush pew, the once-a-week Bible study, and the ten-minute daily devotional?

If our Christianity is little more than a tidy package of extracurricular activities, we are deluded. Are we not still intertwined in the same epic battle between God and Satan? Is there not still a cause?

During more than forty years of ministry, I have encountered many living, breathing witnesses who fit the pattern of the Hebrews 11 heroes and heroines. Throughout the pages of this book, I will sprinkle examples of modern day witnesses I have personally known or heard about from others who were affected by their faith. Their fervent testimony is the crucial link that connects the visible with the invisible. Theirs is authentic heroic faith, the "evidence of things not seen" spoken about in Hebrews 11:1 and it shouts: *Our God is real, and He is here now!*

That I May See Him can be read in several ways. It can be read straight through as a source of inspiration, it can be used as a Bible study tool, or it can be used as a reference during times of trial in your life. At some point, we all go through the doubt of Gideon, the rejection of Joseph or the folly of Samson. Or perhaps we know of someone who is walking through a similar trial. The individual chapters in this book can be used as a source of encouragement and practical counsel for those occasions.

Each chapter focuses on a particular hero or heroine of the faith, delving into his or her experiences, sins, struggles, and relationship with God. I have written from the particular point of view or dominant "set of glasses" through which I believe each character encountered God. I have also outlined several key ways each character overcame challenges, which I hope will also assist the modern day reader to overcome similar challenges. These points are in no way intended to be comprehensive. They are merely my own observations in my effort to understand and apply Scripture.

As first glance, the Hebrews 11 Hall of Fame seems strange. Moses parted the Red Sea. Sarah laughed in the face of God. Noah built an ark and saved the human race. Rahab was a prostitute. On the surface, there seems a tremendous difference between David—the man after God's own heart—and Jephthah, the man who slew his daughter after making a foolish vow. Some of these individuals are allotted only brief mention in the Bible; others dominate entire books. To the human mind, the case of faith seems stronger for some than for others. Yet they are all included in God's lineup.

Clearly, the criteria for a seat in the Hebrews 11 Hall of Fame does not require sinless perfection or exemplary behavior. I find immense relief in this realization. It would be closer to the truth to say that the *eyes* of these heroes and heroines were exemplary. They dared to seek the Invisible on earth as if He were visible. They stretched sight beyond the limit of physical capability.

Today, it is entirely possible for us to pursue God with the same zeal. While we must not tamper with God's inspired Word, I believe God's list is more a pattern than it is a closed club. The latter part of the list focuses on an entire class of people—the prophets—without mentioning a single name. The individuals in Hebrews 11 are representative of God's finest, who became His finest primarily because they doggedly believed "that He is a rewarder of those who diligently seek Him."

At the end of each chapter, I have added a section entitled "Applied Truths." These are practical tools for applying Old Testament Bible lessons to our contemporary lives. Whenever we read about the historic figures of the Bible, it's natural to ask ourselves—what does this mean to me today? How do I apply the lessons I've learned from this Bible character to my life in another century, another culture, another land? What new insights can I take to my workplace with me tomorrow? How can I use these insights to improve my relationship with God and with others? These final applications are designed to make the lessons tangible for today.

Doctors tell me that due to hereditary factors, my heart problems will eventually return. But until then, I desire to actively seek the One I long to know. My life's verse is Philippians 3:10 (KJV)—"That I may know him, and the power of his resurrection, and the fellowship of his sufferings, being made conformable unto his death." If I want to know Him better, I must seek Him actively—in His Word and in His world.

With this book, I hope to intensify a yearning in you to seek God on earth so that you might better know and enjoy our unfathomable God—His love, His grace, His glory, His holiness, the I Am. May your heart ache for Him all the more, as mine does, after having sought Him through the lives of these imperfect heroes and heroines of faith.

—Ralph Wingate, Jr.

FOREWORD

M Y CONTRIBUTION TO this book began as the result of a thank-you note for a bouquet of flowers. In 2003, physicians removed my right eye after a local optometrist, Dr. Jeffrey Huettemann, discovered a malignant tumor during a routine eye exam. My church, Calvary Baptist Church in Normal, Illinois, sent me a bouquet of flowers as I recovered in the University of Iowa Hospital in Iowa City.

I responded with a thank-you note, embellishing it with lofty thoughts as writers often do. From that note, my pastor, Ralph Wingate, Jr., discovered that I like to write. As a somewhat passive member of our large congregation, I had rarely spoken with Pastor Wingate throughout my twenty-five years of attendance. So I was surprised when he approached me one Sunday after church and asked if I would like to help him write a book. He wanted me to adapt a series of eighteen sermons he had preached on Hebrews chapter 11 into a book. Not realizing the magnitude of the project (and Pastor Wingate not realizing the sluggishness of my pen), I answered yes, and a collaborative effort was born. Five years later, I handed him the finished copy.

My driving force while rewriting the sermons originated from tragedy. The prospect of losing my eye and of surviving cancer frightened me. But as I walked through this trial, I discovered God's amazing presence in it. Through the prayers of family and friends, Bible verses, and a host of coincidences too numerous to be mere coincidences, a new awe for God was born. I began to feel like an inside-out version of the blind beggars Jesus healed in the gospels. I longed to run to town to tell everyone what God did for me when He took my eye. Losing my eye became one of the greatest gifts of my life. My new prayer—which is still my prayer today—was that I might see God better with one eye than with two.

Therefore, it seemed providential to me that I agree to help write *That I May See Him*. With the support and understanding of my husband Kevin, my children Gregory and Colleen, prayer uplifter Jane, and a few other praying friends, I immersed myself in the lives of the Old Testament heroes and heroines. It is Pastor Wingate's desire, and my desire, that all who read this book will come away with a deeper longing to see God more clearly, know Him better, and love Him more here on this earth until the day we walk into His embrace in heaven.

—Cammie Quinn

. . . .

CHAPTER 1

ABEL: SEEKING GOD
BEYOND RITUAL

By faith Abel offered to God a more excellent sacrifice than Cain, through which he obtained witness that he was righteous, God testifying of his gifts; and through it he being dead still speaks.

—Heb. 11:4

READING: GENESIS 4

THE LIVES OF the Hebrews 11 heroes and heroines were anything but safe. Their stories rival Hollywood's biggest blockbusters, complete with murder, epic battles, chase scenes, spy scenes, adultery, illegitimate babies, Olympic-sized successes and Olympic-sized failures. We begin with a man who was murdered.

The basics of Abel's story are well-known. Abel presented to God an offering of the firstborn from his flock of sheep while his brother, Cain, gave God the fruit of the ground. God accepted Abel's offering, but rejected Cain's. Angered, Cain murdered Abel.

Two of the most frequently asked questions about the Bible zero in on this story: What was wrong with Cain's sacrifice? Why did God reject it?

And why did God place Abel in the Hebrews 11 Hall of Fame for something as simple as an animal sacrifice? What touched the heart of God about Abel's sacrifice? How can we imitate his sacrifice today?

Lamb or Turnip?

Cain and Abel were not ignorant of God's ways. They knew from their parents, Adam and Eve, that the only acceptable sacrifice was one that required blood in payment for sin. Every time Abel sacrificed a lamb, he humbled himself before a sovereign God by identifying himself with the victim on the sacrificial chopping block. The blood of a turnip simply would not do.

In one sense, these two brothers knew God in a way that we would know a grandfather. Their parents had conversed with God in the Garden of Eden. God had brought the animals to Adam and watched with pleasure as Adam named them one by one. God taught Adam's family how to tend the orchard and instructed them what to eat. In the broad sense of "seeing," Cain and Abel saw God through the testimony of their parents. Possibly, they even heard details from their parents that are not recorded in our Bible.

When Abel sacrificed the lamb, he obeyed God's requirements, humbled himself, and worshipped with wholehearted adoration. Cain, on the other hand, attempted to squeeze in the back door of God's requirement with an offering that was more convenient—the fruit of the ground that God had cursed after Adam and Eve sinned (see Gen. 3:17). On the surface, the difference in the brothers' offerings seems trivial, but the contrast in the hearts that gave the offerings is monumental.

The Bible does not say, but it's conceivable that a shard of malice festered beneath the surface of Cain's actions on the day of sacrifice. Cain may have purposely attempted to circumvent God's requirement in a rebellious outbreak of pride. Cain, the tiller of the ground, may have desired to get a leg up on his brother, the keeper of the sheep, in a move to win God's greater favor. His subsequent reaction to God's disfavor suggests an earlier seed of envy.

Whatever the case, God "had no regard" for Cain's offering. Cain "was very angry, and his face fell" (Gen. 4:5, ESV). God's displeasure should have served as a loud wake-up call to Cain. A truly God-fearing man would have run right out and sought a lamb. After all, this was *God* calling him on the carpet.

God gave Cain ample opportunity to learn from his mistake. He admonished Cain: "If you do well, will you not be accepted? And if you do not do well, sin is crouching at the door. Its desire is for you, but you must rule over it" (Gen. 4:7, ESV). It was not until *after* Cain slew Abel that God punished him and Cain became a "fugitive and a vagabond" (Gen. 4:12).

The question shouldn't be "Why did God reject Cain's sacrifice?" but rather, "Why didn't Cain worship God after God rebuked him?" Cain knew about the merciful character of God from his parents. Cain had a golden chance to draw closer to God after rebuke, just as a child does after a loving father's rebuke. But he clung to pride and dug himself in deeper. He killed his brother, tried to bury his sin, and then cringed in horror when Abel's blood cried out from the ground. No matter how hard he tried to finagle around God's ways, Cain could not get away from the blood.

Stepping Out Beyond Ritual

When Cain and Abel offered their sacrifices to God, they were performing an act of worship similar to our Sunday worship services. Every Sunday, Christians around the world gather to bring their offerings to God. But sadly, many Christians worship with about as much passion as they use to brush their teeth. Their worship has become a habit.

It's all too natural to slip into a ritual of worship, to become theologically house-trained, to settle into a rut, and to not even realize that we've become numbed to our true purpose in God's house. Singing "*I love you*" to God can become just as tinny as "sounding brass" or a "clanging cymbal" (1 Cor. 13:1 KJV).

How can we avoid meaningless worship? More importantly, how can we enlarge the worship we currently offer God? How can we offer a sacrifice as pure and worthy of God's approval as Abel's? Here are some suggestions:

3

1. Start with simple obedience.

Abel was no more privileged than the modern day Christian. He had to coax himself out of bed to offer his sacrifice. He had to don his clothes, attend to personal duties, and walk outside into the cold dawn to fetch the best lamb. Today, the clothing styles may have changed, the shower heads may look different, and our offering may fit into an envelope rather than on a chopping block, but we still follow in Abel's footsteps every Sunday.

Worship starts with simple obedience. However, if we never move beyond obedience, we will never reach true worship. The trick is to open your Bible to see what God has for you before you walk out your front door, pray on the way to your place of worship, and walk inside the sanctuary expecting to see God.

Don. Don is an elderly handicapped member of my church. He routinely passes his hymnal to the next person in the pew, stranger or not, and asks that person to find the page for him. For decades he has ridden our church shuttle to Sunday morning and Sunday evening church services. His shuttle driver—one of a few alternating drivers—is his hero of the week. Until his handicapped wife, Judy, passed away, he brought her with him every week and honored her as if she was the most beautiful lady for miles around. Before every service, he shakes hands with anyone who will shake his, he looks you in the eye, and he makes it clear that he is genuinely glad to see you. It is not an uncommon occurrence to see Don walk up the center aisle during the invitation. His response to the gospel is as regular as the spring rain. Some may think he is seeking attention, but his dearth of pride comes much closer to the throne of God than the intelligent, pew-sitter's stubborn dignity. This man worships.

As simple as obedience may seem, it is as fundamental in God's eyes as His command about blood sacrifice to Cain and Abel. Obedience is the starting gate for heroic faith. It lays the pathway for God to work.

2. Take your worship off the "safe space."

The "safe space" is the place we feel comfortable, where very little is required of us. Many Christians never miss a church service except for illness or unavoidable circumstances. They've chosen a favorite pew, and every member of the church knows it's their spot. They know the words to all the songs without having to think about them. On the surface, they are model Christians. But are they really? That depends.

If we have become too comfortable sitting in our pew or singing a familiar hymn, then we are not worshipping. True worship makes your heart ache. True worship makes it impossible to sit still. True worship makes your soul as antsy as a wiggly child.

Contrary to the commonly held perspective, we are not the audience in church. Sunday services are not performances by a very few for the very many. Neither are they primarily intended for entertainment, comfort, or even instruction. Rather, we are all the performers, the worshippers, the active adorers of our audience of One.

William Temple, Archbishop of Canterbury during World War II, gave the following definition of worship in his book, *Readings in St. John's Gospel*:

> Worship is the submission of all of our nature to God. It is the quickening of conscience by His holiness, the nourishment of mind with His truth, the purifying of imagination by His beauty, the opening of the heart to His love, the surrender of our will to His purpose, and all of this gathered up in adoration to the most selfless emotion of which our nature is capable and therefore the chief remedy for that self-centeredness which is the original, and source of all actual sin.[1]

True worship is a bloodletting of the heart. It is pumped by love and its destination is God's glory. When a true worshipper steps into God's house, he realizes that he's positioned in the center of a bonanza of opportunity. To say the Lord's name in song is suddenly an inestimable privilege, indescribably so in the presence of others who are saying it, too. He calls upon God, sings to Him, seeks answers in His Holy Word, communes with Him, calls and sings and seeks again until he is utterly enraptured with His presence and His holiness. And then he repeats the process throughout the week—in his devotions, in his car, while he is waiting in the supermarket line, on his bed, and at every possible opportunity. Anything less reveals a love problem.

The essence of worship takes us back to the great commandment: "You shall love the LORD your God with all your heart, with all your soul, and with all your mind" (Matt. 22:37). When you love that much, you cannot help but dwell on the One you love. You cannot help but say His name. It is frequently on the tip of your tongue.

Have you ever known someone who goes to an incredible amount of trouble over a birthday gift? A mother, perhaps? A friend? She searches the mall a month ahead of time, finds nothing suitable, locates the perfect gift on the Internet and pays too much for it, buys two cards because she can't decide which one she likes best, picks out special wrapping paper even though she has suitable paper at home, and writes several drafts of a heartfelt message before recording the final draft on the card. Compare this to someone who buys a present on the last day and scrawls a note on a generic card five minutes before the party. The first is love; the second is duty. This is the difference between Abel and Cain. And it is the difference between true worship and ineffective worship.

But what if, in all honesty, we don't love God that much? How do we reach the point of true worship?

Love requires communication, time, and effort. There is no substitute for earnest prayer and Bible reading. Ten minutes a day won't do it. The problem is that many Christians don't believe deep down that the investment is worth it. They are unwilling to risk pulling out all the stops for God for fear that they will not receive an answer from Him and will end up losing the "safe" fellowship they already own. They cling to the "safe space" on the Parcheesi™ board and occasionally dash to the next "safe space." But the truth is this: the greatest fellowship comes when you are in the open and the Enemy ensnares you and you discover that God Himself is there to deliver you. You will never experience this on the "safe space." You can't know God as well there.

When you choose to invest yourself, one day you will experience the God of the universe reach down to personally touch you. From that day on, your worship will take on energy of its own. You will have discovered the momentum that will carry you forward to God again and again.

3. Spend quality time alone with God.

Imagine this test of worship: would you worship God if the entire world had been annihilated by a nuclear bomb and you alone remained alive? If there were no one left to impress, no one to save, no one with whom to share your worship experience, would you do it?

Someday you will be called upon to do this very thing—that is, unless you die suddenly. The deathbed is a solitary place. The people hovering over you will fade. Your hands will gradually lose the strength to grip theirs. Will you worship God even then? If you've practiced a life of wholehearted worship, you will not only worship Him then, but your worship will become a thing of beauty, a point of marvel. To others, it will become "evidence of things not seen" (Heb. 11:1 KJV).

When we focus on our personal relationship with the Lord—when the grand passion of our prayers becomes simply to love Him more—God will answer with a sweet addiction for communion that intoxicates the soul with joy. The term *duty* will soon become obsolete when applied to Bible study and prayer. No longer will it seem strange to pray on your face or to kneel upon soil that soaks your knees. Finding a private place to praise Him will become a daily desperation.

Someone who learns to worship God in private is alone with God even in a crowded church. To that person, God's presence is in sharper focus than the presence of others. When I preach, I should be in the sanctuary alone with God. Butterflies settle in the stomach when you realize that the primary One you need to please is the One who already loves you.

Just when you've come to the point of learning to value your private time with God more than ever, you may discover a fellow churchgoer observing you. After Moses spent time alone with God on the mountaintop, "Moses did not know that the skin of his face shone" (Exod. 34:29 KJV). The brilliance was so great that Moses had to wear a veil to shield the brightness from the people of Israel. He wasn't glowing to impress. He was glowing because he couldn't help it.

It is precisely due to the glowing that even the worshipper most content with solitary worship should never forsake the local church. The rest of the congregation needs the glowing worshipper. And likely as not, due to circumstances and human nature, he will soon stumble and find himself reaching up for the hand of the one who had marveled at him earlier.

4. Learn from rebuke.

God would have opened wide arms to Cain had he admitted his mistake and asked for forgiveness. Cain's biggest failure was not his mistake at the sacrificial block; it was his pride in denying it.

We all fail. We've all been guilty of offering God a turnip. The issue is not whether we will fail, but how we will handle our failure. Hedging with excuses hardens the heart and compounds the problem. There is something heroic about repentance. It presumes that God will not crush us when we lie low and vulnerable. It is as courageous as facing a giant without our armor. And it ultimately plows out a ditch for love to run deeper.

Cain knew what he was losing. He had "seen" God through his parents. Listen to the words of Cain after God banished him: "My punishment is greater than I can bear! Surely You have driven me out this day from the face of the ground; I shall be hidden from Your face; I shall be a fugitive and a vagabond on the earth, and it will happen that anyone who finds me will kill me" (Gen. 4:13-14). I believe that deep down in his soul, Cain realized that the worst punishment of all was banishment from God. Once you have seen God, He outpaces every earthly treasure. There is nothing more devastating than losing Him.

Psalm 119:71-72 says: "It is good for me that I have been afflicted, that I may learn Your statutes. The law of Your mouth is better to me than thousands of coins of gold and silver." Failure offers opportunity for restoration. It is then that God often reveals Himself to us in more intimate ways. The Father embraces prodigal drifters.

A Final Word

It is perhaps appropriate that Abel is the first witness mentioned. His straightforward testimony is uncluttered by other attributes. His simple gift of love and obedience laid bare his heart for all humanity to see. Were Abel living today, he'd be one about whom we'd say: "He fixes his eyes on Jesus."

I am humbled to know that God would count me a hero for simply worshipping Him in faith. It's a sign of our Father's grace that He would extend a red carpet for a simple soul who has little chance of earning earthly accolades. God focuses on the heart. It's our love He desires first and foremost, above all the myriad works of our hands.

Praise God for His perfect simplicity. May we lift our hands to worship Him with gratitude and love.

APPLIED FAITH

1. Every day for a week, take a walk in a private place. Pray and sing aloud to God. If possible, continue this practice indefinitely.

2. On the way to church, turn off your radio or CD player. If you are not alone, ask your passengers to be silent. Ask one of the passengers to pray for the service with the intent that your hearts will be prepared when you walk into the sanctuary.

3. The next time you rebuke a family member or friend, make a point to later embrace that individual in restoration.

4. Place this one request on the top of your prayer list: "Help me to love you more, O Lord."

CHAPTER 2

ENOCH: SEEKING GOD THROUGH THE MONOTONY OF THE MARATHON

By faith Enoch was taken away so that he did not see death, "and was not found, because God had taken him"; for before he was taken he had this testimony, that he pleased God.

—Heb. 11:5

READING: GENESIS 5:18-24; JUDE 1:14-15

OF ALL THE souls who have ever lived, a case could be made that Enoch was one of God's best friends. The Bible states that he "walked with God" and that "he pleased God" (Gen. 5:24 and Heb. 11:5). He was one of only two people—the other being Elijah—privileged to ascend to heaven without dying.

However, it seems strange that even though God distinguished him, the Bible expends only twelve verses on him. The nuts-and-bolts of those verses tell us that he married and fathered children and that he prophesied judgment. Unlike other heroes of the faith, he parted no waters, slew no Goliaths, built no temples, and conquered no armies. For a man who lived 365 years, we know very little about him, yet God singled him out as a hero of the faith.

Why would God spotlight a man for the eyes of all Christendom without giving us many specifics? How can we, as seekers and emulators of God, be satisfied with such generic evidence?

Many Christians living in America today would equate their lives with Enoch's long and potentially monotonous marathon. For those of us approaching middle age or beyond, our children are grown and out of the house, our careers are not as satisfying or lucrative as we'd dreamed, our calendars are marked with doctors' appointments, and there seems little left to anticipate but an occasional vacation and the same-old, same-old. Ungrateful as this attitude is, it can oppress us if we dwell on it.

How do we keep our faith vibrant when we're running on a treadmill? How do we continue running the race of faith when there seems to be nothing new to run for? How do we seek the best of the best when we feel spent at age forty? Fifty? Sixty? Seventy?

Enoch's Weights

Hebrews 12:1 tells us to "lay aside every weight, and the sin which so easily ensnares us, and let us run with endurance the race that is set before us." That's easy for a man like the Apostle Paul to say. Easy for Enoch to say. These men had personally seen God or known men who had seen Him. They lived amid first-generation testimonies.

Whether Enoch walked with God in a tangible way or whether he walked with His Spirit as we do today, Scripture doesn't specify. But nonetheless, the communion was intimate. The Bible indicates that Enoch walked with God for at least 300 of his 365 years.

Did Enoch sin? Scripture records specific sins regarding most of the Hebrews 11 heroes, yet only alludes to it in Enoch's case. We can infer that perhaps Enoch didn't seek God as arduously prior to the birth of his son, Methuselah. Scripture says that "Enoch lived sixty-five years, and begot Methuselah. After he begat Methuselah, Enoch walked with God three hundred years, and had sons and daughters" (Gen. 5:21-22). Possibly something unrecorded happened to Enoch when Methuselah was born, influencing him to walk with God from that day forward. Regardless of what happened when, Enoch was one hundred percent human and therefore missed God's mark for sinless perfection.

What about his burdens? Did Enoch have any? Did he run with any weights? Or did he merely stroll in an Adam-and-Eve-type garden, visiting with God in a carefree manner on grassy pathways for three hundred years?

Enoch lived between Adam and Noah. Noah was Enoch's great-grandson, though Enoch never met him because he was taken to heaven sixty-nine years before Noah was born. However, Adam was still alive and coexisted with Enoch on earth for more than three centuries, dying when Enoch was 308 years old. As the first human on earth, Adam was probably a celebrity of sorts, and it's not out of the question that Enoch conversed with him.

The New Testament book of Jude reveals that Enoch was a prophet and preacher. He prophesied in a bold, probably unpopular manner about the coming of Christ "with ten thousands of His saints, to execute judgment on all, to convict all who are ungodly among them of all their ungodly deeds which they have committed in an ungodly way, and of all the harsh things which ungodly sinners have spoken against Him" (Jude 1:14-15).

The tone of Enoch's message indicates that his contemporaries were not godly people. About four hundred years before Enoch was born, "men began to call on the name of the LORD" (Gen. 4:26), yet God flooded the earth 669 years after Enoch was taken to heaven. Enoch preached in the interim.

As a preacher, Enoch didn't have much to go on. He had no Bible. No story of Abraham. No promise of a Promised Land. No Noah. No Moses. He relied only on his private communion with God and upon a secondhand story about a Creator who made a garden that Adam had walked in, had eaten forbidden fruit in, and had been cast out of. Possibly, Enoch's message was heckled, much like the messages of itinerant preachers who preach judgment on the quads of public universities. "Where is your evidence?" they might have asked him. "Why should we believe you? Who do you think you are? Show us this God of Adam you speak about. Where is He?"

It's not impossible that Enoch took Adam with him when he prophesied. But would the people have believed Adam? After all,

Adam was the man who had perpetrated the fall of mankind. Adam had brought sin into the world.

Certainly, Enoch's preaching did not result in any lasting change. In modern terms, Enoch failed in his ministry. God destroyed almost all of Enoch's remaining congregants with the flood.

Enoch probably married, though the Bible does not tell us his wife's name. He fathered Methuselah, who lived 969 years, as well as an unspecified number of other sons and daughters. His father, Jared, outlived him by 435 years.

As a family man, Enoch no doubt experienced many of the same trials we endure today—family quarrels, financial challenges, diseases, and deaths. As a prophet and preacher of God, he persisted solely by the testimony of a friend and his own personal communion with God. Even without a Bible to nourish his soul, he formed such an intense relationship with God that it pleased God to take him home early.

Three Ways to Energize the Marathon

I know of nothing more physically draining than running a marathon. It takes stubborn determination to keep your body moving forward for twenty-six miles. It takes strength of will and control of mind to keep going, especially when your mind becomes clouded by afflictions or sidetracked by matters that seem more pressing than the race. Inevitably, the runner faces difficult miles when the prize doesn't seem worth the long sacrifice.

As a pastor, my toughest job is endeavoring to keep the flock—including myself—from loitering in the same field for years. In our fast-paced society, the daily cares of this world tend to sidetrack us. In America's relatively affluent society, too much comfort can lure us to forget our purpose. Preoccupied and satisfied with less than the best, we lose momentum and we park, as if we no longer believe that the grass is greener on heaven's side of the fence.

Such "faith-parking" is a silent killer of the soul. After it sits for a while, it begins to sag. It breeds the subtle sins of laziness, self-pity, a critical spirit, gossip, over-indulgence, and apathy. Chaplains tell me that whenever they visit a typical jail, they see at least half the inmates lying in their beds in the middle of the day with the lights off. Churches are not much different.

So how do we keep running mile after mile? How do we keep from becoming weary and faint of purpose when there's no outside stimulation to revive us? How do we seek God with passion when our circumstances aren't passionate?

1. Revolutionize your concept of walking with God.

The common perception of heroic faith spotlights bigger-than-life moments when unusual circumstances collide with unusual opportunities. Ideal settings for heroes and heroines are killer storms, wars, risky expeditions in foreign lands, crime, or sudden disaster. The heroes in our history books usually rose to fame amidst one of these backdrops. In our own lives, we sometimes desire heroic moments so badly that we feel second best and passed over when they don't come.

When the Roman soldiers accosted Jesus at the garden of Gethsemane, Peter played the part of a hero, slicing off a centurion's ear. Though Peter acted out of a desire to rescue Jesus, Jesus didn't want Peter's brand of heroism. Brave as it seemed on the surface, Peter was following his own will rather than God's will. God's plan did not call for overpowering the centurions that night.

For most of us, great boosts of faith usually come on days of quiet revelation. They occur during a walk with a friend who plants a startling seed of faith that you never forget. They occur in a school dismissal line when your child's teacher shows steadfast faith by a simple comment that is ordinary to her but that awakens your faith like a silent torpedo. They permeate a hospital room when your family has gone home and you are left with the sound of steel carts wheeling up and down the hallway, machines beeping, and the murmur of nurses conversing in the hallway, and you open your Bible to a verse that stuns you as if God Himself had walked into the room with your next pill. Moments such as these, uneventful as they seem on the surface, can be life-changing.

15

Sadly, Christians often saddle their concept of spiritual heroism with the world's definition of success. Ambition to excel at school, in a career, and with our personal objectives requires skill, hard work, and dogged perseverance. But spiritual heroism is more a matter of listening than of talking, of waiting than of doing, and of humbling ourselves on our face rather than flying our own flag. While it is never an excuse for shirking our responsibilities, spiritual heroism transfers the bulk of "doing" to the shoulders of an invisible God who can do exceedingly more than our hands can ever accomplish.

Some missionaries, for example, find that even after all their hard work, only one solitary soul comes to Christ in an entire year. Their results look deficient on paper, and they could easily become discouraged if they forget that God is in control. What is to prevent God from using that solitary soul to enlighten a spiritually dark nation? What will stop God from using a missionary's personal journals to encourage multitudes of Christians one hundred years later? Nothing. Absolutely nothing.

No matter how unimpressive our lives may seem to us today, none of us have been dropped off at the bus stop and forgotten. The opportunity for the most heroic offering is at our fingertips. We are already equipped with the highest possibilities for pleasing God. Simple worship is equally attainable by the child, the nursing home resident, the executive, and the homeless man. Worship brings us into the presence of God. When we worship Him, it takes the focus off ourselves and places it on Him. It takes the accountability for results off us and places it on Him. We discover that the only thing left is to drop our eyes and our hands and bow and worship—and that *this* simple, unadulterated offering is, after all, the highest offering.

As we consider revitalizing our spiritual life, let me suggest walking. Walking takes us away from the distractions of telephones and computers, it immerses us in God's creation, and it sets a precedent of momentum on our eternal rendezvous with God.

The Mentor. A friend of mine, Reverend Gerhard Dutoit, tells this story about a spiritual mentor who taught him the importance of literal, as well as figurative, walking. As a young man in theological school in England, Gerhard engaged Dr. J. B. B. Friend as his mentor. Dr. Friend was known as the college's godly vice president who spent a great deal of time in prayer. Every afternoon at 3:30 PM, Dr. Friend walked and prayed. About three-and-a-half years later, after Gerhard had graduated and was in ministry, he passed in the vicinity of Dr. Friend's house in a province of South Africa. Dr. Friend, now in his seventies, had retired and was living with his wife in the cottage of a Christian farmer.

Gerhard yearned to see his old mentor again, so he called and talked to Mrs. Friend, who told him they would love to see him. Though the cottage was a three-and-a-half hour drive away, Gerhard drove there, arriving at about 3:00 PM. The Friends invited him in and showered love upon him until 3:30 PM, when Dr. Friend glanced at his watch and said, "Gerhard, I can't stay any longer. I've got to go. You will stay over tonight, won't you?" Dr. Friend rose from his living room chair and went outdoors for his long walk. Gerhard sat there with Mrs. Friend, who was a tad embarrassed, and said to him, "I guess he hasn't changed a bit." With tears streaming down his cheeks, Gerhard said, "Mrs. Friend, I don't want him to change."

Gerhard realized that Dr. Friend's behavior was the very reason he had chosen him as a mentor years ago. Dr. Friend practiced a tangible relationship with God. He gave an invisible God precedence over a visible, beloved friend. He went forth to meet God as if God was already present at the point of rendezvous, awaiting his arrival. His legs moved with the urgency of a man who is concerned about being late for a crucial appointment. Dr. Friend did not adhere to the commonplace attitude that God has to be cajoled out of the clouds, as if He might not be in a particularly talkative mood or might be occupied with another, more important errand. Meeting God was a sure thing with Dr. Friend—not because he considered himself special, but because he had formed an intimate friendship with God. Dr. Friend's unusual behavior was not lost on Gerhard, who has since become a leader of prayer revivals throughout the world.

Walking with God need not be practiced on a tedious treadmill. Once the walking precedent is set and the connection established, a daily walk can become the source that pumps life into the remainder of the day, breathing new energy into our tasks and into our encounters with others.

2. Walk towards God as if on a ramp.

Just as it's a good idea to walk outdoors, it's also a good idea to think of our Christian journey as taking place on a ramp from earth to heaven. If we are progressing in our relationship with God, we will gradually desire less contact with the ground and more contact with heaven. We will begin to think, as Apostle Paul did, "to die is gain" (Phil. 1:21).

As we age, heaven has a way of becoming more attractive. Friends and family members begin relocating there. Meanwhile, our bodies begin to wrinkle, sag, bulge, and ache. Some days it hurts just to get out of bed. Eventually, we need a knee replacement or some other prosthetic part we never dreamed we'd wear. Our restaurant conversations tend to veer towards health issues. We soon realize that our body won't keep up with our plans. This "earthly house" isn't what it was cracked up to be when we were twenty.

Many people become discouraged as they age, but this need not be the case if we view aging as God's weaning process. He is weaning us away from investing our hopes in the trappings of this world so that we might transfer our hope to our eternal home, where He will give us a new body that will never decay. Why stay here in *this* old body?

Enoch lived in an imperfect body for at least three of our lifetimes. Yet, Enoch was not only *weaning*, but also *leaning*. There was a magnetic pull on his life drawing him towards heaven. Because he chose to walk consistently with God, He grew to view God as an indescribable treasure above everything he desired in life.

Enoch's greatest motivation was not to escape, but rather to arrive. If he could have switched residences in the prime of his manhood, he would have done so. Indeed, perhaps he did, ascending to heaven at age 365 in an era when humans were living 600 years and longer.

Is it possible Enoch might have begged God to take him home? Is that such an improper prayer? I think not. Scripture says that Enoch "was not; for God took him" (Gen. 5:24).

We don't know, but possibly God forewarned Enoch about his imminent departure. The writer of Genesis leaves no doubt that God took him.

While on earth, Enoch pleased God so completely that God recorded His pleasure about Enoch. Before God took him, "he pleased God" (Heb. 11:5).

For those of us who are closer to heaven than to birth, we can trust that if we have walked with an upward gait to God as if on a ramp, it will not be such a difficult stretch to reach our leg over the threshold into heaven. There's no monotony in that.

3. While walking, be bold about sharing your testimony.

One of the few details Scripture records about Enoch is his bold manner of witnessing. "Behold," he told the people, "the Lord comes with ten thousands of His saints, to execute judgment on all" (Jude 1:14-15). While such a bold approach to witnessing is not popular today, Enoch's witnessing pleased God.

As we come to the "way stations" in our journey, God gifts us with opportunities to share our faith with other runners. Like the sweat that pours from a runner's body, our personal testimony need be nothing more complicated than a natural release of the accounts of the journey. It is as simple as telling others how we have seen God work on our own journey. It's as natural as telling a parched runner, "Hey, I found living water over there, and you wouldn't believe what it did for me! Come, I see you are thirsty; let me show you where it is!"

I am convinced that the core problem of neglecting to share our testimony with others is the absence of an ignition spark. Sedentary Christians don't really believe God loves them. They may acknowledge it intellectually, but they don't *know* it. It hasn't soaked into the fiber of their existence to the point that every cell longs to stand up and shout. They end up running the race of faith with sincere intentions, but with the second-rate fuel of duty.

Duty, admirable as it is, does not possess the irresistible thrust of love. It runs out of gas over the long haul. It fixates on practical checklists of do's and don'ts. Duty seeks its affirmation and feedback from people and from rewarding circumstances rather than from God. When people and circumstances don't measure up, duty chokes and falters and sometimes dies.

But how do we make love for God our motivation for witnessing? And how do we find assurance that God loves us? In my experience as a pastor, I have discovered that many Christians want to love God more, but they don't know how.

The process can be compared to the experience of a first-time mother with her baby. Before the baby is born, she might wonder, how do I know I will love this baby? But once she holds the baby and begins to feed him, walks up and down the hallway with him, changes him, and sings to him, the attachment becomes so tangible that she may wonder why she cannot see the rope that binds her heart to her baby's heart. When that baby begins to respond with smiles and hugs, the mother experiences love she never imagined possible. The same thing happens in our relationship with God.

When we make the effort to walk with God every day as if He is visible, we soon discover—with a shock at first, and increasing awe thereafter—that the Creator of the universe personally responds to us. He might speak through a Bible verse or a coincidence that cannot possibly be mere coincidence, or even in a more dramatic "burning bush" experience. As He responds, we become amazed that He would love someone as undeserving as us, and consequently our love for Him grows, sometimes almost to the point of bursting. We become addicted to His voice and so over-filled with His love that our first instinct is to run home and tell someone else about it. This kind of love begs for an outlet. Witnessing is no longer a problem. It's a relief.

Depending upon our circumstances, some of us will testify before crowds, while the majority of us will testify one-on-one along our journey. Some, like the thief on the cross, may never be granted an opportunity to testify except, perhaps, by legacy. But what a legacy that thief has left for the final-hour converts of this world!

Whether we testify to one or to many, our testimony ultimately is before Almighty God. In a broad sense, our testimony is our attitude, our lifestyle, and our worship, as well as our evangelical outreach. Testifying with our actions and our words is a form of worship. Our main audience is our invisible God—not mankind. Were we the last human alive on earth, our testimony should go forth full-force. Enoch pleased *God*.

There are many ways to share our testimony, some of which are quite unique. I am particularly encouraged by those who share their faith without any special talent, intelligence, or charisma.

Glenn Yuille. Glenn was an elderly man confined to a wheelchair. He had endured some horrific trials in his life, but God used those trials to draw Glenn closer to Him. Glenn was so thrilled with his salvation that he wrote and printed a Bible tract. The cover was bright red and black, flames outlined, with one word emblazoned across the front—*Hell.* Inside eight folded panels, the gospel message stressed the consequences of rejecting Jesus Christ.

Before Glenn distributed the tract, he called everyone in the Pontiac, Michigan phone book to tell them he was sending them a gift. He mailed the tracts, and literally hundreds of people came to Jesus as a result of his desire to share his excitement about his new life in Jesus. Even a judgment-message, offered out of love for Jesus, reaped amazing results.

Sharing our testimony is nothing more complicated than a simple outpouring of the love God has poured into us. Our ways of expressing it are as limitless as our imagination.

Enoch's "Translation"

Of all the Hebrews 11 heroes of the faith, we cannot point to a burial ground for Enoch. He was not buried. His bones were not carried out of Egypt. In a mode more direct than camel or oxcart, more streamlined than supersonic jets or rockets, his bones were instantaneously transported to the ultimate Promised Land of all.

A Final Word

Monotony is never boredom when it is consistency on a quest for God. It is, rather, a single-minded, upwards journey towards an ultimate residence with God. There is no need to be bored on a quest that promises companionship with God and offers opportunities to spill testimonies of that companionship upon others desperate for sustenance. Each day becomes an open road with endless encounters and possibilities.

Enoch walked with God for three centuries. I believe his life exemplifies the sentiments of David found in Psalm 27:4. He longed to "behold the beauty of the LORD, and to inquire in His temple." Enoch was so overwhelmed as he beheld the attributes of God that it affected every aspect of his life. I often wonder how he must have appeared to his contemporaries. He was truly "one of a kind."

APPLIED FAITH

1. As frequently as possible, walk alone outdoors on a rendezvous with God.

2. Ask God for unique new ways to share your testimony.

3. Look for unusual men and women of faith like J. B. B. Friend and learn from them.

. . . .

CHAPTER 3

NOAH: SEEKING GOD ACROSS THE CHASM TO THE UNSEEN

By faith Noah, being divinely warned of things not yet seen, moved with godly fear, prepared an ark for the saving of his household, by which he condemned the world and became heir of the righteousness which is according to faith.

—Heb. 11:7

READING: GENESIS 6-9

THE ACCOUNT OF Noah's ark is one of the most familiar stories in the Bible. We accept it without batting an eyelid. Yet to the people of his day, Noah must have seemed delusional. Rain as we know it didn't exist yet. The earth was watered with a mist that rose from the ground (see Gen. 2:6). Noah's prediction of a catastrophic flood defied science.

Yet God clearly ordered Noah to "make yourself an ark of gopherwood" to be used as an escape vessel for Noah and his family (Gen. 6:14). The order was no less preposterous to Noah than if God were to order me to build a spaceship in my back yard and invite my family to escape in it. To his peers, Noah must have seemed like an eccentric fear monger, a Chicken Little who squawked for over a century, "The sky is falling, the sky is falling."

What convinced Noah to carry out such a far-fetched plan? How did he get to the point of following the commands of an invisible God?

In today's world, how do we get to the point of sacrificing the visible to pursue the invisible? How do we pull up stakes from a comfortable job and relocate our family to a mission field across the world? How do we turn down a lucrative position in favor of a lower paying job in full-time Christian service? How do we get to the point of tossing off comfortable practicality to follow Christ down a precarious road?

The Brewing Storm

Noah was born into a situation that no sensible Christian would envy. The hearts of men had turned rotten at the core. Until now, whenever God observed anything He'd made, it was always "good" or "very good." But now, "the LORD saw that the wickedness of man was great in the earth, and that every intent of the thoughts of his heart was only evil continually. And the LORD was sorry that He had made man on the earth, and He was grieved in His heart" (Gen. 6:5-6).

But Noah "found grace in the eyes of the LORD" (Gen. 6:8). Like Enoch, he was a man who "walked with God"(Gen. 6:9). He was "a righteous man, blameless in his generation" (Gen. 6:9, ESV). Though Noah was a sinner just like every other human, he chose to serve God wholeheartedly even in the midst of a corrupt world. To his peers, he was already an oddity before God ever told him to build an ark.

One day, God informed Noah that He intended to destroy all flesh upon the earth with a catastrophic flood. He gave Noah verbal blueprints for the ark and a list of passengers: himself, his wife, his three sons and their wives, and a specific list of animals. Scripture is not entirely clear, but Noah was to spend from one hundred to one-hundred-twenty years building the ark (Bible scholars vary on the exact number of years).

If anyone was ever born on the ledge at the end of the world, Noah was. While everyone around him basked in indifference,

Noah hammered away diligently on the only escape vessel on the planet. He exemplified the New Testament words: "Because narrow is the gate and difficult is the way which leads to life, and there are few who find it" (Matt. 7:14).

Five Steps for Crossing Over the Chasm to the Unseen

How did Noah maintain faith in a vision that no one else shared? How did he walk to the edge of his sanity and stay there for one-hundred-twenty years? How do we find the faith to venture over the chasm to the unseen today?

1. Use God's Word as your guide rope.

Let your mind wander back for a moment. Can you imagine Noah's thoughts when God gave him the blueprint for the ark? The ark was to be approximately four-hundred-fifty feet long, seventy-five feet wide, forty-five feet high, three decks high, one door, one window, made out of gopherwood, with pitch tar slathered inside and out. Basically, it was a waterproofed floating box.

Okay God, Noah must have thought, I don't so much like the design of this thing. First of all, I'd rather build this thing out of pine. There are a lot of pine trees around my house, so why should I go out of the way to get the gopher wood? And what about the safety features? There's only one door. And couldn't I cut more windows so we can air this thing out as we're going? And God, how am I going to steer this thing without a rudder? And what about lifeboats? Didn't You forget a few things?

And then, imagine the scene in Noah's back yard as he began to build the ark. The scenario might have gone something like this:

"Noah, what are you building?" a neighbor asked as a crowd congregated around the piles of gopher wood.

"A boat," he replied, whacking a nail.

"A boat? There's no water around here. The closest lake's a day away."

"God's going to send a flood."

"What's a flood?"

"Water is going to destroy the earth," Noah said, peering up from his work.

"Water? What water? You mean the mist that comes up from the ground?"

"A *flood* of waters. I'm escaping in the ark with my family and two of every kind of animal. Want to come?"

They slapped their knees and howled. But day after day, they heard the chink of Noah's hammer and every time they looked out their windows, they saw a wooden monstrosity that had begun to cast a shadow over their gardens. Word traveled, and the small inquiring group told others who came to gape. In between the whacks of his hammer, Noah could hear their ridicule. But he kept on hammering.

It's impossible to accurately recreate the scenes from Noah's experience, but it's clear that God's orders took precedence in Noah's mind above the approval of his peers. Even when God's instructions seemed incomplete, Noah refused to alter the plans to his own logical specifications. He didn't bargain for a detailed itinerary or a backup plan. He obeyed long before he understood. Instead of changing God's plans, he allowed God's plans to change *him*. He picked up his axe, kissed his wife, went out the door, and the vision took over.

Scripture describes Noah as being "moved with godly fear" (Heb. 11:7). His was a holy fear sustained by love, a fear that chose to jump feet-first into the belief that God "is a rewarder of those who diligently seek Him" (Heb. 11:6). He gave equal weight to God's blessings and His judgments. He heeded God's solemn warning. Man's words, though, couldn't stop him—not doubts, not ridicule, not threats. Scripture never records a single word about Noah fearing man. Rather, Scripture tells us that Noah became a "preacher of righteousness" (2 Pet. 2:5) as he was building the ark, while God waited with longsuffering for men to turn their hearts to Him (see 1 Pet. 3:20).

As in Noah's day, God's Word is the standard for our spiritual works today. It separates the self-serving from the God-serving. It weeds out those who seek power, attention, self-gratification, and material gain. It isolates those whose motive is God's glory. Noah understood that God's plan was infinitely larger than he and his family. He kept walking, day after day through storms of doubt, hanging onto the guide rope of his intimate, direct communication with God.

2. Spend time alone with God.

God's Word is never two-dimensional to those who have learned to fellowship with Him. Yet, finding time for fellowship with God is a challenge in a demanding world. If you have a family, there are children's ball games and school activities to attend. For those who live several miles away from school, extra hours are required for driving back and forth. Our spouse deserves a portion of our time, as do our grandchildren. Our jobs require an even larger chunk of time. Even for those who are single, the day is packed with responsibilities.

Our time with God must be planned. If we expect it to just "become available," we will never enjoy quality time alone with the Lord. It may seem illogical to create a space of time for an invisible God when so many visible people need our time, but doing so is life-changing. The benefits spill over into all portions of our lives.

Spending quality time with God is like walking with a best friend. Unlike a human friend, God is sovereign, but some similarities can be noted. When you're walking with a friend, you're moving alongside him or her, you're able to speak freely and easily because you're frequently in agreement, you're not moving too fast, and you're making everything enjoyable. You notice the cloud formations, the shooting star, and the butterfly. You're in tune with one another, and you've grown to know each other so well that you can anticipate each other's words before they're even spoken. Sometimes even a shared look is enough to convey a thought. I believe this is the kind of intimate relationship Noah enjoyed with God.

Noah learned to walk alongside God in complete trust. Picture a child learning to ride a bicycle as his father steadies the seat with one hand. After a few trial runs up the street, the father releases his hand for a few seconds at a time. The child learns to trust that his father is still beside him even though his father's hand isn't consistently on the bicycle. His father has caught him before, and he trusts that he can do it again. As the child matures and transfers the connection to God, he eventually learns to trust that God is present even when he falls and scrapes his knees. Yet, he still chooses to hop back on the bike for the sheer joy of more time with his Companion. It is then that he is ready to walk on water.

3. Be willing to say "yes" to the different drummer.

Author Henry David Thoreau wrote in his book, *Walden*: "If a man does not keep pace with his companions, perhaps it is because he hears a different drummer. Let him step to the music which he hears, however measured or far away."[2]

There's no question that God called Noah to march to the beat of a different drummer. Even Noah's family must have questioned his sanity.

But when Noah was done explaining his actions, he lived them. Nothing else was off-kilter about his life. His daily example of integrity and faithfulness earned his family's admiration. I'm amazed that they went along with his strange request. But he was so consistent, they trusted him. In the end, they entered the ark with him.

Noah was at the right place at the right time when God required a man to preserve the human race. To those of us who are relegated to an office cubicle or a kitchen or a fast-food counter, it doesn't seem fair. The "different drummer" job sounds much more appealing.

But was Noah's day-to-day life *really* that much different than ours? After all, hammering nails for one-hundred-twenty years isn't such a glorious task. The curiosity seekers no doubt eventually grew accustomed to the fruitcake down the street and went back to their own business. Noah hammered nails for one-hundred-twenty inglorious years before he finally became a ship's captain for one year.

If Noah had skipped the years of common work, he would have never ridden the high seas. The same is true today. If we neglect the common roads God asks us to walk, we will miss God's best plans for us. If we actively embrace a deep faith in God, our feet will eventually walk on paths they would have missed otherwise.

Throughout the world, Christians are engaged in a variety of everyday activities that require only a nod from God to turn the mundane into the heroic. Businessman Todd Beamer led a group of airplane passengers who foiled terrorists from crashing it into a government building on a day that began as ordinary but now lives in infamy as 9/11. Heroes and heroines were born all over the United States in the aftermath of Hurricane Katrina in 2005. The disciple of Christ who regularly stokes the Spirit of God with prayer and communion is only one circumstance away from surmounting human fear. Though he may not even consciously think about it, he is a prime candidate for heroism.

Whether the world casts a spotlight on us or not, if we follow Jesus Christ, we will invariably make decisions that will distinguish us from the crowd. We will walk on paths we would not have chosen otherwise, and those paths will lead to other paths. Whether we like it or not, we will become counter-cultural. In a sense, today's serious followers of Christ are all "different drummers" waiting for marching orders.

4. Take the first step.

One of the problems of stepping off the beaten path is that it goes against the "norm" that many of us have practiced in our Christian journey. If it doesn't feel safe, we stay away.

But once you take the first step, God begins to fill in the gap between Point A and Point B until the impossible becomes nothing more complicated than the next logical step. David, the Psalmist said: "You enlarged my path under me, so my feet did not slip" (Ps. 18:36). In our churches today, timid Christians who have never received a traffic ticket serve in prison ministries. The blind write hymns about seeing. The wheelchair-bound organize marathons. The grief-stricken become counselors. Daily faithfulness is the essential element that bridges the chasm from possible to impossible, plank-by-plank. Five or six steps across the bridge and the chasm no longer seems so deep. On the other side, you turn around and see that the miracle that brought you across is nothing more complicated than a long series of faithful footprints.

Abraham Lincoln. Our sixteenth president was a common farmer's son with less than a grade school education. As a young man, he failed miserably in the grocery business. But his passion to halt the spread of slavery led him step by step down the road to postmaster, lawyer, state representative, senator, and finally president of the United States. As civil war erupted, he simply kept walking faithfully forward, making tough decisions each day while chaos broke loose all around him. He steered a straight course through the windstorm, refused to get sidetracked, and kept his vision. It was God's circumstances that gave Lincoln's vision momentum. God's blueprint made a self-educated, faithful man great in the annals of history.

5. Keep "hammering nails" for the long haul.

Every morning for one-hundred-twenty years, Noah had to lift his head off the pillow and say, "Lord, please give me strength to accomplish Your will today." Every morning he had to recommit to his decision. Would he pick up the hammer again or not?

How did Noah keep going? What drove him?

Noah had to come to the point of being willing to build the ark even if it were never used. He had to allow his relationship with his invisible Master to surpass his attachment to his God-given, visible task.

When we think of Noah, we usually picture him on the high seas. But it was not Noah's victorious ride on the ark that made him great in God's eyes. It was the hammer stroke years beforehand that said, "I believe You will enable me to build this massive ark" and the hammer stroke on another equally uneventful day that said, "I believe You will alter science by creating rain" and the stroke the

30

next day that proclaimed, "I believe You will carry me safely away on the crest of a trillion raindrops."

I like to imagine Noah standing at the foot of his three-story ark at the break of dawn, raising his arms in worship to the One who had gifted him with yet another day to ring out his love with his hammer. His relationship with God deepened with every proclamation of his hammer: "I love you, I love you." By the time the flood came, Noah knew God so intimately that he did not need the flood to prove God true. And God did not need the flood to prove Noah true. Their bond of love was imprinted with the oil of years upon the handle of Noah's hammer.

In the end, Noah would have fallen prostrate to worship God even if God had cancelled the flood. Noah was not a hero in God's eyes because he built an ark, but because his love was grand enough to build an ark.

Noah's Relocations

For approximately one year, Noah and his family rode out the flood. They witnessed the ultimate storm story. After the flood subsided, Noah and his family and the animals walked out onto dry land to colonize a new world. Borrowing the words of Neil Armstrong, the first man on the moon, Noah's first step was truly "one small step for [a] man, one giant leap for mankind."[3]

When he disembarked, Noah built an altar and worshipped God. As dark as his last days on the former earth had been, his first days on the new earth eclipsed the past, bright with promise. Man and beast multiplied, replenishing the earth. God created yet another phenomenon of science that Noah had never seen. Noah beheld a rainbow in the clouds, a sign of God's covenant with man that He would never again destroy all flesh with floods.

Noah lived 350 years after the flood. The remainder of his life reads like the script of today's average, troubled Christian. Despite his exemplary faith, he was as susceptible to the temptations and the ups and downs of life as we are. He died at age 950, relocating yet again to another new world—heaven.

A Final Word

Noah was an amazing example of simple faith in a complex God. Though he couldn't understand God's plan or see the end result, he steered a straight course using nothing more complicated than the faithful swing of a hammer.

He exemplified the verses in Hebrews 12 that summarize the faith of the Hebrews 11 heroes: "Let us run with endurance the race that is set before us, looking unto Jesus, the author and finisher of our faith" (Heb. 12:1-2). For Noah, running the race meant picking up the hammer each day no matter how futile the work seemed.

Noah's sphere of belief went far beyond what he could see—so far that he spent over a century conquering doubt that would have defeated most modern day men and women in a week or two. For love of God, he became an eccentric fool who doddered away at a carpentry project in his back yard.

Board by board, Noah built a bridge from the seen to the unseen. After a few boxes of nails, his hammer no longer seemed so heavy. Defying science no longer seemed so preposterous. For Noah had learned that knowing God in solitude supersedes human language. He fell in love with God, the chasm faded out of focus, and Noah walked on water before the first drop of rain ever fell. And then one day, God sent the storm, and the common man, Noah, captained the ship that saved mankind.

Applied Faith

1. As you walk alone with God each day, build your own "ark" of faith. Choose an item—a nail, a leaf, or a stone—and offer it to God each day as a symbolic accumulation of your love and service.

2. Send a card or encouraging word to an unsung hero or heroine who faithfully "hammers nails."

3. The next time you run across a "different drummer," be willing to see him or her through a fresh perspective in a nonjudgmental attitude of acceptance.

CHAPTER 4

ABRAHAM: SEEKING GOD WHEN IT SEEMS HE IS BREAKING HIS PROMISE

By faith Abraham obeyed when he was called to go out to the place which he would receive as an inheritance. And he went out, not knowing where he was going. By faith he dwelt in the land of promise as in a foreign country, dwelling in tents with Isaac and Jacob, the heirs with him of the same promise; for he waited for the city which has foundations, whose builder and maker is God. By faith Sarah herself also received strength to conceive seed, and she bore a child when she was past the age, because she judged Him faithful who had promised. Therefore from one man, and him as good as dead, were born as many as the stars of the sky in multitude—innumerable as the sand which is by the seashore.... By faith Abraham, when he was tested, offered up Isaac, and he who had received the promises offered up his only begotten son, of whom it was said, "In Isaac your seed shall be called," concluding that God was able to raise him up, even from the dead, from which he also received him in a figurative sense.

—Heb. 11:8-12, 17-19

READING: GENESIS 11-25

GOD GAVE ABRAHAM one of the greatest and most far-reaching promises of all time. When Abraham was about seventy-five years old, God told him: "I will make you a great nation; I will bless you and make your name great; And you shall be a blessing....And in you all the families of the earth shall be blessed" (Gen. 12:2-3).

But Abraham's wife, Sarah, was barren. Finally, twenty-five years later, when Sarah was ninety years old and Abraham was one hundred, Sarah miraculously bore Abraham's son, Isaac, only to have God approach Abraham a few years later with a bombshell: *Sacrifice him to me as a burnt offering.*

What must Abraham have thought? Why would God ask him to destroy the first seed of His promise? What made Abraham continue to serve and obey such an unpredictable God?

Today, what should we do when we've placed all our trust and effort in a specific God-given promise and it doesn't come to pass? Or even worse, what if it comes and it's snatched away, or it fails? Why should we keep walking with a God who seems to break promises?

The Promise

God's promise to Abraham was so huge that He used the enormity of nature to describe it. God told Abraham: "I will multiply your descendants as the stars of the heaven and as the sand which is on the seashore" (Gen. 22:17). And "I will make your descendants as the dust of the earth; so that if a man could number the dust of the earth, then your descendants also could be numbered" (Gen. 13:16). And "To your descendants I will give this land [the land of Canaan]" (Gen. 12:7). Through Abraham, God would one day form the nation of Israel. One of his descendants would be Jesus, the Messiah.

Abraham lived in Haran in the Ur of Chaldees with his family until God called him forth into the land of Canaan. Before journeying into Canaan, he had married Sarah, a woman ten years younger than him—a woman who turned out to be barren. Abraham's name was initially *Abram*, which means "exalted father." After God gave Abraham the promise, He changed his name to Abraham, which means "a father of many nations" (see Gen. 17:5).

Abraham was seventy-five years old when God instructed him to leave his home for Canaan. He departed with his barren wife, with Lot (his nephew), and all their goods and servants. Abraham pursued God's promise by leaving familiar ground. He left his home and his supporters, and he ventured onto dangerous, uncharted land with a barren woman to birth a kingdom. He placed all his bets on a promise, even when it meant walking away from safety, familiarity, and comfort to find answers. Like an explorer in nineteenth century America, he headed west across the Mississippi with a barren wife to populate the West.

Three Ways to Keep the Promise Alive

How do we follow a God-given promise when all practical evidence points to the contrary? How do we cling to God's invisible promise when waiting no longer seems sensible? When the promise seems dead, how do we revive it?

1. Keep walking forward with blind trust and obedience.

Just keep walking. As simple as it sounds, it's one of the most profound solutions to faith problems. Abraham's whole life was about walking—journeying out of his country, walking up the mountain to sacrifice Isaac, walking through the land God promised Abraham's descendants. "Arise," God told him, and "walk in the land through its length and its width; for I will give it to you" (Gen. 13:17).

When God first called Abraham, Scripture says that "By faith Abraham obeyed when he was called to go out to the place which he would receive as an inheritance. And he went out, not knowing where he was going" (Heb. 11:8). At a time in life when most of us would prefer to retire, he stepped out on God's appointed journey with blind trust.

The greatest steps of faith often border on insanity. By its very definition, faith deals with things "not seen" (Heb. 11:1). Those who are serious about faith embrace the invisible. They are deeply in tune with the voice and character of God and His Word to the point

35

of sacrificing the visible. They take unusual steps that sometimes bypass logic. We watch them and marvel.

Ralph Wingate, Sr. When I was twelve years old, I watched my father take a step of faith after God called him to preach. I remember my mom and dad gathering us together in our home to pray. As we knelt, my dad prayed: "God I'm willing to go where you want me to go." In mid-life, with a family to support, my dad quit his job to attend seminary. At age thirty-three, he pulled up stakes even though he didn't know how he would support us. As a result, he became a pastor (still preaching today in his eighties), my brother and I became pastors, and my sister and her family all became involved in the Lord's work.

Obedience, however, doesn't guarantee a trouble-free journey. Abraham endured famines, separation from his kinsmen, war, and the destruction of nearby Sodom and Gomorrah. Even worse, he faced bumps of his own making. Twice, he told kings that his beautiful wife was his sister, for fear that they might murder him to take his wife (see Genesis 12 and Genesis 20). His lies endangered the lives of the kings, who hurriedly returned Sarah untouched once they comprehended the powerful hand of God upon Abraham's life.

About ten years after God gave Abraham the promise, Sarah approached her husband with a better idea. Why not conceive an heir with Hagar, her handmaiden? After all, God's promise was getting stale and Sarah was getting long-in-the-tooth. Why not help God out a little? Abraham followed Sarah's advice, and Ishmael was born to Abraham and Hagar when Abraham was eighty-six years old.

About fourteen years after Ishmael was born, when Sarah was ninety and Abraham was one hundred years old, Isaac was miraculously born to Abraham and Sarah, just as God had promised. Abraham and Sarah's answer to the promise, along with God's answer to the promise, inhabited the same house.

Abraham's life became a soap opera. Sarah and Hagar were at each other's throats, and Abraham was at his wit's end. And though

Abraham loved Ishmael, he had to come to terms with God's will that Ishmael would never be the recipient of God's initial, grand promise.

Abraham's sin was unusual in the sense that it wasn't driven by the more common motivations of lust or greed, but by a blip in his faith. When God didn't intervene according to his expectations, Abraham attempted to manipulate circumstances to fit inside a box of human proportions. His blip cost him dearly.

But Abraham kept walking, two steps forward, one step back, two steps forward, gradually growing in his faith. When he fell, he got up, shook himself off, and sought God again. He was never satisfied with status quo faith. While some of his peers might have labeled him a hypocrite, he was instead a fallible human being who chose not to stay wrecked, but believed God was big enough to recast wrecks into incurable promise-seekers.

Through it all, Abraham sought God relentlessly. He built altars, he obeyed God's command to circumcise the males in his household, he beseeched God for mercy upon his kinsman Lot, and he sought God for the well-being of Ishmael. Through it all, he yearned to see God. His eagerness is evident when "he ran from the tent door to meet them [three heavenly visitors], and bowed himself to the ground" (Gen. 18:2).

Abraham was able to keep walking faithfully through the un-known because God would not let go of him. God never abandoned him after giving him a command. He reappeared to him again and again in the form of visions and in the form of the three heavenly visitors. God even tenderly took him outside to look at the stars to remind him of the promise (see Gen. 15:5).

Abraham had seen God, and he knew Him intimately. He sought God, and God sought Abraham. It was a relationship of devoted companions who do not let go.

2. Be willing to sacrifice everything—*even* the promise.

One day, God confronted Abraham with a test that reigns supreme as one of the greatest tests of all time. God said to Abraham: "Take now your son, your only son Isaac, whom you love, and go to the land of Moriah; and offer him there as a burnt offering on one of the mountains of which I shall tell you" (Gen. 22:2).

Isaac was probably a young boy by then, past the precarious age of infant mortality, able to walk alongside his father. All of a sudden, God was asking Abraham not only for his beloved child, but He was asking for the promise back. Imagine what Abraham must have thought: What?! Offer up Isaac? The seed of promise? How can You require Isaac's life and still fulfill Your promise?

The promise and the new command were diametrically opposed. Abraham had to make a choice: either trust his own common sense or obey God's bizarre command. How could he slaughter the seed of God's own promise, brought forth by a miracle? Was this a trick? Abraham didn't know the answer. But he had seen God, and he trusted Him.

He rose early in the morning, saddled his donkey, took Isaac and two servants with him, and split the wood for the burnt offering. For two days they traveled to the mountain God had designated. On the third day, Abraham parted ways with his servants and the donkey. He and Isaac climbed the mountain side-by-side—Isaac with the wood on his back and Abraham with the fire and knife. Their conversation went something like this:

"Father, I see the fire and the wood, but where is the lamb?"

"My son, God will provide himself a lamb for a burnt offering."

When they arrived at the mountain, Abraham arranged the wood in a pile, bound Isaac, and laid him on the wood. Knife in hand, he stretched forth his hand, ready to slit the throat of his son. Suddenly, an angel called out from heaven: "Do not lay your hand on the lad, or do anything to him; for now I know that you fear God, since you have not withheld your son, your only son, from Me" (Gen. 22:12). Abraham looked up and saw a ram caught in the thicket. He released Isaac and offered the ram as a substitution in place of Isaac.

Throughout his sojourns with God, Abraham had learned a valuable truth: *Since God could not give up His faithfulness, Abraham could give up his son.* He trusted more in the immutable character of God than he did in his own human understanding. How Abraham must have wept when he saw the ram in the thicket!

Today, just as in Abraham's day, God is dead serious about the first commandment: "You shall love the LORD your God with all your heart, with all your soul, and with all your mind" (Matt. 22:37). God, in other words, says: your love for Me must outpace your love for all your beloved ones who may seem like living, breathing promises I granted to you.

One day, God asks a parent to part with a daughter who He calls to the mission field. Another day, He asks a wife to temporarily part with a husband who leaves to undertake humanitarian work in an unsafe environment. Still another day, He asks two best friends to part paths for various ministries. Name your dearest human companion. He or she is fair game for God.

Sometimes when God calls upon us to make a sacrifice, the sacrifice makes no earthly sense. It is during those times that we must strap on a "but if" faith. When facing death in a fiery furnace, Shadrach, Meshach, and Abed-Nego said, "Our God whom we serve is able to deliver us from the burning fiery furnace, and He will deliver us from your hand, O king. But if not, let it be known to you, O king, that we do not serve your gods" (Dan. 3:17-18). Job, when afflicted with the death of all his children and with boils from head to foot, said, "Though He slay me, yet will I trust in Him" (Job 13:15). When the promise fades, there is nothing better to do than simply hold onto the invisible hand of the Promise Giver.

One of the most striking examples of a shattered promise is the crucifixion of Jesus Christ. What must the apostles have thought? Their friend and mentor, the One who walked on water, the One who healed the sick, the One who raised Lazarus from the dead, the One who claimed to be the Son of God, died with just as much pain and blood as any other mortal man. Surely they must have questioned their devotion to Him. Had they sacrificed everything to follow someone less than divine? Had they been fools to give up so much for Him?

Just when they thought Jesus was dead, He arose. And so He will for us. Even when all seems lost, God's promises to His faithful children inevitably lead to resurrection and life.

3. Enlarge your perspective.

Helen Keller was once asked what would be worse than being born blind. She responded: "The most pathetic person in the world is someone who has sight, but has no vision."[4] Spiritual vision is the ability to see hoped-for answers to God's promises beyond human boundaries. Vision beckons feet over chasms where the seeker might fall at any moment, but where the payoff is unparalleled.

As humans, we naturally envision our grand plans as a straight line to an expected goal at a reasonable deadline. But Scripture says: "'For My thoughts are not your thoughts, nor are your ways My ways,' says the LORD. 'For as the heavens are higher than the earth, so are My ways higher than your ways, and My thoughts than your thoughts'" (Isa. 55:8-9). God beckons us upon the zigs and zags and switchbacks of life. L. B. Cowman records these thoughts from F. B. Meyer and from her own addendum in the April 16 entry of *Streams in the Desert*:

> O glorious faith! Your works and possibilities are these: contentment to set sail with the orders still sealed, due to unwavering confidence in the wisdom of the Lord High Admiral; and a willingness to get up, leave everything, and follow Christ, because of the joyful assurance that earth's best does not compare with heaven's best....You must also be willing to take your ideas of what the journey will be like and tear them into tiny pieces, for nothing on the itinerary will happen as you expect.[5]

Abraham had the right idea when he "looked for a city which hath foundations, whose builder and maker is God" (Heb. 11:10, KJV). Even though he was a wealthy man, he knew that the end of his journey would not be a comfortable dream home overlooking the sea. He lived in a tent. The Greek word for *tabernacle* in Hebrews 11 means "tent" or "cloth hut." A tent is characteristic of a person who is seeking, who dares not sink roots lest his master give marching orders.

Though today most of us don't live in a tent, we must ask ourselves: *Is God the true quest of my life?* God grants spiritual vision to people who are desperate for Him. Scripture promises those who seek God: "You will find Him if you seek Him with all your heart and with all your soul" (Deut. 4:29). Scripture speaks of Him as being so near that we can touch Him. God made man "so that they should seek the Lord, in the hope that they might grope for Him and find Him, though He is not far from each one of us" (Acts 17:27).

If you've sought the Lord long enough and hard enough, you already know that spiritual vision is difficult to maintain. Vision killers await us like insidious traps. They ambush us and attempt to shake off our spiritual glasses. Sin shelves our vision by making us feel unworthy. Self-sufficiency makes us complacent. The responsibilities of everyday life stifle spiritual passion until we become too tired to pursue God. Critics tempt us to doubt our mission, often precisely at the time when we are serving the Lord wholeheartedly. And perhaps the most cunning and common of all, discouragement douses our vision by whispering to us: *Who are you kidding? You are a nobody. This will never work!*

Abraham was no stranger to these traps, but he realized that his mission was far bigger than his narrow world. God's promise to him was similar to the promise the angel would deliver to the Virgin Mary—that she would conceive a child who would "reign over the house of Jacob forever; and of His kingdom there will be no end" (Luke 1:33).

Was God's promise *for* Abraham? Was it *about* Abraham? Was it *for* Mary? Was it *about* Mary? Mostly, no, but in small measure, yes. Yet the promises overlapped their lifetimes, as well as the lifetimes of many to come. Abraham and Mary held in their mortal hands the seed that would save humankind from sin. God's promise was an unmatured seed in the womb, awaiting the playing out of Abraham's and Mary's faith that would give it birth. It would mature far beyond anything they could have ever seen in one lifetime.

The significance of Abraham's sacrifice on that lonely, windswept mountaintop went beyond the three flesh-and-blood characters who enacted it (see Romans 4 and Galatians 3). Abraham's faith that day foreshadowed God's plan to offer grace through faith in Jesus Christ.

41

The ram was a sinless, substitutionary offering to please a holy God. It was primarily for God—not for Abraham, though Abraham benefited. Isaac, the seed of promise, had to be sacrificed that day just as Jesus would be sacrificed centuries later. All of man's reasoning had to be slaughtered on Abraham's mountain. Faith alone had to reign in order for grace to be unveiled. It is no mistake that Abraham had to sacrifice the promise.

Eventually Abraham's sacrifice would make perfect sense in reverse. Like rewinding a movie after watching it in its entirety, Abraham's part would become illuminated by the whole. So, too, will our part make perfect sense in God's plan. We must never discount the far-reaching effects our seemingly little steps of faith might have. While God's specific promise to us may not lead to anything as epic as the birth of a Savior, there is ample ground in between our limited vision and God's immense purposes. We simply must trust His plan, as Abraham did.

Hebrews 11 points out that divine promises often exceed human life spans: "And all these, having obtained a good testimony through faith, did not receive the promise, God having provided something better for us, that they should not be made perfect apart from us" (Heb. 11:39-40). Though most of the heroes and heroines of the faith died almost empty-handed, they demonstrated an unusual outlook that is characteristic of great faith. They were "assured" of the promises, and they "embraced" them as if they'd already received their bestowment in full (Heb. 11:13).

Whether God's promise to us comes to fruition in our lifetime or not, we can trust that our contribution will prove to be an integral, inseparable part of God's plan. It is right to cling to a God-given promise, even when it seems impractical and unprofitable to do so.

Abraham's Latter Days

Sarah died when Abraham was 137 years old. Not long after she died, Abraham confronted the reliability of God's promise once again. Was it still in force, or had it grown stale with time? Isaac needed a wife. Without a wife, the promise was no good and the sacrifice on the mountain was for naught.

Possibly too old to make an arduous journey by camelback, Abraham entrusted the sacred lineage of God's promise to his personal servant. Abraham trusted that his faith could do what his legs could not do—even when the messenger was a fallible human being. He instructed the servant to travel to his homeland to find a woman among his kindred, assuring him that God would "send His angel before you" (Gen. 24:7). The servant brought back Rebekah to marry Isaac. Isaac and Rebekah would later bear Esau and Jacob.

Abraham soon remarried. Keturah bore him six children. He died at age 175, "an old man and full of years" (Gen. 25:8). Isaac and Ishmael buried him alongside Sarah.

A Final Word

God blessed Abraham throughout his life because he walked faithfully forward in blind trust and obedience. God testified of him: "Abraham obeyed My voice" (Gen. 26:5). He kept walking even when his accumulated intellect, his sage judgment, and his common sense told him to quit. Like a toddler who falls repeatedly, he picked himself up off the ground, dirty and bruised, reset his vision, and walked onward.

Abraham didn't need to see the goal line in order to keep walking. His obedience was fueled by his relationship with the One who was forever faithful to him. He understood that God's promise was more precious than his stake in it. He rejoiced in it as if he could already see its fruition. Jesus later honored Abraham with these words, spoken to the Pharisees: "Your father Abraham rejoiced to see My day, and he saw it and was glad" (John 8:56).

One of the most endearing phrases ever written about a man in the Bible is found in this passage of Scripture about Abraham: "And the Scripture was fulfilled which says, 'Abraham believed God, and it was accounted to him for righteousness.' And he was called the friend of God" (James 2:23).

May we, too, aspire to become the "friend of God."

APPLIED FAITH

1. Slip a picture of a tent into your Bible as a reminder that we are sojourners on this earth, on a journey to our home in heaven.

2. Make a list of people you would find agonizing to release even if God personally asked you to do so, as He asked Abraham to surrender Isaac. Surrender each of them in prayer regularly.

3. Tear a map into tiny pieces and place it on a box near your place of prayer to signify your willingness to follow God's pathway for your life.

CHAPTER 5

SARAH: SEEKING GOD IN THE SHADOW OF ANOTHER

By faith Sarah herself also received strength to conceive seed, and she bore a child when she was past the age, because she judged Him faithful who had promised. Therefore from one man, and him as good as dead, were born as many as the stars of the sky in multitude—innumerable as the sand which is by the seashore.

—Heb. 11:11-12

READING: GENESIS 11-23

SARAH WAS NEVER blessed with a vision of God. In fact, Scripture offers very little proof that she even sought God. But Sarah's husband, Abraham, saw God on several occasions. Even his concubine heard the voices of angels.

It seems no wonder that God didn't appear to Sarah. She tempted Abraham to conceive a child through a servant, and then she vexed the servant until the servant fled. A few years after Sarah and Abraham finally gave birth to their own child, she evicted her servant and servant's child into the wilderness.

But in her defense, she lived a difficult existence, following and obeying a rich husband who chased an invisible God and provided her with nothing more luxurious than a tent. On two occasions, he willingly surrendered her to kings for less-than-honorable purposes.

On the surface, Sarah was an unfortunate shrew who was never blessed with a vision of God or of His angels. She is one of the more questionable members of the Hebrews 11 lineup who doesn't seem to fit among the others. Why did God include her?

Today, how do we continue seeking God when He shows Himself to others, but never to us? How do we seek God in the shadow of another?

Sarah's Burden

When Sarah married Abraham, she had no inkling of the rough ride ahead. Her husband began hearing God's voice—messages from Almighty God that not only quickened his faith, but also moved his feet. He uprooted Sarah from their home in Ur of the Chaldeans and moved to Canaan, traveling from place to place, living in a tent, following an invisible God.

Sarah was a woman of such "beautiful countenance" that Abraham commanded her to pose as his sister lest any man in the course of their travels kill him for her (see Gen. 12:11-13). In truth, she was his half-sister (see Gen. 20:12-13), but the plan was nevertheless a deception. When a famine deflected their journey to Egypt, the Pharaoh abducted Sarah until God plagued his household with "great plagues" and he released her (Gen. 12:17). Scripture is not clear whether she was sexually misused or not.

Yet despite the indignity she bore, Sarah remained loyal to Abraham. She knew her husband was special. God had given him a magnificent promise: "I will make of thee a great nation" (Gen. 12:2, KJV). And later God told him: "I will make your descendants as the dust of the earth" (Gen. 13:16). Then God told Abraham that his seed would be as numerous as the stars (see Gen. 15:5). It would stand to reason that Sarah would be intimately involved in this promise. Yet Sarah remained barren.

The pressure must have stretched Sarah to the snapping point. The weight of kings and of nations rested upon her ability to bear a child. She was the stopper plugging up a promise designed to carry down through the annals of Christianity. It had been ten years since God's first promise to Abraham, and she was seventy-five years old. And still no baby.

During the entire ten years, God had never appeared to her, but always to Abraham. God had never given *her* the promise. Sarah not only faced her physical inadequacy, but she stared God's seeming indifference full in the face. Did God care about her part in this plan, or did she even belong in it at all?

Suggestions for Seeking God in the Shadow of Another

What enabled Sarah to remain faithful in the shadow of a man who seemed to receive all the attention from God? How do we endure in our walk with God when we must do it alongside a privileged "other" who enjoys God's fellowship despite his or her imperfections?

1. Anticipate jealousy and push it away.

One day when Sarah was seventy-five years old, she decided she'd had enough. She approached Abraham and said, "The LORD has restrained me from bearing children" (Gen. 16:2). She offered Abraham her handmaiden, Hagar, to produce the offspring that she could not produce. Ishmael was born of this ill-advised union when Abraham was eighty-six, Sarah seventy-six.

It was a soap opera in the making. When Hagar realized she had conceived Abraham's child, she began to despise Sarah. Sarah, in turn, blamed Abraham. She dealt so harshly with Hagar that Hagar ran off into the wilderness, pregnant and homeless. While Hagar was resting by a well, an angel of the Lord spoke to her, saying: "Return to your mistress, and submit yourself under her hand" (Gen. 16:9). The angel also said, "I will multiply your descendants exceedingly, so that they shall not be counted for multitude" (Gen. 16:10). (Indeed, Ishmael would father many of the Arab nations that are home to the modern day Muslims.)

Hagar immediately returned to Abraham's household. Whether she told Sarah about the angel, Scripture doesn't say, but no doubt doing so would have heaped an extra helping of vexation upon Sarah's soul.

Not until fourteen years later, when Abraham was ninety-nine and Sarah eighty-nine, did God mention Sarah as part of His plan. He appeared to Abraham and said: "And I will bless her [Sarah] and also give you a son by her; then I will bless her, and she shall be a mother of nations; kings of peoples shall be from her" (Gen. 17:16). He even changed her name from Sarai to *Sarah*, meaning "princess" instead of "my princess," signifying the broadening scope of her influence. All of Sarah's jealousy was for naught. Isaac was miraculously born to Abraham and Sarah the next year, when Ishmael was fourteen years old.

The facts of the story read like a Hollywood script. There was one father and two mothers, and there were two sons. There was one son born the ordinary way, and one son born through God's intervention. There was one son born by spiritual compromise, and one son born by God's promise. Ishmael was born according to works, by trying to solve the problem through human effort. Isaac was born by faith when Abraham and Sarah trusted God's promise.

Having it both ways created friction that would raise sparks for years. Even Ishmael and Isaac would quarrel. Jealousy would divide the household in such a way that the words of Jesus (see Matt. 12:25) and Abraham Lincoln come to mind: *A house divided against itself cannot stand.* Sarah—perhaps rightly, though cruelly—vexed Abraham until he permitted her to evict Hagar and Ishmael, resulting in anguish for all parties involved.

Sarah's jealously should be no surprise, for throughout the Bible, jealousy lurks in close proximity to the birth of divine plans. Eve believed God was keeping something from her in the garden. Joseph presumed Mary was carrying a child conceived by another man. The Pharisees feared Jesus was usurping their ministry. The presumption of the tempted is this: God (or God's representative in my life) doesn't love me enough. The challenge always becomes pushing away the jealousy in order that God's plan might go forth.

Ishmael's birth was the result of Sarah's fall over jealousy. Even though God blessed Ishmael, the deviation from God's plan could have been avoided if Sarah had observed the following two principles of faith.

- **Wait longer.** For years, Sarah was not sure what God was doing. What was God up to? Why wouldn't He spark life into her barren womb? She waited, but her patience ran out. Sarah gave her handmaiden to Abraham and informed him that "the LORD has restrained me from bearing children" (Gen. 16:2), as if she had come to the conclusion that God had purposely closed her womb. She was correct. But she incorrectly presumed that in doing so, God was rejecting her.

  Sometimes circumstances don't make sense unless we think of them in terms of God purposely holding back the blessing. It's as if God bolsters His shoulder against the mechanisms of events in our lives because He is meticulously unfolding His own perfect plan. Patience is key in faith.

- **Remember that God uses unlikely people.** God specializes in using unremarkable and imperfect people. Jesus was the son of a carpenter. The apostles were fishermen. Paul was a persecutor of Christians. Mary Magdalene was demon-possessed.

  God's touch never diminishes in proportion to mortal inferiority or weakness. Rather, the opposite is often true. Consider 1 Cor. 1:26-29:

  For you see your calling, brethren, that not many wise according to the flesh, not many mighty, not many noble, are called. But God has chosen the foolish things of the world to put to shame the wise, and God has chosen the weak things of the world to put to shame the things which are mighty; and the base things of the world and the things which are despised God has chosen, and the things which are not, to

49

bring to nothing the things that are, that no flesh should glory in His presence.

The church widow. When I was pastoring in Connecticut, an elderly widow who lived in a tiny makeshift house in our community impacted our church in a mighty way. God had been prospering Emmanuel Baptist Church to the point that our growing congregation eventually needed a larger auditorium. We needed property, and we needed to build. Nearby was a church that Emmanuel had split away from sixty years ago—long before I was born. The membership of that church had shrunk to about a dozen people, with no pastor. One day representatives from that church approached me and said, "We would like to merge back with Emmanuel. We don't have any bills and we have just a small amount of money in our checking account." We decided to proceed with the merger.

At the same time, the elderly widow—a member of that tiny church—became terminally ill. She willed Emmanuel $100,000 for the purchase of new property. We purchased a beautiful spot on the summit of a hill where the church can be seen prominently from around the community. The faith of this unassuming lady in a dwindling church encouraged our entire congregation. (See Chapter 10 for more details about this story.)

2. Respect God-given authority, even when it falters.

Almost every modern day woman I know would have considered leaving Abraham. Though he was a prophet of God who personally conversed with the Almighty on several occasions, he faltered as a leader and as a husband. Yet Sarah stuck with him.

In fact, Sarah was so obedient that the New Testament cites her as a role model for today's women in the area of subjection and obedience to husbands—"as Sarah obeyed Abraham, calling him lord" (1 Pet. 3:6).

But why did Sarah stick with him? Abraham not only surrendered her to the Pharaoh of Egypt early in their marriage, but he pulled the same stunt about 24 years later, soon after God had specifically promised him a son through Sarah "at this set time next year" (Gen. 17:21).

Abraham couldn't possibly have relinquished Sarah to another man at a worse time. What was this mighty man of God thinking? Where was his faith? In all fairness, probably Abraham lacked the power to prevent King Abimelech from abducting Sarah, but Scripture is clear that his words gave the king the green light: "She is my sister" (Gen. 20:2). Both Abraham and Sarah repeated the same lie—Sarah because Abraham had asked her to lie, and Abraham because he feared he would be slain for his wife (see Gen. 20).

A lie is lie, and in this regard, both Abraham and Sarah sinned. But is it possible that in the larger scheme of things, Sarah went along with Abraham's plan out of extraordinary faith? After all, she had already seen God rescue her out of the first captive situation. She had tasted the unlikely, the impossible. Perhaps she had developed a hunger for divine intervention on her behalf from the One who spoke to her husband.

And then, just when God's plan seemed most in jeopardy, God delivered her again. In a dream, God told King Abimelech, basically, "If you touch her, you're a dead man, for she's another man's wife." The king quickly restored Sarah to Abraham untouched, along with gifts of livestock, servants, and silver.

Despite Abraham's sin, God's plan moved forward. Like a divine magnetized puzzle whose movements were preprogrammed before the existence of earth, Abraham's sin set the next pattern in motion. God was well aware that Sarah was at the brink of conception. It was no surprise to Him that the paternity of Isaac teetered in imminent peril. The moment Sarah entered the king's domain, God closed the wombs of every female in the household. After she exited, He reopened them. Sarah's womb would be preserved for Abraham's seed, and for Isaac. Psalm 109 speaks of the sovereignty of God's plans: "He rebuked kings for their sakes, saying, 'Do not touch My anointed ones, and do My prophets no harm'" (Ps. 105:14-15).

What if Sarah had refused to go along with Abraham's plan? What if she had told King Abimelech she was Abraham's wife?

Possibly, she would have never witnessed God's hand of protection upon her. God's protection may have been the very thing that explains her silence in Scripture regarding Abraham's sacrifice of Isaac. We can only surmise, but it's plausible that Sarah trusted that the same God who could open and close wombs could also slay her son and raise him up again.

Today's Christians are rarely abducted by kings, but occasionally we may face situations where a godly authority will ask us to follow an imperfect plan. When that day comes, we will need to make a choice, knowing that continuing to faithfully follow a godly authority may mean stepping over the boundary into gray areas. No one can give us a license to sin, nor should we use Sarah's lie as a precedent. But I believe that keeping the larger picture in mind is paramount. God clearly honored Sarah's decision to follow Abraham's long-range pursuit of God's promise.

No prophet of God is perfect. No leader or mentor is perfect. But would we turn our backs on Moses because he struck the rock when God commanded him to speak to it? Would we excommunicate David because he committed adultery with Bathsheba? Would we ban Peter from establishing the church because he denied Christ? How much of our Bible would remain if we tore out all the pages where sin and heroes coexist?

Today, will we not grant even an inch to the authority figure standing beside us? Will we not wait and pray for the backslider to stand again? We must never forget that kings and kingdoms, that the lineage of Jesus Christ, and that the salvation of all mankind rises and falls upon grace.

3. Humble yourself enough to seek God through His revelation to others.

About a year before Sarah gave birth to Isaac, she was going about the routines of the nomadic life, dusting out the tent, shooing out the flies, when suddenly she heard three strangers conversing with her husband outside the tent. Abraham called one of them "My Lord" (Gen. 18:3).

Moments later, Abraham hastened inside and instructed Sarah to prepare cakes for his guests, then hurried back outside. She heard him instructing a servant to kill and prepare a calf. Later, as the men sat down outside to eat, Sarah heard one of the strangers say her name. Possibly, she may have peeked through the tent door to view the visitors, but Scripture doesn't say. We only know that she heard them.

> "Where is Sarah your wife?"
> So he [Abraham] said, "Here, in the tent."
> And He [one of the three visitors] said, "I will certainly return to you according to the time of life, and behold, Sarah your wife shall have a son."
>
> —Gen. 18:9-10

One tent flap away, Sarah's heart thudded. Her nervousness was evident. She laughed when they mentioned a baby—a baby at *her* age. Despite God's repeated promises to Abraham, her wrinkled skin told her otherwise. Every day lived was another day in the life of a geriatric woman, far past the age of fertility. But why were these strangers here? And how could they know about God's promise unless they were messengers from God?

Her hands must have trembled as she resumed her chores. It must have taken all her restraint to remain in the tent. She wanted to burst outside, but doing so would not be proper. Once again, Abraham was in the presence of angels. Once again, God was speaking directly to her husband, and *not* to her.

She could have thrown every dish outside the tent in a colossal temper tantrum. But I believe that it was enough for Sarah that God had spoken her name. As humbling as it must have been, she stuck with a husband who was God's chosen recipient for rendezvous and revelations.

Throughout history, God has spoken to believers through other believers. What is the Bible but the inspired record of God's revelations to mankind, channeled through prophets and apostles? What are the biographies of missionaries and preachers but the testimony of mortals who have seen the unmistakable work of God in their lives? Would we throw out our Bibles, our libraries?

When immersed in daily life on the ground level, our spiritual discernment tends to lose focus. We are too close; life blurs. Jesus suffered partially due to proximity distortion. When He taught in His home territory, His listeners said, "Where did this Man get this wisdom and these mighty works? Is this not the carpenter's son?" (Matt. 13:54-55). They tried to dismiss His authority, as if the real Jesus should have materialized by magic. "However, we know where this Man is from," they said, "but when the Christ comes, no one knows where He is from" (John 7:27). They dragged down the miraculous to the mundane.

Today, what of the man or woman standing next to us who claims to have heard from God? What of the sinner in our office who is thunderstruck with a revelation of God? Familiarity is not grounds for dismissal.

If God chooses to speak through a comrade or coworker, we are blessed to be within a tent's flap of His voice. Though God's confidante may not be perfect, His plan always is.

God's Blessings Upon a Shrew

Did God leave Sarah unrewarded for her faithfulness? After all, the Bible never specifically says that she saw God.

When Isaac was conceived, the Bible tells us, "And the LORD visited Sarah" (Gen. 21:1). God may have never appeared before Sarah's eyes, but God touched Sarah. Much like the blind men in the gospels, Sarah received her sight through the touch of God.

If you think Sarah was dissatisfied, listen to her comments after Isaac was born: "And Sarah said, 'God has made me laugh, and all who hear will laugh with me....Who would have said to Abraham that Sarah would nurse children? For I have borne him a son in his old age'" (Gen. 21:6-7). Sarah named him Isaac, meaning laughter. As almost every new mother will attest, laughter at this crossroads is synonymous with unspeakable joy.

In many ways, Sarah was as blessed as Mary, the earthly mother of God in the flesh. Though they could hardly have been more dissimilar in age or in character, God used each of them in similar ways at the opposite ends of the lineage of Jesus Christ. The parallels are astonishing.

God made both wombs bear impossibilities, one without a mortal man's participation and one that was barren and past age. Genesis 18:14 says of Isaac's birth, "Is anything too hard for the LORD?" Luke 1:37 says of John the Baptist's and Jesus' births, "For with God nothing will be impossible." Both births were foretold by angels. God providentially protected the seed of both wombs from mistaken identity by clear-cutting a path of misinterpretation around them. Both were born in humble estate: Jesus in a stable, and Isaac probably in a tent.

There is no question that God blessed Sarah. Abraham received the promise, but Sarah bore the promise in her own flesh.

Sarah died at age 127. Abraham wept for her and purchased a special resting place in a cave in Hebron in Canaan, where he would be buried beside Sarah thirty-eight years later. Isaac, too, mourned deeply for his mother, finally finding solace in his marriage to Rebekah after his mother's death.

A Final Word

It would be ideal to say that Sarah transformed into a sweet, angelic mother after the miracle of Isaac's birth. But she remained as temperamental as ever. Years later, when jealousy flared up in the household again, she banished Hagar and Ishmael into the wilderness. An intent study of Scripture leaves the reader wondering just how loud and ugly her fits must have been.

But it is encouraging to know that even a woman with shrewish qualities can be counted a heroine by God. Despite her quirks, we know from the words of Hebrews 11 that Sarah's heart was steadfast—for "she judged Him faithful who had promised."

God focused on the intent of Sarah's heart, on her obedience, on her steadfast walk alongside an imperfect leader in the long pursuit of God. God looked past Sarah's bad behavior, peering deep beneath her layers of defenses, and He chose Sarah.

APPLIED FAITH

1. Read a biography of a missionary or preacher, and view God through His revelations to this Christian.

2. List all the imperfections and sins that could potentially disqualify you from a leadership position in your church if they were spotlighted for your congregation to see.

3. Ask a Christian leader if he or she has ever experienced God's presence in an evident way. Then ask God to reveal Himself to you.

4. In a small group setting, share with one another your unfulfilled desires to see God's presence in your lives. Pray for one another.

CHAPTER 6

. . . .

ISAAC: SEEKING GOD
FROM THE MIRE OF
A TROUBLED HOME

By faith Isaac blessed Jacob and Esau concerning things to
come.

—Heb. 11:20

READING: GENESIS 21-28, 35

I F EVER THERE was a poster child for a dysfunctional family,
it was Isaac. As a newborn, he gazed up into the wrinkled faces
of geriatric parents. His older half-brother, Ishmael, despised
him. When Isaac was a boy, his father took him away from his
mother on a short journey. When they arrived at their destination,
his father tried to kill him and claimed that God instructed him
to do it.

After Isaac married, he and his wife, Rebekah, remained
childless for twenty years. Finally, Isaac's long-awaited heir was
born—not one son, but two. It should have been cause for joy, but
Isaac's twins were at each other's throats from the womb. As adults,
Jacob coaxed Esau out of his birthright. Years later, Rebekah urged
Jacob to trick Isaac into giving him Esau's inheritance. When Esau
discovered the deception, he threatened to murder Jacob.

Isaac could hardly be called the holy father of holy sons. This hero of the faith was mired in serious family troubles that today would result in prison sentences.

Since childhood, Isaac knew he'd been chosen to carry forth the covenant God had made with Abraham—to birth a great nation for God's people and to possess the land of Canaan for their home. Isaac knew that the future of God's plan hinged on his fatherhood and ultimately upon one of his sons. But his life didn't seem to mesh with God's calling upon it.

These children? Isaac must have cried out to God. You want to bless Your people with *these* children?

How did Isaac become a hero of the faith in the midst of such depressing circumstances? How did he keep faith in a divine plan when the recipients were so unworthy?

Today, how can God accomplish divine purposes in our lives when our own family depletes our spirit? How can we pour holy oil into fractured pots?

Isaac's Tall Boots

Isaac was born with a set of "tall boots" sitting beside his bed. His father, Abraham, was the founder of a new nation. Abraham was rich in land and livestock, he'd initiated the ordinance of circumcision, and even kings acknowledged that the hand of God was upon him. Abraham was the George Washington of his day, and much more.

But Isaac was no Abraham. He was a meek and passive man. He mourned for his strong-willed mother for years after she died. He meditated in a field, he never went to war, he humbled himself in the presence of his enemies, and he spent the final decades of his life blind. He was so easily deceived by his own family that at surface glance, he seems somewhat of a patsy.

Neither was Isaac a paragon of virtue. Like his father, he lied to King Abimelech, claiming that Rebekah was his sister for fear they would kill him for her. Just as sons today repeat the sins of their fathers (such as drunkenness, physical abuse, and others), Isaac parroted his father's sin of lying.

Bible scholars often characterize Isaac as the mediocre son of a godly father and the mediocre father of a godly son. His position was somewhat like a middle child's—upstaged on both sides by his father and by two impetuous sons.

If his bland personality diminished his chances at heroism, so, too, did his home life. Sparks flew between his father and mother regarding Abraham's concubine, Hagar, the mother of his half-brother, Ishmael. One day, his mother ejected Hagar and Ishmael into the wilderness. Isaac remained as the sole child in a household tainted with bitterness.

Three Steps for Conquering the Mire

How did Isaac fill his father's tall boots? What positive steps did he take to seek God in the midst of negative circumstances?

Today, how do we seek God when we are bogged down in the mire of too much reality at home?

1. Revisit God's past blessings in your life.

God did not leave Isaac without footholds. Isaac's life itself was a miracle. None of his other relatives or friends had been born to a ninety-year-old mother and a one-hundred-year-old father. His birth was a physical impossibility.

When Isaac was a boy, God bestowed another unforgettable foothold. His father took him on a three-day journey to a mountain in the land of Moriah. Little did Isaac know that God had commanded Abraham to slaughter him on an altar. Little did he know that his obedience would later serve as a picture of the sacrificial death of the Messiah.

Young Isaac carried his own firewood just as Jesus would carry His own cross. With each step, he grew increasingly puzzled. In the past, he had watched his father perform animal sacrifices with the same knife he carried today. As they hiked closer to the place God had designated, and as the winds swept across the desolate heights, Isaac inquired of his father. "Where is the lamb for the burnt offering?" His father answered simply: "My son, God will provide for Himself the lamb for a burnt offering" (Gen. 22:8).

At their destination, Abraham bound Isaac and laid him on the firewood. Then, as Abraham poised the knife above him, a voice called out from thin air: "Do not lay your hand on the lad, or do anything to him; for now I know that you fear God, since you have not withheld your son, your only son, from Me" (Gen. 22:12).

In a nearby thicket, a ram jerked and struggled, tangled by its horns. It would be a ram Isaac would never forget, a voice he would never forget. His father untied him and sacrificed the ram in his place.

Only two humans, one ram, and one angel were present on this desolate mountain. The occurrence could have easily been dismissed as a mini-pilgrimage with a happy ending. But God recorded the story of the private events of a troubled family in His Holy Word, and for thousands of years it has encouraged millions of Christians. Isaac obeyed with a childlike faith that adults strive to attain. He trusted his father and the God of his father on a lonely mountain when nothing seemed to make sense.

But God did something more for Isaac that day. He began preparing him for a difficult decision that he would make years later. Scripture doesn't tell us, but possibly Isaac struggled with the idea that his father loved God more than him. It would be tough to erase the image of his father's knife poised above him. Would his father *really* have killed him? It would be a lesson he would revisit years later with his own sons.

When Isaac was forty years old, God provided him with a wife through a faithful servant's obedience and an angel's leading. Twenty years after Isaac and Rebekah married, God granted twin sons, Esau and Jacob, to formerly barren Rebekah in answer to Isaac's prayers. God's blessings would come decades apart, but they became undeniable evidence of His hand upon Isaac's life. They became footholds Isaac could rest upon when the ground ahead seemed too difficult to tread.

2. Walk forward even when your situation seems fruitless.

As a pastor, I often encounter Christians who feel as if wet sand has been dumped upon their dreams. The bliss of marriage has worn off, their children are grown and gone, and their jobs are uninspiring. Nothing promising seems to lie on the road ahead. Instead, responsibilities and problems compound, and they grow so weary they feel tempted to quit.

It's not unusual to feel this way as we get older, particularly as we realize that friends and family will seldom meet our expectations. Many Christians abandon their God-given callings or veer towards alluring substitutions that temporarily deaden their disappointments. They become spiritually powerless.

Isaac was no stranger to this sort of disappointment. History records Isaac as a hero of the faith, but he, too, lived a daily grind, battling a disheartening variety of both people and events:

- **Feuding children.** Isaac's children vexed him. Before they were born, God warned Isaac's wife: "Two nations are in your womb, two peoples shall be separated from your body; one people shall be stronger than the other; and the older shall serve the younger" (Gen. 25:23). They wrestled in the womb, jockeying for position—a battle that would continue for a very long time.

  Esau and Jacob couldn't have been more different. Esau was a "hairy man" but Jacob was a "smooth-skinned man" (Gen. 27:11). Esau became a hunter in the fields, but Jacob preferred to dwell in tents. Unwise favoritism would further split the household. Isaac loved Esau, but Rebekah loved Jacob.

  One day, Esau arrived from the field, famished and weak. Jacob seized the opportunity. He coaxed Esau out of his birthright in exchange for a pot of stew. Yet Scripture aims its harshest words at Esau, calling him a "profane person" and one "who for one morsel of food sold his birthright" (Heb. 12:16). Why?

Esau understood the spiritual significance of his birthright, just as Cain, centuries earlier, understood the significance of the blood sacrifice. They were sacred bestowments centered on God, much like a marriage vow is today. The birthright and the subsequent blessing went to the firstborn male, with the honor and promise of the birthright pointing forward to the promise and inheritance of the blessing. Those in the line of Abraham also inherited the promise of the Messiah.

Esau bartered his spiritual birthright to satisfy his temporal hunger. He gulped down the stew, and basically said, "So what, it's only a birthright. I need food to survive, don't I? Go ahead and take the birthright!" Because he was a Jewish boy raised in a Jewish family, he understood the gravity of the situation, but in a selfish moment, he chose to dismiss a divine endowment and its accompanying responsibilities.

Esau chose the seen above the unseen. His carelessness that day would strain the relationships in a household already fractured by bitterness.

- **Drudgery.** Isaac's problems were not limited to his sons. Famine struck. Isaac considered moving his family to Egypt, but God appeared to him and said: "Do not go down to Egypt; live in the land of which I shall tell you. Dwell in this land, and I will be with you and bless you; for to you and your descendants I give all these lands, and I will perform the oath which I swore to Abraham your father. And I will make your descendants multiply as the stars of heaven; I will give to your descendants all these lands; and in your seed all the nations of the earth shall be blessed" (Gen. 26:2-4).

  As a boy, Isaac had heard the voice of God's angel on Mt. Moriah. He had listened to his father's testimonies of encounters with God. But today, Isaac beheld God for the first time with his own eyes.

I once heard a scientist on a documentary state that even if all the dinosaur bones mankind has ever found could be assembled into life-size reproductions, they could never match the experience of beholding a single living dinosaur. So it must be with beholding God. His Word and the testimonies of others, while necessary and preparatory, can never match seeing Him face to face.

Isaac obeyed God. Despite the famine, God blessed him in Gerar with abundant livestock and servants. But his problems did not end. Soon Isaac's Philistine neighbors envied his wealth. King Abimelech ordered him to leave. Isaac moved to the valley of Gerar. There he located the wells his father had dug long ago. The Philistines had clogged them with dirt. Isaac re-dug them and christened them anew with the same names his father had given them.

When the herdsmen of Gerar noticed a fresh spring of water spouting from Esek, they claimed the well as their own. Isaac allowed them to take it. He moved on and dug Sitnah. They took it, too. He dug Rehoboth and began to feel a breath of relief when they did not take it.

At nearby Beersheba, patient Isaac rested in the evening. No doubt he suffered from the same type of up-and-down, back-and-forth weariness that has assailed mankind since Adam and Eve. That night, God appeared to Isaac again and said: "I am the God of your father Abraham; do not fear, for I am with you. I will bless you and multiply your descendants for My servant Abraham's sake" (Gen. 26:24). It was the reassurance Isaac needed. He was so moved that he built an altar on the spot. There, his servants dug another well.

King Abimelech appeared on the scene. (This Abimelech is probably not the same Abimelech that Abraham knew. Abimelech was a common name for Philistine kings.) Isaac must have been dismayed, expecting another takeover. But the king's words astonished him: "We have certainly seen that the LORD is with you" (Gen. 26:28). Abimelech requested a peace covenant.

Enemy sat with enemy, eating and drinking and making peace—the king who had evicted Isaac from his neighborhood alongside the wealthy herdsman who had lied to Abimelech about his wife. The same day, Isaac's servants came running with news of the new well: "We have found water"(Gen. 26:32).

Scripture doesn't say how long Isaac's trials in Gerar lasted—whether years or just a season. But his responses to his trials represent his faith. The man with stars on his mind spent his days digging in the mud. The man who wanted to venture to Egypt sojourned in a dry place that must have seemed fruitless at times. The man who had been deeded the land of Canaan by the Creator of the universe walked in submission to greedy landowners and a jealous king. Valor was not his way, but this peacemaker walked forward, building altars in a dry land and sacrificing personal desires as his father had taught him on Moriah. As a result, he softened the heart of a king and glorified the King of kings in the eyes of all who observed him.

3. Bless the hard-to-bless.

Sometimes, even though it seems like a waste of breath to bless a wayward family member, it's possible that our blessing will come to fruition in the years to come. This was Isaac's experience.

When Isaac felt it was time to bestow the all-important blessings on his sons, he summoned his favorite son, Esau, to his bedside. As the firstborn, Esau was slated to receive a double portion of the multi-faceted blessing. Isaac would 1) recommend God to his son for a lifetime, demonstrating to the entire family the significance the father placed on the Lord; 2) pray for his son; and 3) prophesy concerning future events. The prophecy included the inheritance and in the case of the Abrahamic line, it included paternity to the direct lineage of the coming Messiah.

Isaac was old and blind the day he summoned Esau. Though he would actually live for decades, he feared he was near death. Little did he know that this long-awaited day of sacred blessing would be tainted with deception that would ironically fulfill God's sovereign will.

Isaac's wife instigated the deception. Rebekah sent Jacob into Isaac's bedchamber to claim the favored blessing. Through lies and trickery, Jacob impersonated Esau. Isaac bestowed Esau's blessing upon Jacob:

> Therefore may God give you of the dew of heaven, of the fatness of the earth, and plenty of grain and wine. Let peoples serve you, and nations bow down to you. Be master over your brethren, and let your mother's sons bow down to you. Cursed be everyone who curses you, and blessed be those who bless you!
>
> —Gen. 27:28-29

When Esau returned from hunting, he discovered the deception, wept, and begged his father to give him a blessing, too. Custom forbade Isaac to rescind the first blessing. Isaac had made a solemn promise before Jacob *and* before God. The only remaining option was for Isaac to give Esau a secondary blessing that must have seemed more like a curse than a blessing to Esau:

> Behold, your dwelling shall be of the fatness of the earth, and of the dew of heaven from above. By your sword you shall live, and you shall serve your brother; and it shall come to pass, when you become restless; that you shall break his yoke from your neck.
>
> —Gen. 27:39-40

Esau despised the blessing and vowed to kill Jacob. Despite the heartbreak Isaac must have felt for Esau, he summoned Jacob back to his bedside and blessed him a second time, restating the blessing in full knowledge and understanding. This was perhaps Isaac's finest hour—the pinnacle of his faith.

What gave him the strength to do it? How could he comply with the plans of a son who would deceive, a son with murder in his heart, and a wife who lied? Were *these* the seed of Abraham? Were *these* the seeds from which all the nations of the earth would be blessed?

Possibly God's message to Isaac's wife at the birth of his children—that "the older shall serve the younger" (Gen. 25:23)—raced to the forefront of his mind on this day. But more importantly, Isaac had learned to believe more in God's promise than in the bearers of the promise. Because of the sin in his own life, he knew humans are fallible, that they pass through seasons of sin, that even the best of them are sometimes sifted as wheat (see Luke 22:31). He trusted God above the circumstances.

This day, Isaac, the peacemaker, sacrificed his personal desires in order to pursue the big picture—God's plan for the entire nation of Israel. A century after the sacrifice on Moriah, his father's decision to choose God foremost made perfect sense, even to the point of "sacrificing" a son.

Blind Isaac looked to the future. He peered across generations with long-range vision. He saw the fulfillment of God's promise "afar off" and was "assured" of it and "embraced" it, sacrificing his desires for "things to come" (Heb. 11:13, 20).

God's Blessings Upon Isaac

Isaac lived the final decades of his life blind. Yet God granted him previews of His divine plan. Isaac would see God's wisdom in the choice of Jacob to continue the line to God's promised seed.

By now, Esau had manifested recklessness regarding spiritual matters, including marrying two pagan Hittite women who were a "grief of mind to Isaac and Rebekah" (Gen. 26:35). After Isaac's "deathbed" blessings, Jacob wisely departed to Paddan-aram to escape Esau's wrath and to obey his father's entreaty to avoid pagan women (unlike Esau had done). Out of a misplaced effort to please his father, Esau took a third wife, a daughter of the same Ishmael who had been evicted from Abraham's home. He consistently chose temporal solutions to his problems.

After Jacob left home, God appeared to him one night in a dream and bestowed upon him the Abrahamic promise of offspring and land. Jacob's walk with God began in earnest this night. Jacob said: "Surely the Lord is in this place; and I did not know it" (Gen. 28:16). Jacob would encounter God again and again, and Isaac would live long enough to hear about it.

Isaac would also live long enough to hear about the reconciliation of Esau and Jacob (see Gen. 33). He would know about the births of his many grandchildren.

Isaac died at age 180, "old and full of days" (Gen. 35:29). Jacob and Esau buried him.

A Final Word

Scripture records a quiet moment in Isaac's life that is particularly characteristic of his faith. When he was about forty years old, his father's servant brought Isaac's intended bride to him on camelback. Unaware of her approach, "Isaac went out to meditate in the field in the evening; and he lifted his eyes and looked, and there, the camels were coming" (Gen. 24:63).

Of all the preparations and pursuits Isaac could have been engaged in while he awaited his bride, he was praying in a field. Dull and boring as he may have seemed, Isaac understood the potent importance of the quiet virtues—reflection, patience, and prayer.

As a peacemaker, Isaac preferred to avoid trouble rather than to stir it. His greatness does not lie in the fact that he performed colorful acts of heroism. He tended livestock. He dug wells. Basically, only two monumental historic events occurred in his long life—his trip to Mt. Moriah as a boy and his family's deception at his bedside. Both events were thrust upon him.

Isaac is characteristic of the unsung heroes and heroines in our lives. More often than not, it is not the big acts of splitting the sea or killing the giant that influence us in our walk of faith. It is the "being there," the quiet dependability of a faithful servant through thick and thin, that strengthens our faith without us ever marking the moment on a calendar. It is the memory of the unassuming, steadfast faith of the deceased that makes us weep at graves, when the curtain opens on a loved one's lifetime and we begin to realize how much our loved one split the sea for us.

The familiar phrase, "the God of Abraham, the God of Isaac, and the God of Jacob" appears numerous times throughout Scripture. Without Isaac, there would be no chain. He was a solid link in the Messianic chain from Abraham to Jesus.

In our world today, there are vastly more Isaacs than there are Davids and Moseses. I am thankful that God breathes Isaac's name in the same breath as Abraham's and Jacob's. Our God is a lover of the lowly and the majestic, for our God, in the flesh, was both.

APPLIED FAITH

1. Write about a spiritual milestone in your life. Consider printing and binding your story at a local copy shop for your family as a lasting memorial of God's blessings in your life.

2. Display a picture of a spiritually influential individual from your past in a prominent place inside your home to remind you of God's Isaacs in your life.

3. If you have children, bless them by recommending God to them and praying for them in their presence.

4. If you do not have children (or even if you do), select an unrelated child in your church and pray for and encourage that child.

5. Pray in a field or in another outdoor location of solitude.

CHAPTER 7

JACOB: SEEKING GOD THROUGH BROKEN RELATIONSHIPS

By faith Jacob, when he was dying, blessed each of the sons of
Joseph, and worshipped, leaning on the top of his staff.

—Heb. 11:21

READING: GENESIS 25, 27-33, 35, 37, 46-49

DOWN THROUGH THE corridors of Old and New Testament Christianity, Jacob is regarded as one of the greatest patriarchs of the faith. His name is mentioned repeatedly throughout the Bible in the "starting lineup" of the founding heroes—Abraham, Isaac, and Jacob.

But Jacob's life was plagued with broken relationships. His brother, Esau, vowed to kill him. His father-in-law, Laban, tricked him out of his bride. His wives bickered over him. His favorite son, Joseph, was abducted by jealous siblings who sold him into slavery. For decades, Jacob believed that Joseph had been killed by a wild animal.

Most of Jacob's tragedies stemmed from his own selfish choices. He stole Esau's birthright and blessing. He retaliated against Laban's deceptions with schemes of his own. He played favorites with his wives and his sons.

Jacob's given name means "deceitful." In modern day terms, he played the role of an unscrupulous Wall Street executive who waits for an opportunity to make a killing on the market, no matter who gets hurt in the process. It wouldn't be too far off base to label Jacob as a "con man."

Yet this con man became a hero of the faith. During the course of his long line of broken relationships, God changed his life so radically that He renamed him "Israel," or "prince of God." As he lay dying, Jacob blessed his children and grandchildren, and he worshipped God.

How did Jacob change from a con man to a hero of the faith who not only worshipped God, but who imparted blessings? Did he ever repair the broken relationships in his life? If so, how?

Today, how can we repair the broken relationships in our lives? And how can we find the strength to impart blessings upon others while vital relationships in our lives remain shattered?

The Shattering Day

Young men often leave home for a bright future, but Jacob left home running for his life. On an otherwise ordinary day, Jacob ended up committing an offense against his brother that in today's world could result in a lawsuit.

Trouble had been brewing in the home of Isaac and Rebekah for years. As a twin born last, Jacob missed the firstborn status by the space of a heel. According to custom, the birthright and a double portion of the blessing would go to the firstborn twin, Esau. Jacob's near loss was like an Olympic runner who misses the gold medal and all its trappings by a tenth of a second.

But despite the natural order of birth, Jacob's mother and father disagreed about the future of their sons. Rebekah favored Jacob, and Isaac favored Esau. In Rebekah's opinion, God fully intended a usurpation of power. As the boys struggled in her womb, an angel told Rebekah that "the older shall serve the younger" (Gen. 25:23). Rebekah, therefore, honored God's sovereignty in her desire to see Jacob prevail, though she also simultaneously enacted the dishonest workings of her own will—probably for selfish motives—to bring about God's intended usurpation.

One day, Jacob gained ground. Esau came in from the field, famished. Jacob convinced Esau to accept a pot of stew in exchange for Esau's birthright. The swap was made, though Scripture doesn't indicate whether the boys ever told anyone.

The birthright was not the coveted "gold medal," but it was a first step. It was similar to today's parent/child dedication ceremony, in which the parents promise to bring up their children in the nurture and admonition of the Lord. The "gold medal" would come later in the form of the blessing, which would include the inheritance of material possessions, predictions concerning the child's future, and the father's spiritual blessing upon the new family leader. In the Abrahamic line, it carried the additional benefit of a position in the direct lineage of the Messiah.

The swapped birthright set the stage for the overthrow. It came on a day when Isaac, old and blind, felt it prudent to complete his paternal responsibilities prior to his death, though he would actually continue living for decades to the age of 180.

Isaac called Esau to his side and asked him to fetch fresh venison for a celebratory meal to accompany the blessing. While Esau obediently went out hunting, Rebekah sprang to action. She coached Jacob, something like this:

"Hurry! Go fetch two young goats from our own flock so you can present them to your father for the blessing."

"But Father will know it's me," Jacob protested. "I'm smooth and Esau is hairy. He will curse me instead of bless me."

"Let me worry about that. Now go!"

When Jacob returned, Rebekah cooked the meat, disguised Jacob in Esau's clothing, and covered his hands and neck with the hairy skins of the young goats Jacob had killed.

In his bedchamber, blind Isaac called out. "Who comes here?"

"It's Esau, your firstborn," Jacob lied.

"How did you kill your game so quickly?"

"Oh, well, um… because God brought it to me."

"Come closer, son." Isaac caught his hands. "The voice sounds like Jacob's, but the hands feel like Esau's. Are you really Esau?"

"I am, Father."

Satisfied, Isaac ate and drank, then said, "Come kiss me." When Jacob kissed him, Isaac said, "Ah yes, your clothes smell like the field of Esau." And then he blessed him with the all-important blessing:

> Therefore may God give you of the dew of heaven, of the fatness of the earth, and plenty of grain and wine. Let peoples serve you, and nations bow down to you. Be master over your brethren, and let your mother's sons bow down to you. Cursed be everyone who curses you, and blessed be those who bless you!
> —Gen. 27:28-29

The deed was done. Jacob walked away with it all, including Esau's position in the direct lineage of Jesus Christ.

Jacob's deception, instigated by his mother, waxed larger than he had perhaps intended. In the space of an hour, sin fell like dominoes, sin upon sin. Lies. Impersonation. A traitor's kiss.

The consequences landed hard and fast upon Jacob. Esau vowed to murder him. Isaac insisted that Jacob depart for Haran. Suitcases had to be packed in a hurry. The heir of the Abrahamic promise, Isaac insisted, must not choose a wife from the nearby Canaanite women. No, the heir must travel to Haran to marry a daughter of Rebekah's brother, Laban. Jacob's mother took the more practical approach. "Go, or Esau will kill you!" She promised to send for him when Esau's anger cooled.

Jacob would not return for twenty years. Everything he took with him that day was stolen. Figuratively, his pockets were filled with silver and gold and Abraham's deeds to the Promised Land. He'd inherited a fortune, but he'd shattered his life. Like a prisoner fresh out of jail, he faced a whole new world alone.

Would God honor a man who had stolen a spiritual inheritance? Would God pass down the promise to a liar?

Four Steps for Mending Broken Relationships

How did Jacob overcome the sin that marred his life? How did he mend his broken relationships, even to the point of bestowing blessings?

Today, how do we overcome our own mistakes when the consequences have already settled in and taken root? Is it possible to repair hopeless rifts in relationships? Following are some steps we can take:

1. Learn from your mistakes.

Personally, I wouldn't hand over any important responsibilities to a thief like Jacob. A man who tells lies cannot be trusted. Yet God graciously appeared to Jacob during his fugitive flight and handed him a windfall of opportunity.

One night, as Jacob laid his head on a stone pillow, God appeared to him in a dream. Angels ascended and descended a ladder to heaven. God stood above the ladder and gave Jacob the promise he had given Abraham so many years before:

> I am the LORD God of Abraham your father and the God of Isaac; the land on which you lie I will give to you and your descendants. Also your descendants shall be as the dust of the earth; you shall spread abroad to the west and the east, to the north and the south; and in you and in your seed all the families of the earth shall be blessed. Behold, I am with you and will keep you wherever you go, and will bring you back to this land; for I will not leave you until I have done what I have spoken to you.
>
> —Gen. 28:13-15

Jacob was shocked! It wasn't as if he had been seeking God. "Surely the LORD is in this place; and I did not know it," he said (Gen. 28:16).

But he responded well. He set up his stone pillow as a pillar, anointed it with oil, and called the place *Bethel* (or "the House of God"). He made a vow: "If God will be with me, and keep me in this way that I am going, and give me bread to eat and clothing to put on, so that I come back to my father's house in peace, then the LORD shall be my God" (Gen. 28:20-21).

The key that day was not Jacob's worthiness, but rather, God's sovereignty. God chose to pursue imperfect Jacob. Jacob did nothing to deserve it. Possibly for the first time in Jacob's life, God caught his attention.

It was the commencement of a new and long journey for Jacob, both literally and figuratively. He would spend the next twenty years blundering forward.

Middle Ground. In my years of pastoral counseling, I have become well acquainted with the type of "middle ground" Jacob inhabited during these formative years. It's the land between blatant sin and wholehearted worship, where many Christians live. It's a land of excuses, of righteous manipulation, of playing "human chess" in a socially acceptable way. It's a safe place for those who have experienced the hand of God in their lives, but are not yet wholly committed. It's a land of small spiritual steps that don't cost too much. It's a time of moving forward while holding back.

Nonetheless, in this adolescent stage of his spiritual walk, Jacob learned several important lessons:

- **You reap what you sow.** Soon after he ran from home, Jacob met his wife-to-be, Rachel, the daughter of his Uncle Laban. For seven years, he labored for Laban to earn the right to marry her, but on the wedding night he found Rachel's older sister, Leah, in his bed. Shocked, he confronted his uncle. Laban explained that he preferred that his firstborn, Leah, marry first. If Jacob wanted Rachel, too, he'd have to work another seven years.

  Laban cheated Jacob out of the most important treasure in his life—Rachel. It was the same brand of deception and sibling-switch Jacob had practiced on Esau. The deceiver had been deceived.

- **The important things in life are worth working for (rather than stealing).** Perhaps one of the most endearing things ever said about Jacob are these words from Genesis 29:20: "So Jacob served seven years for Rachel; and they seemed only a few days to him because of the love he had for her." Jacob ended up serving Laban for fourteen years so he could marry his first love, Rachel. He learned to struggle for what was important to him.

    During the twenty-year period Jacob worked for his uncle, his children were born. Though he loved Rachel with a legendary love, Jacob was certainly no paragon of virtue, even considering the traditions of the times when the priority of descendents overshadowed God's intended purpose of monogamy. Jacob fathered six sons and one daughter by Leah, two sons by Rachel, two sons by Rachel's maid when Rachel was barren, and two sons by Leah's maid when Leah was barren.

    Jacob played favorites with his wives and his children, just as his parents had played favorites with him and Esau. Jacob's children would eventually detest the young sibling, Joseph, because he was their father's clear favorite, firstborn of Rachel. Jacob did not love his first wife, Leah, despite her continued efforts to win his affections, year after year (see Gen. 29:31). He made no attempt to hide his preference for Rachel. Consequently, Leah and Rachel quarreled over their husband's affections. God responded by temporarily closing Rachel's womb, granting children to Jacob through Leah. It would be Leah's son, Judah, who would become the heir of the Abrahamic promise.

- **Selfish manipulations do not produce long-term happiness.** As a clever and resourceful manager, Jacob increased Laban's livestock to a "great amount" (Gen. 30:30). But after his son, Joseph, was born, he decided it was time to return home. Long ago, God had promised to bring him back home again, and Jacob had vowed to return.

But Laban convinced him to tarry, offering him a larger share of the livestock. Jacob tarried, and Laban cheated him. Jacob retaliated by manipulating the breeding. He was so successful that Laban's "countenance" soured towards him (Gen. 31:2). Laban's sons turned envious and bitter. Though wealthy in material goods, Jacob was weary. He wanted out. There was no true peace or happiness here.

One night, an angel spoke to him in a dream and ordered him to return home. It was the push he needed. He gathered his large family and his flocks, and he left Laban without saying good-bye. His wife, Rachel, complicated matters by stealing her father's images of gods, which Bible scholars think were icons made of precious metals.

When Laban caught up with them, an ugly encounter ensued. Like a storm cloud that builds silently for a prolonged period, it fueled the sort of awkward blowup that all relatives and friends dread. Both men voiced legitimate grievances. Laban finally agreed to release his daughters after securing a promise from Jacob that he would not harm them or marry more wives. When they parted, Laban kissed his daughters and grandchildren, but there is no mention of even a handshake between the two men who had met twenty years earlier with embraces and kisses.

The lessons Jacob learned during his years in Haran were practical, moral lessons. They were common-sense steps for success that even nonbelievers would find profitable. But Jacob's hands were still dirty, and his relationship with God was shallow. Scripture does not mention a broken spirit or any effort to seek forgiveness from anyone he'd hurt. Figuratively, his pockets were still crammed with Esau's stolen inheritance.

Fresh out of the school of manipulations, Jacob left the protective umbrella of his Uncle Laban. Jacob went home.

2. Humble yourself with a "prodigal son's" heart.

Jacob's road home led straight through Esau's territory. It was an ominous road, much like the famous yellow-brick road in the popular film, *The Wizard of Oz*. It's not hard to imagine Jacob tiptoeing, reciting: *Lions and tigers and bears, oh my, lions and tigers and bears.*[6] Did Esau still want to kill him? Was it a big mistake to come home?

Scripture says that as "Jacob went on his way" that "the angels of God met him" (Gen. 32:1). The vision lent him the shot of courage he needed. Once again, God led a man who did not necessarily deserve to be led. Jacob proceeded carefully, sending messengers to advise Esau of his presence. They returned with startling news. Esau was coming to meet Jacob—with four hundred men.

On this night, Jacob stood at a crossroads of monumental significance. He could retreat to a comfortable life of more games with Uncle Laban, or he could move forward as God had directed him, headlong into danger. His old sin lay on the pathway between him and Esau like a giant, felled, rotting tree. In twenty years, it hadn't washed away.

In the darkness of night, alone, he called out to God with a desperate prayer:

> I am not worthy of the least of all the mercies and of all the truth which You have shown Your servant... Deliver me, I pray, from the hand of my brother, from the hand of Esau; for I fear him, lest he come and attack me and the mother with the children. For You said, "I will surely treat you well, and make your descendants as the sand of the sea, which cannot be numbered for multitude."
>
> —Gen. 32:10-12

Jacob, the con man, humbled himself. He was weary of the old games. The "old Jacob" would've attempted to outmaneuver or outwit Esau. But this time, Jacob's tone rings similar to the words of the New Testament prodigal son: "I will arise and go to my father, and will say to him, 'Father, I have sinned against heaven and before you, and I am no longer worthy to be called your son. Make me like one of your hired servants'" (Luke 15:18-19).

And then, Jacob went a step further. He prepared a peace offering of several hundred head of livestock and sent them ahead with his servants to Esau as a gift. With his gift having gone out before him, he moved his wives and children to a position of safety. And he waited for the encounter.

3. Actively seek encounters with God.

But before he could meet Esau, another encounter occurred that night—one of the most unique and bold encounters in history. Genesis 32 describes it:

> And Jacob was left alone. And a man wrestled with him until the breaking of the day. When the man saw that he did not prevail against Jacob, he touched his hip socket, and Jacob's hip was put out of joint as he wrestled with him. Then he said, "Let me go, for the day has broken." But Jacob said, "I will not let you go unless you bless me." And he said to him, "What is your name?" And he said, "Jacob." Then he said, "Your name shall no longer be called Jacob, but Israel, for you have striven with God and with men, and have prevailed." Then Jacob asked him, "Please tell me your name." But he said, "Why is it that you ask my name?" And there he blessed him. So Jacob called the name of the place Peniel, saying, "For I have seen God face to face, and yet my life has been delivered."
>
> —Gen. 32:24-30, ESV

This night, Jacob wrestled with what many Bible scholars believe was the pre-incarnate Christ. Hosea, chapter 12, refers to Jacob's opponent as an angel. Commentator Matthew Henry writes: "The angel he wrestled with is called *God*, and therefore is supposed to be the *Son of God*, the angel of the covenant."[7] Jacob identifies his opponent in Genesis 32:30: "I have seen God face to face."

Jacob knew that he needed something he could get *only* from God. He was no stranger to hand-to-hand combat, having wrestled

Esau in his mother's womb. God, in a sense, graciously met Jacob on Jacob's own turf with Jacob's own choice of weapon.

But when Jacob wrestled on this night, his attitude was different than it had been in the past. It was as if he was saying, "This time I'm going to get the blessing from God instead of wrestling it from my brother. This time I'm going to get it from the right place."

God's personal blessing was the missing puzzle piece in Jacob's spiritual growth. It was the antidote to the sin that had plagued him all his life. It was much like our own need for salvation today. The blessing he'd stolen from Esau was polluted by sin. Even though it was not without power, it was a counterfeit that did not satisfy. He needed the blessing anew straight from God, unpolluted and pure. He needed to know that in spite of his sin, God loved him enough to give him the blessing, God-to-man, face-to-face. When his opponent released it to him, he held an authentic blessing in his hands. It was truly *his* now to keep or to give away.

Jacob's battle is epic, yet personal. It is the mini-story of every seeking Christian. When you choose to reach out and grab a bigger piece of God, you take a risk. If you lack the perseverance to hold on, you run the risk that He'll slip through your fingers and disappear as if He never existed at all. If you hold on half-heartedly, you might be crushed by the struggle. Either way, you end up throwing the substandard faith you already possess into the pot. Potentially, you might lose it all. Desperation, as Jacob possessed that night, is a valuable accessory.

As Jacob fought, God fought against him. Or so it seemed. With a single touch, God dislocated Jacob's thigh. Yet Jacob wanted a piece of God so badly that he continued to fight in spite of his injury. Even when the angel said *Let go!* Jacob persevered. As with the woman in the New Testament who persisted in her entreaties for help even after Jesus insinuated that she was a dog (see Matt. 15:22-28), God seemed to be saying to Jacob, "Do you really, really want Me? If you want Me, it's going to hurt."

When we decide to seriously seek God, we must be willing not only to weather earthly obstacles and our own besetting sins, but we must be willing to endure the challenges of God Almighty

Himself. Inevitably, Jesus will ask us in the heat of battle, "Do you love Me?" again and again and again, just as He interrogated the apostle Peter, until we feel quite insulted. It will seem as if He is pushing us away at the same time He is gathering us in.

Faith does not come cheap. Yet, despite the cost, I believe God fixes the fight. Jacob could never have held his own against the Creator of the universe all night long. I imagine that as Jesus wrestled with Jacob, He was also shouting to him, *Hang on, hang on, I'm going to bless you!*

Scripture says Jacob "struggled with the Angel and prevailed; he wept, and sought favor from Him" (Hos. 12:4). By the end of the long night, God blessed him. He also gave him a new name. Jacob was now "Israel." The deceiver was now a "prince of God."

Later, after Jacob purchased land and built a house, God blessed him a second time, just as Jacob's father had confirmed the blessing upon Jacob a second time. God appeared to him, re-dubbed him "Israel," and reaffirmed the Abrahamic promise of offspring and lands. After God "went up from him in the place where He talked with him," Jacob set up a pillar of stone and poured oil over it as a memorial (Gen. 35:13).

4. Wait.

When Jacob awoke the next day to face Esau and his troop of 400 men, he was a new man with a new heart and a new name. As he led the way, with his wives and children behind him, he "bowed himself to the ground seven times, until he came near to his brother" (Gen. 33:3). It was an outrageous risk. As far as Jacob knew, Esau was preparing to slaughter him.

But instead, Esau "ran to meet him, and embraced him, and fell on his neck and kissed him, and they wept" (Gen. 33:4). Jacob was so moved that he told Esau, "'I have seen your face as though I had seen the face of God, marveling that you were pleased with me'" (Gen. 33:10). Jacob must have felt that God was pleased with him, too, on that day of reconciliation with his estranged twin brother.

One of the most interesting things about Jacob's restored relationship with Esau is that Jacob had very little to do with it.

God softened Esau's heart behind the scenes. The Bible doesn't tell us when or how. But somehow, a man with murder on his mind became a gracious host, eager to forgive. Their relationship was not only repaired, but also improved, because from the womb the brothers had never gotten along. Scripture is silent about their relationship after their reconciliation except to mention that they would later bury their father, Isaac, together, after which Esau and his family would move away to Seir because the land could not support the livestock of both brothers.

Jacob's story does not end here. As his sons grew to manhood, he would suffer anguish from yet another severed relationship. One day, Jacob's favorite son, Joseph, failed to return from the fields after Jacob had sent him out to check on his brothers. Joseph's jealous brothers had waylaid him and thrown him into a pit, then reconsidered and sold him into slavery to a band of passing Ishmaelites. When the brothers showed Joseph's coat (which they had dipped in goat's blood) to their father, Jacob presumed that his son had been killed by a wild animal. Though all his children endeavored to comfort him, Jacob "refused to be comforted, and he said, 'For I shall go down into the grave to my son in mourning'" (Gen. 37:35). (See the full story in this book's Chapter 8, "Joseph: Seeking God After Rejection.")

But as in the case with Esau, God restored Joseph to Jacob many years later through no effort of Jacob's. It is doubtful that Jacob even prayed for a reunion: he thought Joseph was dead. The reunion came gloriously at God's appointed time in the unraveling of God's will through life's daily circumstances. It was all God's doing.

Even today, God gives us hope for seemingly hopeless reunions, in these ways and more:

- **Restoring our broken relationships on the "earth" side of heaven.** For those of us who are hoping for restoration, it is right to continue hoping. Even when none of our efforts or prayers seem to be making a difference, there is yet hope. Just as with Jacob and Esau, and with Jacob and Joseph, the entire story is not yet written. Whether due to sin or separation or other factors, relationships shift into unplanned hibernations and fluctuations, sometimes through no fault of our own. But God is able to restore, even when years of silence pass in the interim.

In America's capitalistic society, it is normal to think of achieving our goals one step at a time as we climb the ladder to success. But this is not usually God's way. In a single day, without any effort from Jacob's hands, Esau reunited with him. In a single day, without any of Jacob's best-laid plans, Joseph was returned to him. God's whims take precedence over years of the will and work and grief of man. God's grace takes precedence over man's most stellar efforts. When there seems to be no hope, there is yet hope.

- **Coping with relationships that cannot be restored.** But what if your loved one *never* reconciles with you? What if he (or she) dies first? What if you die first?

  What about Jacob's wife, Leah? Scripture indicates that he did not love her, though she longed for his favor. There is no record that he ever reconciled with her. And what about Laban? Did Jacob ever mend fences with him, or was their relationship left in a state of half-repair, crippled by unconfessed injustices? We simply don't know. What about Jacob's father? Jacob visited Isaac before Isaac died, but there's no mention of forgiveness sought or forgiveness granted. From one end of his life to the other, Jacob was encompassed by broken fences.

  It seems amiss for a "hero of the faith" to be lauded amid such spiritual clutter. But even heroes and heroines are not immune to the shattering of relationships. No doubt they would admit, just like us, that nothing is ever ideal about abandoning a relationship. But sometimes, even when we desire to make amends, we run into a "No Trespassing" sign that cannot be crossed. Observing the sign is no crime. Abandoning hope is the crime.

If nothing else, we can cling to this thought: to have loved and lost in this life is not necessarily utter loss. For to have loved someone to the point of experiencing their rock-bottom faults that no one else sees, and then to have forgiven them when no one else sees, is to have known and loved them with a fullness that imitates Christ's love for us. To have loved and forgiven is to have accepted the whole person, which is a marathon most humans abandon.

But what if the subject of our affection resides in heaven? Obviously, in such a case we cannot experience reconciliation on earth's soil. The Old Testament character, Job, lost his first set of children in a windstorm. Though the loss was not Job's fault, he was permanently separated from them on earth. God blessed him with a new family, but no matter how much Job longed to see his deceased children, they were still gone.

Why? Is not God the great restorer? Does He not delight in raising the dead?

Listen to the words of Jesus: "My God, my God, why have You forsaken Me?" (Matt. 27:46). Even Jesus had to die before being reunited with His family. A rift of adopted sin and a gulf of death lay between Him and His Father. But afterwards, after all the suffering had ended, Jesus sat at His Father's right hand.

Ultimately, some restorations will wait until heaven, where we are told that the lion and the lamb will lie down together, and where all is made right. Make no mistake: this is no second-best solution. There will be nothing inferior about this reunion. For we know that our Father breaks out His best robes and rings and fatted calves for reunions. Even today as we wait, I believe He is preparing them.

The Day of Worshipping

Jacob learned to worship God with the rare kind of purity that comes only after having seen a holy God intervene personally in his life. As Jacob bestowed the blessing on the sons of Joseph, he worshipped with an outpouring that was as pure and vital as the thin, lung-piercing air of high mountain altitudes, way above the clogged and tangled considerations in the pews of dormant Christianity. Jacob had sought God and faced Him. Now, more than ever before, he understood that pure worship is nothing more complicated than a response to a personal revelation of God. When authentic, it is as unstoppable as a knee-jerk reaction. It longs to express itself.

The words recorded about Jacob in Hebrews 11 make sense only as a culmination of his experiences. They are undergirded with a caliber of joy that cannot be captured by human language: "By faith Jacob, when he was dying, blessed each of the sons of Joseph, and worshipped, leaning on the top of his staff" (Heb.11:21).

It was no small thing for Jacob to give away the blessing. He had spent his life grasping for it. He wrestled for it in the womb, bargained for it, stole it, and then wrestled God for it. To give it away was the pinnacle of his spiritual journey. The one who stole the blessing became the blesser.

Listen to Jacob's heart spill over with gratitude as he blessed his two grandsons:

> God, before whom my fathers Abraham and Isaac walked, the God who has fed me all my life long to this day, the Angel who has redeemed me from all evil, bless the lads; let my name be named upon them, and the name of my fathers Abraham and Isaac; and let them grow into a multitude in the midst of the earth.
>
> —Gen. 48:15-16

While bestowing the blessing, Jacob switched hands, blessing the youngest first. Scripture seems to breathe an inaudible gasp at this juncture. All of a sudden, we as readers seem taken aback. Was Jacob up to his old tricks again?

But the opposite is true. Probably Jacob had been given prophetic vision concerning the boys. But perhaps Jacob had also learned to cease manipulating, even to the point that he believed

God could circumvent his switched hands. Switching hands was an act of faith that said, "Deception no longer holds dominion over me. I know now that Your providence is stronger than anything good or evil my flawed hands can steal or bless."

With the switching of hands, Jacob took his worship to an unconventional level precisely because he had experienced a holy confrontation with God. Later, Jacob would bless all of his sons, including Judah (Leah's son), who would carry forth the Abrahamic covenant through the lineage of Jesus Christ.

Jacob died at age 147. In accordance with Jacob's request, Joseph took him back to Canaan to be buried next to Abraham, Isaac, and Leah.

A Final Word

Jacob, the former con man, could also accurately be called a liar, a thief, and a polygamist. But God used him anyway. He pursued and confronted Jacob until Jacob responded. Unlike some of the other heroes and heroines of the faith, Jacob never truly sought God until he got a good dose of Him. God sought him first until Jacob wouldn't let go.

If Jacob is responsible in any way for his position in the Hebrews 11 lineup, it is because he became so dissatisfied with his self-serving agenda that he let go of it in order to grasp a dangerous God. Desperate, he refused to let go even when he'd sustained an injury, and even when God seemed to be fighting against him. He struggled past the barrier of common sense, past the brink of human limitations, and he risked everything. He came away with the greatest prize that any fighter could ever win. He saw God face-to-face, he touched Him, and he was touched by Him.

In the midst of Jacob's long journey of faith, God graciously restored two of his most treasured relationships. Jacob experienced joyous reunions that he hadn't even dreamed possible. One day, he embraced a brother who had planned to murder him, and on another day, he embraced a son he presumed was long dead.

Sometimes, as Jacob learned, God fixes the fight, and in His own perfect time and place on a matchless, one-of-a-kind day, He arranges unforeseen encounters that result in reunions that formerly seemed impossible. No executive secretary or international negotiator could arrange such reunions. They come suddenly as a gift from behind a curtain newly opened after a prolonged intermission in God's perfect scenario.

In spite of the broken shards that mar each of our lives, may we learn to grab hold of God in a new and bold way. He will grant us the strength to bless others and to worship Him with a heart that cannot be silenced.

APPLIED FAITH

1. Ask God to meet you in a holy confrontation.

2. Offer a gift of peace to someone with whom you wish to reconcile.

3. Pray anew for reconciliation of a relationship you have previously discarded as hopeless.

. . . .

CHAPTER 8

JOSEPH: SEEKING GOD
AFTER REJECTION

By faith Joseph, when he was dying, made mention of the departure of the children of Israel, and gave instructions concerning
his bones.

—Heb. 11:22

READING: GENESIS 30, 37, 39-50

THE STORY OF Joseph is one of the most well-known and best-loved stories in the Bible. His life is the epitome of the frequently quoted verse: "And we know that all things work together for good to those who love God, to those who are called according to His purpose" (Rom. 8:28).

But Joseph paid a high price for his faith. In stark contrast to the life of his father Jacob, Joseph's hardships did not stem from his sins, but from his obedience. Though he sported a youthful arrogance that provoked his brothers, he honored God consistently, even when it cost him dearly to do so. His name, appropriately given, means "May God increase."

The crux of Joseph's ministry was centered around his God-given gift. God empowered him to interpret his own dreams and the dreams of others. But Joseph's father rebuked him for his interpretations. Joseph's half-brothers were so jealous of him that they sold him into slavery. To say that his talents were not appreciated is an understatement. Joseph not only suffered rejection from his family, but he was cast out for exercising the very ministry with which God had gifted him.

Unlike his patriarchal forefathers—Jacob, Isaac, and Abraham—Joseph never saw or heard God, at least as far as the Bible reveals to us. How, then, did he find the strength to hold onto such a troublesome gift when it cost him so much to use it? How did a man who had been rejected by his own family open his arms to deliver them from famine a decade later? And what does Joseph's request regarding his bones have to do with heroism?

Today, how do we continue to seek God when we've been rejected by someone whose Christianity we once admired? How do we continue serving Him when the talents He gave us are criticized or snubbed? How do we survive the sting, especially when it comes from Christians?

The Day of Rejection

If there's anyone who might have rebelled against God, it was Joseph. Members of his own family, integral links in the Messianic line, threw him into a pit, and then sold him into slavery for no good reason.

It happened on a day when Joseph honored his father's request to travel to Shechem to check on his brothers as they tended the family's livestock. At age seventeen, he was the next-to-the-youngest of twelve sons, all half-brothers except for his younger full brother, Benjamin. Scripture indicates that on a previous occasion, Joseph had brought his father a bad report about his older brothers. He was his father's unofficial "private eye," and his older brothers no doubt saw him as a goody-two-shoes who was too big for his britches.

Not only was Joseph his father's obvious favorite, but God's gift to Joseph set him another peg above his brothers. His prophetic gift to interpret dreams was invaluable in its warnings to prevent calamity, but it intimidated those who did not appreciate its forecasts.

Not long before Joseph's brothers threw him into a pit, Joseph announced the details of a recent dream to his family. In his dream, each of his brothers was represented by a sheaf of wheat, but Joseph's sheaf stood upright, while his brothers' sheaves bowed in submission to him. His dream was not appreciated in the least. Perhaps it was youthful exuberance, but Joseph seemed tactless when it came to relating to his brothers. He soon shared another dream with them. This time, the sun, moon, and eleven stars bowed to him.

His father rebuked him: "What is this dream that you have dreamed? Shall your mother and I and your brothers indeed come to bow down to the earth before you?" (Gen: 37:10). Joseph's brothers "hated him" and "envied him" (Gen. 37:8, 11).

When his brothers saw Joseph approaching to snoop on them, they jumped at the chance to ambush him. "Look, this dreamer is coming!" they said (Gen. 37:19).

They seized him, stripped off a special multicolored coat his father had made for him, threw him into a dry pit, and then sat together around a picnic meal to discuss his fate. Scripture says he "pleaded with" his brothers in the "anguish of his soul," but they "would not hear" (Gen. 42:21). One of the brothers, Reuben, convinced the others to spare his life. After much discussion, they hauled him out of the pit and sold him to a company of passing Ishmaelites for twenty pieces of silver. Later, they dipped Joseph's coat in goat's blood to trick their father into thinking he'd been devoured by wild animals.

In a single day, Joseph's charmed life came crashing down. Could it have been a joke? Were his brothers trying to teach him a lesson? But as mile after dusty mile passed by, and no one came to fetch him from the Ishmaelite camel caravan, the reality of betrayal descended upon him. Strangers took him far away, to another country. With every mile, his home and family faded into the distance.

Is there any worse abasement than being cast out, of realizing you are unwanted by those you thought loved you most? Joseph's very own family, anointed by God in its heritage, had done the severing—not heathens or strangers, but people he had trusted. Possibly, the thought even occurred to him that his father had set it up from the beginning. After all, Jacob had once used an elaborate deception to steal his brother, Esau's, blessing, hadn't he?

Joseph unexpectedly found himself trashed by the people he loved the most. As a boy of seventeen, he could have easily cried out, "Why would I want your God when you treat me this way?" He could have cast off his faith and joined a band of rebels. In today's world, he would seem an ideal candidate for a gang member.

Five Steps to Overcome Rejection

What kept Joseph from turning against God? How did he overcome his disappointment to the point of walking forward to become a hero of the faith?

How do we climb out of our own pits of rejection? How do we continue to actively seek God when the weight of undeserved oppression threatens to drown our once-eager soul?

1. Continue moving forward on your God-given pathway.

The Ishmaelites sold Joseph to Potiphar, an officer of the Egyptian pharaoh. If there's any question that God sustained Joseph in his brokenness, one look at his new situation should dash all doubts. Who would expect this account about a man who had just been sold into slavery?

> Now Joseph had been taken down to Egypt. And Potiphar, an officer of Pharaoh, captain of the guard, an Egyptian, bought him from the Ishmaelites who had taken him down there. The LORD was with Joseph, and he was a successful man; and he was in the house of his master the Egyptian. And his master saw that the LORD was with him and that the LORD made all he did to prosper in his hand. So Joseph found favor in his sight, and served him. Then he made him overseer of his house, and all that he had he put under his authority. So it was, from the time that he had made him overseer of his house and all that he had, that the LORD blessed the Egyptian's house for Joseph's sake; and the

blessing of the LORD was on all that he had in the house and in the field. Thus he left all that he had in Joseph's hand, and he did not know what he had except for the bread which he ate. Now Joseph was handsome in form and appearance.

—Gen. 39:1-6

God blessed Joseph in an unlikely place. Even Joseph's master "saw that the LORD was with him." Joseph must have sensed it, too, for it flowed forth from his obedience and the initiative of his hands. As Potiphar's overseer, Joseph became a productive manager who not only sustained the estate, but also prospered it.

Though the pain of his family's rejection must have weighed like a millstone on his heart, Joseph moved forward in the place God set him. If he had immobilized himself into a quagmire of self-pity, he would have never been in a position to save his family years later.

Today, many Christians carry unseen millstones, yet even so, we must continue moving forward despite our attachments to the past. Our greatest example, Jesus, always moved forward during the years of His ministry. He never fixated in a benumbing way on family or friends beyond the period God loaned them to Him. Surrendering them was part of the journey, even to the point of seeming harsh. Who can forget His remark to His worried parents after they found their missing Son conversing with teachers in the Temple: "Did you not know that I must be about My Father's business?" (Luke 2:49).

Like Jesus, we must shift our attention to the tasks on the pathway in front of us and upon the souls on the road nearest us. Would we begrudge those who are ahead of us because we are dwelling on those behind us?

The admonition of Hebrews 12 might well have been written with Joseph in mind:

Let us lay aside every weight, and the sin which so easily ensnares us, and let us run with endurance the race that is set before us, looking unto Jesus, the author and finisher of our faith, who for the joy that was set before Him endured the cross, despising the shame, and has sat down at the right hand of the throne of God. For consider Him who endured such hostility from sinners against Himself, lest you become weary and discouraged in your souls....Therefore strengthen the hands which hang down, and the feeble knees, and make straight paths for your feet, so that which is lame may not be dislocated, but rather be healed.

—Heb. 12:1-3, 12-13

At Potiphar's house, life seemed on the upswing for Joseph—that is, until Potiphar's wife eyed him, and his world came crashing down again. When she tempted him, he resisted. He explained his gratitude for the position God had given him in her husband's household and said to her, "How then can I do this great wickedness, and sin against God?" (Gen. 39:9). But she persisted, and when he continued to evade her, she outmaneuvered him by stealing one of his garments and lying to her husband. Potiphar took her word as truth and cast Joseph into the king's prison. In the space of a day, Joseph lost everything his faith and good will had gained. He found himself behind bars, shamed as an adulterer. He must have wondered, "Why, God, why? I was obeying You. What are You doing?"

2. Continue using your God-given gifts.

But God sustained Joseph again. Who would expect this account about a man who had just been imprisoned?

But the LORD was with Joseph and showed him mercy, and He gave him favor in the sight of the keeper of the prison. And the keeper of the prison committed to Joseph's hand all the prisoners who were in the prison; whatever they did there, it was his doing. The keeper of the prison did not look into anything that was under Joseph's authority, because the LORD was with him; and whatever he did, the LORD made it prosper.

—Gen. 39:21-23

God not only prospered Joseph in prison, but He brought Joseph another opportunity. Into his charge, the captain of the guard placed two out-of-favor newcomers—the butler and the baker of the pharaoh of Egypt. Both promptly experienced dreams, and both came to Joseph for interpretations of their dreams.

The butler, Joseph predicted, would be restored to the pharaoh's service. The baker would be hanged. As Joseph interpreted their dreams, in a weak moment of opportunism, he entreated the butler: "But remember me when it is well with you, and please show kindness to me; make mention of me to Pharaoh, and get me out of this house. For indeed I was stolen away from the land of the Hebrews; and also I have done nothing here that they should put me into the dungeon" (Gen. 40:14-15).

Within three days, the interpretation of both dreams proved true. "Yet the chief butler did not remember Joseph, but forgot him" (Gen. 40:23).

For two years, the butler forgot him. What must Joseph have thought? How did Joseph survive for two more years in prison without giving up his faith?

I believe that Joseph "saw" God through his gift of interpretation. Whenever God gave Joseph a new opportunity, Joseph experienced God working through him. This seems evident in a statement he made before interpreting the butler's and baker's dreams: "Do not interpretations belong to God?" (Gen. 40:8). Joseph was fully aware that God's power was streaming through him. It was the primary means through which Joseph saw and sought God. Though God did not rescue him, Joseph knew that God counted him worthy of use. And the more it happened, the more Joseph yearned to "see" God again and again. Each "sighting" carried him to the next.

In my own life, I've discovered that I yearn for God's power. I want the power of God streaming through me in order that I might experience His presence more intimately. The danger, however, is that it's a heady business. It's easy to forget that His power is reserved for His own glory—not for my best-laid plans, no matter how God-honoring my motives might be.

His power is an aggressive tool, like a GPS device with a pre-programmed route. If I choose to hang on, it will inevitably pull me through the mire before it will ever take me up the mountain.

In fact, as the author of Hebrews points out, it may never take me to a mountaintop at all, instead reserving the unveiling of God's promises for others who come after me (see Heb. 11:13, 39-40).

When God gave young Joseph the dream about the sheaves, I doubt Joseph ever imagined God would require him to bow low as a slave and a prisoner before he would ever see his brothers bow. God's gift to Joseph sent him on a pathway through bottomlands of humility he never knew existed. The crucial point is that he kept using his gift even when it seemed to get him nowhere.

3. **Realize that your walk of faith is not primarily about you or your feelings.**

The next sentence in Scripture about Joseph's journey is enough to send a shiver of anticipation down the reader's spine: "Then it came to pass, at the end of two full years, that Pharaoh had a dream" (Gen. 41:1). He slept and dreamed a second time.

Pharaoh's dreams vexed him so much that he sought an interpreter. When the magicians of his kingdom failed to provide interpretations, the butler finally remembered Joseph. Pharaoh summoned him from prison. Joseph was handed a change of clothes and a shaver, then given audience before the royal throne.

Pharaoh basically said to Joseph, "I heard you have power to interpret dreams. No one else can understand my dreams. Can you?"

"No, I can't," Joseph replied. "But God can. Tell me your dreams."

Pharaoh recounted two dreams, both dreamt on the same night. In the first dream, seven attractive, plump cows emerged out of the Nile River. Seven ugly, thin cows emerged to devour them. In the second dream, seven plump ears of grain grew on a stalk. Seven thin, blighted ears grew and swallowed the plump ears.

When Pharaoh had finished, Joseph replied, "The dreams of Pharaoh are one" (Gen. 41:25). Listening to Pharaoh's dreams must have wrenched Joseph's soul. His own double-dream of the wheat sheaves and the stars, dreamt thirteen years ago, had never come to pass.

Joseph explained to Pharaoh that the seven plump cows and seven plump ears of grain represented seven years of plenty throughout the land of Egypt. The seven lean cows and seven blighted years represented seven years of famine. For the next seven years, Egypt would experience abundance, followed by seven years of famine. Joseph advised Pharaoh to appoint overseers to store one-fifth of the harvests during the abundant years in preparation for the famine.

Finished with his interpretations, Joseph had no reason to expect anything but a swift return to his prison cell. But once again, God blessed Joseph. Who would expect this account of a prisoner recently summoned from a dungeon?

> And Pharaoh said to his servants, "Can we find such a one as this, a man in whom is the Spirit of God?" Then Pharaoh said to Joseph, "Inasmuch as God has shown you all this, there is no one as discerning and wise as you. You shall be over my house, and all my people shall be ruled according to your word; only in regard to the throne will I be greater than you." And Pharaoh said to Joseph, "See, I have set you over all the land of Egypt." Then Pharaoh took his signet ring off his hand and put it on Joseph's hand; and he clothed him in garments of fine linen and put a gold chain around his neck. And he had him ride in the second chariot which he had; and they cried out before him, "Bow the knee!" So he set him over all the land of Egypt.
>
> —Gen. 41:38-43

All of a sudden, Joseph's years as an overseer in Potiphar's house and in prison came into focus. Within the bonds of slavery and behind the bars of a prison, God had been grooming Joseph to oversee Egypt.

The famine would strike not only Egypt, but worldwide. Joseph's gift of interpreting dreams became the means of deliverance for the entire known world. For seven years, Joseph stored the overabundance of the harvest. When the famine struck, "all countries came to Joseph in Egypt to buy grain; because the famine was severe in all lands" (Gen. 41:57).

What if Joseph had been released from prison two years earlier, as he'd requested? Two years less suffering for this man might have translated into a disaster for the world. Joseph's day-to-day faithfulness in a dungeon became an integral part of God's epic plan.

After his elevation to power, Joseph could have used his power to apprehend and punish his Hebrew family. But instead of dwelling on his losses, he looked forward, and he set his mind on accomplishing God's plan in his life. It was as if he carried this precious promise from the book of Isaiah in his pocket:

> If you take away the yoke from your midst, the pointing of the finger, and speaking wickedness, if you pour yourself out for the hungry and satisfy the desire of the afflicted, then shall your light rise in the darkness and your gloom be as the noonday. And the LORD will guide you continually and satisfy your desire in scorched places.
> —Isa. 58:9-11, ESV

In the midst of Joseph's difficult journey, God comforted him with new blessings. Pharaoh gave Joseph a wife, Asenath, who bore him two children before the famine began. In naming them, Joseph proclaimed God's goodness. His firstborn he called Manasseh—meaning, "causing to forget." I like to imagine him holding his firstborn's tiny hand, saying with joyful tears, "God has *Manassehed* me. God has removed the sting of my family from my memory. He has given me a new life, a new family." His second son he called Ephraim—meaning "double fruit." With Ephraim, he must have said, "God has *Ephraimed* me. He has given me twice as much. He has blessed me with a second son."

Just when we think God does not care about our feelings, He brings along a new, unexpected set of blessings—enough to keep us walking forward no matter how difficult the journey.

4. **When given the opportunity, forgive those who have rejected you.**

Despite his unprecedented rise in Pharaoh's government, Joseph must have continued to wonder about his initial double-dream. It had never been fulfilled like his other dreams, though his interpretation of it had cost him more than any other dream. Not only had it gone unanswered, but its fulfillment seemed more remote than ever. The borders of country and of culture, as well as the schism of betrayal, had separated Joseph from his family. For all he knew, his father and brothers might be dead by now. How could his God-given dream have strayed so far off the mark? Had he done something wrong? Was God punishing him for his pride?

One day, ten men from Canaan walked into his presence, asking to buy grain. It wasn't unusual for Joseph to be approached by groups of travelers asking to buy food. But this time when he looked up, his own brothers (except for young Benjamin) bowed before him. Though they did not recognize him, Joseph recognized them immediately.

A wide range of emotions churned inside him. His brothers had been counting twenty pieces of silver the last time Joseph saw them—slave payment from the Ishmaelites for Joseph. This day, they came unwittingly before a brother with whom they had shared a home and a beloved father, a brother they had betrayed and cast out of their lives and their country. Joseph could have had them executed on the spot.

The question in Joseph's mind this day had nothing to do with the grain. It was not "Should I give my brothers food?" but rather, it was "Do my brothers feel any remorse about what they did to me? Do they care about me? Are they genuine followers of the God of Abraham?" His entire walk of faith hinged on the God of Abraham, perpetuated through the seed of the very family who had rejected him. Until Joseph knew the truth about the state of their souls, he could not reveal his identity to them. His position of power would have compromised the test.

So Joseph zeroed in on Benjamin, the absent brother, his only full brother, the remaining favored son of his father's favored wife, Rachel. Though Scripture does not say, Benjamin was probably not present the day his brothers sold seventeen-year-old Joseph into slavery. Possibly, Benjamin was only a young boy then.

In Joseph's mind, Benjamin became a surrogate of himself. If given the chance, would his brothers sell out Benjamin, too? If so, they would in theory sell Joseph again. Joseph had to know.

He sent his brothers through a gauntlet of tests. First, he demanded to see Benjamin. As collateral, he seized Simeon, one of the half-brothers. The remaining nine brothers traveled back home, not to return for a while. When the family finally ran out of food and convinced Jacob to part with Benjamin, they returned to Egypt and presented Benjamin to Joseph. Moved, but still not convinced, Joseph maneuvered circumstances so that Benjamin was caught red-handed with Joseph's silver cup. The penalty for theft was slavery.

The moment of truth had come. Judah, the brother who would carry the Abrahamic seed through the Messianic line, stepped forward: "Now therefore, please let your servant remain instead of the lad as a slave to my lord," he begged (Gen. 44:33). If not, he said, Jacob "will die" of sorrow (Gen. 44:31). The brothers all "fell before him [Joseph] on the ground" (Gen. 44:14). Joseph's double-dream of the sheaves and stars materialized before his eyes.

In an instant, the years of rejection dissolved. Joseph broke down and wept. Ordering everyone to exit the room except his brothers, he "made himself known to his brothers. And he wept aloud, and the Egyptians and the house of Pharaoh heard it" (Gen. 45:1-2). After much weeping and embracing, the brothers returned to Canaan to tell their astonished father the news and they, along with the entire extended family, came to dwell in Egypt where, after a joyous reunion, Joseph sustained them through the famine.

In a true spirit of grace, Joseph set his remorseful, embarrassed brothers at ease: "Do not therefore be grieved," he said, "or angry with yourselves because you sold me here; for God sent me before you to preserve life." Again, he reaffirmed that spirit: "But as for you, you meant evil against me; but God meant it for good, in order to bring it about as it is this day, to save many people alive" (Gen. 45:5, 50:20).

Joseph was able to forgive his brothers because he witnessed God's eternal purpose in their role. Their rejection had not been everlasting, nor had it signified a permanent turning away of the souls of godly men, but rather it had served as a vehicle for accomplishing God's higher purposes. Had Joseph been gifted with a dream about Jesus, he would have seen that even God, the Father, would take on the role of a rejector in order to redeem the souls of men.

Possibly the most poignant question ever asked in history was Christ's: "My God, My God, why have You forsaken Me?" (Matt. 27:46). It implies the forsaking was done without provocation. For years, Joseph had felt the same brand of forsakenness.

I believe that his tears on the day of reconciliation were not as much due to the fact that he was being reunited with his brothers, but due to the fact that Joseph was "seeing" God again. His double-dream was finally being fulfilled. God was real, God was there, and God was good. His troubled journey was worthwhile, after all.

I would like to suggest that the deepest rift between Joseph and his family was not their rejection of him, but rather God's delay in fulfilling his initial double-dream. Joseph longed to know that God completely loved and accepted him just as surely as he needed to know that his family still loved him. This new unveiling from God about his costly dream was, to him, like an ovation.

5. Identify yourself with God in a tangible way.

When the famine ended, Joseph was still relatively young by the standards of the day—only in his mid-forties. He would live to be 110, spending the latter half of his life in Egypt, settling his family upon land Pharaoh had given them, and revamping the nation's system of land ownership after the famine had shifted all resources to the crown.

Joseph's father, Jacob, died seventeen years after relocating in Egypt, having first blessed each of his twelve sons, as well as Joseph's sons Manasseh and Ephraim. Joseph honored Jacob's request by carrying his remains to Canaan and burying him next to Abraham and Sarah, Isaac and Rebekah, and Jacob's first wife, Leah.

Joseph lived several decades longer—long enough to see his great-grandchildren. Before he died, Joseph requested that his family carry his bones to the Promised Land. "God will surely visit you," he explained, "and bring you out of this land to the land which He swore to Abraham, to Isaac, and to Jacob" (Gen. 50:24).

His family embalmed him temporarily in a coffin in Egypt. Years later, during the Israelite exodus from Egypt, Moses took the bones of Joseph with him to the Promised Land, where they were buried (see Exod. 13:19 and Josh. 24:32). Before his death, in a speech to the Israelites, Moses gave this tribute to Joseph: "Let the blessing come on the head of Joseph, and on the crown of the head of him who was separate from his brothers" (Deut. 33:16).

In an era when one's choice of burial seemed to signify allegiance, Joseph tangibly sealed his allegiance to the Hebrew God with his bones, choosing to be buried in the land of the family who had betrayed him, doing so despite all the anguish they had caused him. He cast his lot with the seekers of the Promised Land rather than with the Egyptians, who had treated him like a prince.

Joseph's request sums up his conclusions about his turbulent life, as if he were saying, "The Hebrew God of my imperfect fathers is my God, and I know He shall lead my family back to the Promised Land, and I shall follow Him even with my decaying bones."

A Final Word

Joseph is honored as a hero of the faith because he consistently chose to follow the God of the people who had rejected him, believing God's invisible manifestations despite all visible evidence to the contrary. Joseph is the epitome of a victim who could have become hard as nails, yet Scripture goes to the trouble to record his tears again and again. He stayed tender when most men would have become bitter.

Without Joseph, there may not have been a Jesus. Joseph's half-brother, Judah, the direct link in the bloodline to Jesus Christ, might have perished in the famine. God chose to use a sidelined offspring to salvage the Abrahamic promise and the coming of the Messiah.

How did Joseph do it? What gave him the strength? I believe the answer lies in an addiction: with each trace of God he collected from his prophetic dreams and their interpretations, his craving for God revived and intensified. From one location to another, he continued seeking God through the use of his gift because he understood that it was God's chosen avenue for him, and thus it was the best place to see God again. Never once did God abandon him. In each new location, God consistently brought Joseph opportunities to use his gift.

Though all heroes and heroines of the faith do not survive to see the results of their sacrificial suffering, Joseph saw spectacular results. Through God's divine arrangement of epic events and personal circumstances, he enjoyed a joyous reunion with his family, and he played the key role in saving his family and an entire nation from a devastating famine.

And it all started with a teenage dream that no one believed...

APPLIED FAITH

1. Reestablish contact with a friend or family member with whom fellowship has been broken.

2. Pray for someone who has spitefully used you, knowing God is able to restore fellowship.

3. Pray for new opportunities to serve God in unlikely places.

4. Serve a meal or send a gift to someone who has hurt you.

5. In a special place, identify yourself with God in a tangible way.

. . . .

CHAPTER 9

MOSES: SEEKING GOD BETWEEN MOUNTAINTOPS

By faith Moses, when he was born, was hidden three months by his parents, because they saw he was a beautiful child; and they were not afraid of the king's command. By faith Moses, when he became of age, refused to be called the son of Pharaoh's daughter, choosing rather to suffer affliction with the people of God than to enjoy the passing pleasures of sin, esteeming the reproach of Christ greater riches than the treasures in Egypt: for he looked to the reward.

By faith he forsook Egypt, not fearing the wrath of the king: for he endured as seeing Him who is invisible. By faith he kept the Passover and the sprinkling of blood, lest he who destroyed the firstborn should touch them. By faith they passed through the Red Sea as by dry land, whereas the Egyptians, attempting to do so, were drowned.

—Heb. 11:23-29

READING: EXODUS 2-5, 11-12, 14, 19-20, 24, 32-34; NUMBERS 20; DEUTERONOMY 4, 31, 34

HAVE YOU EVER known someone who had a spiritual mountaintop experience but then languished because the spotlight moved on? Most of us know someone who flared briefly and brilliantly and then burned out to a cold existence.

They speak of their experience as if it were a one-time fluke. They sit back and sigh as if it could never happen again.

To study Moses is to study a man who enjoyed one spiritual mountaintop after another. To the modern Christian hungry for God's intervention, Moses seems to have been granted more than his share of spiritual opportunities.

Is God unfair? How many spiritual summits should one human be allowed to experience? Moses witnessed the burning bush, he defeated Pharaoh, he parted the Red Sea, he received the Ten Commandments atop Mt. Sinai, and he led the Israelites across the wilderness to the Promised Land.

As mighty as Moses seems, it is remarkable to me to read in Numbers 12:3 (KJV) that Moses "was very meek, above all the men which were upon the face of the earth." And it is equally interesting to realize that his walk with God was far from a stroll down Glory Lane. He spent forty years in exile tending sheep, he weathered more complaints than any leader should have to endure, he suffered betrayal at the hands of his spiritual comrades, and he stumbled so badly that God refused to allow him to enter the Promised Land.

How did the meekest man on earth manage to usher millions through a gateway of walled-up waters, and then through the wilderness for forty years? And how did Moses keep walking from one spiritual mountaintop to another despite discouragement and difficulties?

For us today, how is it possible to continue climbing to another spiritual mountaintop when the drudgery and thankless tasks of everyday life drag us down? How do we seek summits in the real world?

Born in the Valley

Moses began his life in a shadowed valley of slavery and infanticide. By law, he should have been drowned in the Nile River. He drew his first breaths as far away from a spiritual mountaintop as life could remove him.

For 430 years, the Egyptians had dominated the Israelites. The Israelites dwelt as a displaced people in Egypt, descendants of Joseph and his brothers who had sojourned there in time of famine. The Egyptian pharaoh oppressed them with hard labor and pronounced death by drowning upon every newborn male baby. Like Jesus, Moses' life was in danger from its very inception.

When his godly mother, Jochabed, decided she could no longer safely hide Moses, she set her three-month-old baby adrift in a basket of bullrushes in the very river that Egyptian law would've utilized to kill him. His sister, Miriam, watched the basket from afar to see what would become of her baby brother.

I like to imagine Miriam comforting her brother as the basket bobbed in the reeds by the river bank. When Pharaoh's daughter spotted the basket, she ordered her handmaids to fetch it. As she opened it, I think God must have whispered to Moses, "All right, Moses, let 'er rip!" Scripture says that "she saw the child, and behold, the baby wept. So she had compassion on him" (Exod. 2:6). Miriam emerged and offered to find a nursemaid, then returned to fetch Jochabed to nurse Moses.

God honored Jochabed's faith by catapulting her son from a death sentence to a royal position in the household of the king of Egypt. God planted the unlikely savior of the enslaved Israelites under the very nose and provision of the man whose mission it was to destroy them.

Moses became "learned in all the wisdom of the Egyptians, and was mighty in word and in deeds" (Acts 7:22). Scholars suggest that as the adopted son of Pharaoh's daughter, Moses may have been in line for the throne of Egypt. There is no doubt that he possessed the privileges and powers of princes. Moses mingled among an elite circle of men who built pyramids, wrote hieroglyphics, and discussed the proverbs and philosophies of men. He became a learned man with ample training that would later enable him to write the first five books of the Bible. God arranged the circumstances of Moses' life in such a way that he was in a strategic position to accomplish God's purposes.

Four Steps for Climbing Modern Day Summits

We all desire to reach spiritual summits, but where exactly are they when the clothes need to be laundered, the grass cut, your son's homework checked, supper prepared, the bills paid, and the next day planned around a similar list of chores? Life has accelerated to such a pace that there is little opportunity to go mountain climbing. Is it possible to reach multiple spiritual summits in our modern world? If so, how?

1. Choose God's way, even if it sidelines you.

Life in the king's court came to a crashing halt one day when Moses observed an Egyptian beating a Hebrew slave. Moses killed the Egyptian and hid his body in the sand, hoping his deed would not be discovered.

Why did Moses choose to align himself with the Hebrews when it meant risking his royal position? Listen to the words of Heb. 11:24-26:

> By faith Moses, when he became of age, refused to be called the son of Pharaoh's daughter, choosing rather to suffer affliction with the people of God than to enjoy the passing pleasures of sin, esteeming the reproach of Christ greater riches than the treasures in Egypt; for he looked to the reward.

Moses was a Hebrew at heart. He remembered that his mother's faith had sustained his life and that his mother's God had transported him into the company of a king. Her godly influence on him stood the test of time. Of all the riches he'd gained in Egypt, his faith was the real treasure deep within him. In the seen world it held no value, but Moses nurtured it deep within his soul.

When Pharaoh heard about Moses' traitorous act, he set out to kill him. In one moment, the fate of Moses had been hurled back forty years. Once again he was under a death sentence of the ruler of Egypt.

2. Make the most of your current position.

Moses fled to the land of Midian, where he soon became a family man and a common shepherd. His new life was anything but fulfilling to a man who had enjoyed the social life of a prince. He lived and breathed animals and dust and weather. He was forty years old and would spend the next forty years—the prime of his life—as an uncelebrated shepherd.

How many times do you suppose Moses second-guessed himself? What place was there in Midian for all the high learning he'd gained? Surely he must have thought of all the ways he could have helped the Hebrews if he'd only turned his back when the Egyptian was beating the Hebrew. Had he wasted his life?

But there was something more in Midian. Moses soon formed a crucial relationship with his father-in-law, Jethro. Jethro was a devout worshipper of Jehovah. Once again, Moses encountered his mother's God. In Jethro, Moses found a spiritual mentor (see Exod. 18).

Even more important, Moses learned the vital importance of seeking God in solitude. He tended his sheep in the vicinity of Horeb, the "mountain of God" on the backside of the desert. I believe he kept communion with God here.

Moses discovered a spiritual gold mine in Midian. Whenever he led the sheep across a river or found food for them, he was unknowingly preparing to lead the Israelites across the wilderness. Whenever he sought a wayward lamb, he was preparing to gather souls who strayed to worship idols. Whenever he prayed on his face over his flock, he was preparing to intercede for his people. Whenever he paused to worship near Mt. Horeb, he was preparing for Mt. Sinai.

What had seemed like banishment in the beginning was in reality a superlative boot camp of the spirit. Here in Midian, in the midst of solitude, he learned the joy of touching God daily. Here, Moses learned to adore God.

My "mountain" in Michigan. During the summer after my junior year in high school in Pontiac, Michigan, I lived with my football coach. My dad had graduated from seminary and was working temporarily as an assistant pastor in Toledo, Ohio before starting a church near Steubenville, Ohio. Down the street from my football coach's house was an open field. Someone had dumped truckloads of dirt near the back of the field in a mound that stood about six feet high and twelve feet wide. It was overgrown with weeds, but it became a special place to me. Every day I walked down the street and climbed my little "mountain" to pray. I didn't realize the full import of it at the time, but God used my time at my football coach's house to teach me to fellowship daily with Him on my special "mountain."

One day out of the blue, God called Moses off the bench. Moses noticed that a bush had caught on fire near Mt. Horeb, but strangely enough, it wasn't consumed. When he moved closer to investigate, a voice called out to him: "Do not draw near this place. Take your sandals off your feet, for the place where you stand is holy ground" (Exod. 3:5). Moses hid his face, and God continued: "Come now, therefore, and I will send you to Pharaoh that you may bring My people, the children of Israel, out of Egypt" (Exod. 3:10).

With one *poof!* of a bush, Moses' rash action against the Egyptian forty years ago came racing to the forefront. God had purposely chosen someone with a propensity for saving the Israelites. In His own time, God exposed the pearl of faith Moses had been nurturing quietly for so long.

Moses was astounded at the presence of God. After forty years of prayer in the dust of mundane Midian, *Moses saw God.* From this, Moses would never recover.

Revelation always demands a response. It is like a lightning bolt that wields tremendous power that must go somewhere. Moses bid farewell to Jethro, packed up his family, and headed to Egypt to face the most powerful man on the planet. The meekest man on earth was now a mighty force with which to be reckoned.

3. Continue climbing despite the obstacles.

Have you ever heard the phrase: "He died climbing"? It poses the idea of not only enduring, but of enduring on the climb. This kind of enduring assumes an ongoing quest. One of the remarkable character traits about Moses is that he kept climbing despite multiple obstacles that would have turned back most prudent men:

- **Personal inadequacy.** Moses was a mere shepherd and a hunted exile—not a diplomat. "I'm not eloquent," he complained to God.

  God replied by granting Moses special signs. He empowered Moses' rod to transform into a serpent and back again; He gave him the ability to turn his hand leprous and to restore it again; and He gave him the ability to turn river water into blood.

  God also assured Moses that He would teach him what to say. He appointed a spokesperson for Moses—Aaron, his own brother. It's interesting to note that later Aaron would become a detriment to Moses. This is perhaps an instance of God granting a request that was not in the best interest of Moses. Moses was a man of faith, but not perfect faith.

- **Opposition from both foe and friend.** God administered ten plagues through Moses and Aaron. Modern horror films could never outdo the Pandora's box that Moses unleashed—water turned to blood, frogs, gnats, flies, death of livestock, boils, hail and fire, locusts, pitch darkness, and death of the firstborn. Despite the horror of it all, Moses obeyed God. He returned to Pharaoh again and again, asking him to free the Israelites, even when God Himself tugged on the other end of the rope by hardening Pharaoh's heart.

  The minute Moses began to work, his own people undermined his efforts. When Moses approached Pharaoh the first time, Pharaoh not only said "no," but he saddled the Hebrew slaves with more labor than they could possibly accomplish in the allotted time. The Hebrew foremen marched straight to Moses and Aaron and blamed them. Momentarily discouraged, Moses cried out to God: "O LORD, why have you done evil to this people? Why did you ever send me?" (Exod. 5:22, ESV).

Opposition often came to Moses in more subtle, deceptive ways. Pharaoh engaged sorcerers to mimic Moses by using their secret arts, diminishing God's miracles with facsimiles, sowing doubt. He also tried tossing Moses "carrot sticks." He offered to free the Hebrews without their livestock. Though the idea seems worthy of consideration on the surface, it posed a spiritual compromise. The demand Moses had always put to Pharaoh was not merely "Let my people go," but "Let my people go so they may sacrifice to the Lord." Their freedom was not simply a matter of relief, but of worship. To settle for anything less, Moses would have had to dishonor God. He wisely resisted temptation.

Of all the plagues, the tenth must have turned Moses' stomach, for he, too, had drawn his first breaths under an edict of terror—"Kill every Hebrew male baby" (see Exod.1:22). This time, God Himself was sending the destroyer: "Thus says the LORD: 'About midnight I will go out into the midst of Egypt; and all the firstborn in the land of Egypt shall die, from the firstborn of Pharaoh who sits on his throne, even to the firstborn of the female servant who is behind the handmill, and all the firstborn of all the animals'" (Exod. 11:4-5). Only those households with the sacrificial blood of a lamb upon the doorposts would be spared.

When Pharaoh refused to release the Hebrews, Scripture says that Moses "went out from Pharaoh in great anger" (Exod. 11:8). By this time, Moses had become "very great in the land of Egypt, in the sight of Pharaoh's servants and in the sight of the people" (Exod. 11:3). Kill their firstborn? How could Moses order *that*? Moses was tired.

Reluctantly, he obeyed. Hebrews 11:28 says: "By faith he kept the Passover." The lambs were gathered and slain, the doorposts marked with blood. At midnight, the Lord moved across the land and struck dead all the firstborn unprotected by the blood. The deed was done, and Pharaoh finally capitulated.

On that night, God's will triumphed over all the power and riches of Egypt. Six hundred thousand men and their families and livestock filed unhindered out of Egypt. Along with the plunder from Egypt, the Hebrews carried a special treasure—the bones of Joseph. The bones signified the faith of Joseph, who'd clung to God's covenant with Abraham, now being fulfilled with every footstep of the Israelites (see Gen. 50:24-25).

I like to imagine Moses standing under the stars, clutching his rod, watching the dust rise above the tramping feet of God's redeemed, too overwhelmed to speak. He had been right, after all, to leave Midian.

And then, just when it seemed safe, God said to Moses: "And I will harden Pharaoh's heart, so that he will pursue them" (Exod. 14:4). *What!* Moses must have thought. Pharaoh's army, including six hundred of his elite chariots, charged after them.

The Israelites cried out to Moses in terror. "You mean we came all the way out here to die in the wilderness? This is all your fault! We should have stayed in Egypt!" (See Exod. 14:12.) It was the same cry Moses would hear repeatedly for the next forty years.

As Moses studied the rising clouds of dust from the chariots, his faith was stripped down to the bare wood. God hadn't revealed a solution. Moses knew only God's purpose: "that the Egyptians may know that I am the LORD" (Exod. 14:4).

He turned to his host of terrified followers: "Do not be afraid. Stand still, and see the salvation of the LORD" (Exod. 14:13). *Now, Lord!* he must have cried on the inside, *Now!*

In the nick of time, God answered: "Lift up your rod, and stretch out your hand over the sea and divide it. And the children of Israel shall go on dry ground through the midst of the sea" (Exod. 14:16).

In an instant, the man who had once been condemned to drown in the Nile controlled the waters. Using the same rod God had empowered back at the burning bush, Moses split the sea while the Israelites passed through on dry ground. He wielded the rod again to return the waters, and the Egyptians drowned. Scripture says, "Thus Israel saw the great work which the LORD had done in Egypt; so the people feared the LORD, and believed the LORD and His servant Moses" (Exod. 14:31).

- **Betrayal of comrades.** Three days after the miracle at the Red Sea, the Israelites complained about bitter water. So God showed Moses how to make the waters sweet. Next they grumbled about food. So God created a special bread called *manna* that tasted like honeyed wafers and reappeared on the ground every morning for the next forty years. God provided manna for His people day by day, and not before.

  Rarely was Moses free from complaints. He needed great draughts of God to keep going. And God knew it. Again and again, Moses climbed Mt. Sinai for the refreshment he gained from being alone with God.

  On one of these climbs, God ordered Moses to bring Aaron and Aaron's two sons, Nadab and Abihu, and seventy of the elders of Israel. When they arrived partway up the mountain, God rewarded them with a stunning vision rarely granted to human eyes. They saw the God of Israel:

  > And there was under His feet as it were a paved work of sapphire stone, and it was like the very heavens in its clarity. But on the nobles of the children of Israel He did not lay His hand. So they saw God, and they ate and drank.
  >
  > —Exod. 24:10-11

  It was as if God had invited them to a picnic. And then God called Moses up higher, alone. By himself, Moses entered the center of God's storm cloud of glory. It was a privilege unequaled in human history.

  For forty days he soaked in God's intimate presence without interruption, receiving laws as well as instructions for a sanctuary and an ark for the covenant. When he descended the mountain, he carried precious treasure—two tablets of stone written with the finger of God—ten priceless commandments to guide the Israelites in their walk with God. Moses carried the only copy of fresh pages of truth from God.

Horror met him at the bottom. A false-god party was in progress, centered around a golden calf Aaron and the Israelites had built. Tired of waiting, they had resorted to worshipping a more tangible god.

In one of the biggest displays of temper in history, Moses picked up the stone tablets and smashed them on the ground. His people had pulled out the rug from beneath everything he had done. They had undermined the whole reason for leaving Egypt. They had violated the first commandment on the tablets. They had sampled sin at its very core. Why shouldn't God just destroy them all? In fact, God stated His intention to Moses: "Now therefore, let Me alone, that My wrath may burn hot against them and I may consume them" (Exod. 32:10).

That day, I suspect Moses was a weary, lonely man. Even his brother, Aaron, had betrayed him. But Moses knew God intimately enough to hang his hat on the invisible when the visible proved unstable. Instead of lying down, Moses regrouped and chose to seek God all the harder.

- **Sin.** One day after wandering for forty years in the wilderness, Moses heard the same old complaint one too many times. "No water! Why have you brought us out here to die? We'd be better off in Egypt!"

Moses and Aaron fell on their faces and sought God for help. God instructed them to gather all the people, then take the rod—the same rod used to initiate the plagues and split the Red Sea—and *speak* to the rock for water.

Moses obeyed until he came to the moment. In a temper, he shouted to all: "Hear now, you rebels! Must we bring water for you out of this rock?" (Num. 20:10). He smote the rock twice. Water flowed out abundantly for man and beast.

Moses' anger seems understandable. But Moses had exhibited more than just anger. "Must we bring water for you out of this rock?" he'd demanded. It was never supposed to be *we*. Moses had elevated himself on par with God. He took a share of God's glory. The leader who prayed so often on his face exhibited pride, and even worse, he did it before the eyes of an entire nation.

God's hammer fell. He said to Moses and Aaron: "You shall not bring this assembly into the land which I have given them" (Num. 20:12).

- **Discouragement.** On any given normal day, Moses was inundated with a mind-boggling mass of regulations that could rival any government job. His work was interrupted with nonstop complaints, he was obliged to carry out God's fierce judgments, and he did it all in the body of a man with eighty-plus-year-old bones.

  But in his daily struggles, Moses drew upon the lessons of Midian. He fell upon his face before God fervently and often. He sought God's mercy on behalf of his people whenever they sinned. He built altars for worship and sacrifice. And he led the people in the construction of a mobile tabernacle, designed for God's dwelling place among men.

  Whenever Moses hit a brick wall, God intervened. Whenever he got tired, God sent comfort. God rained manna from heaven, spewed water from rocks, and He sent Moses' father-in-law, Jethro, to offer wise counsel. He transferred some of the Spirit on Moses over to seventy handpicked leaders in order that they might share Moses' burden. Again and again, He revealed Himself to Moses when Moses sought Him.

4. Seek the true prize at the summit.

The key to climbing mountains is in the seeking. The average Christian's problem is not the absence of God in our modern day world, but rather a vision problem.

Moses offered this advice to his people: "But if from thence thou shalt seek the LORD thy God, thou shalt find him, if thou seek him with all thy heart and with all thy soul" (Deut. 4:29, KJV).

Moses "endured as seeing Him who is invisible" (Heb. 11:27). He sought with the stubbornness of an eccentric blind man who dares to believe he can still see. He took his faith overboard. Seeking God carried his feet into new places he would have never ventured otherwise.

When Moses climbed Mt. Sinai three months after departing Egypt, he climbed an inferno. The entire mountain shuddered. Moses struggled one step at a time up the mountain, eighty-year-old knees aching, smoke stinging his eyes, lungs straining in cinder-filled air. He had seen God in the burning bush, and he desired a greater portion of His holiness. He needed it; he ached for it. He understood that it wasn't what God could do for him that mattered most; rather, the greater reward was in the revelation of His character and what *that* would inject into Moses and his ministry.

Perhaps Moses' most desperate cry for God came after the Israelites built the golden calf. Humanly speaking, Moses needed an embrace from God to remove the wedge that sin had driven through the heart of their fellowship.

As Moses entered the tabernacle outside the camp, we read one of the most amazing statements in Scripture: "So the LORD spoke to Moses face to face, as a man speaks to his friend" (Exod. 33:11). Moses begged God to maintain His presence on their journey. He basically said, "If You don't come with us, there's no sense in us going. How will anyone know we're Your people if You're not with us?"

God agreed and answered, "I will also do this thing that you have spoken; for you have found grace in My sight, and I know you by name" (Exod. 33:17).

And then Moses dared to ask for the one thing he'd been holding back, the one thing he yearned for more than anything else: "Please, show me Your glory" (Exod. 33:18).

And Almighty God said *Yes!* He sheltered Moses in the cleft of a rock and then passed by, turning backwards. He unveiled a small slice of His glory for His beloved friend, Moses. Moses gives no description in Exodus of what he saw. There is a gap, a strange silence, as if words could not capture the vision. Whatever Moses saw, it would sustain him for a long time.

Then God instructed Moses to "cut two tablets of stone like the first ones, and I will write on these tablets the words that were on the first tablets which you broke" (Exod. 34:1). Moses communed with God for forty more days on Mt. Sinai, gathering laws and instructions to build a tabernacle, and returning with freshly inscribed tablets. It was the trip he had longed for the first time. God gave it to him, along with a countenance that reflected His divine glory with such a sheen that Moses had to wear a veil to cover his face.

Opportunities to see God are just as available today as they were in Moses' day. It is a cop-out to believe that we have been limited to a more sophisticated, subdued New Testament replica of divine manifestations. The problem is not the era; it's our negligence in asking. How often do we ask God, "Please, show me Your glory" (Exod. 33:18)? Jesus promises us: "And he who loves Me will be loved by My Father, and I will love him and manifest Myself to him" (John 14: 21).

Among those of us who choose to pursue a mountaintop experience, there's a danger in parking soon thereafter. The glorious moment fades, cars need to be cleaned and bills need to be paid, and we adjust our vision back to "reality." It is the same feeling as exiting the doors of the sports arena after watching the greatest game you've ever seen. While we may genuinely desire to stay in the moment, we gradually readjust our focus upon the mundane matters of life.

Moses never parked. He was driven by a yearning to see God on earth. His true prize was in God, not in the crowds who followed God. He waded through all the muck and disappointments of life, never losing his passion to see God again.

The Final Ascent

Before he died, Moses commissioned Joshua, "a man in whom is the Spirit," to shepherd the people (Num. 27:18). Joshua would take his place and lead the Israelites into the Promised Land. Perhaps one of Moses' most stunning statements is contained in his final message to his people: "for the LORD your God is a merciful God" (Deut. 4:31).

The Hebrew word for *merciful* means "full of compassion." This from a dying man. This from a man who had unleashed God's plagues. This from a leader disqualified from the finish line at the end of a forty-year marathon.

In a deeply human moment before he died, Moses asked God to reconsider—to allow him to cross the Jordan into Canaan. God not only said no, but He told Moses that after his death, the Israelites would turn to other gods and that He would forsake them (see Deut. 3:23-28 and 31:16-18).

If there was any time for Moses to turn away from God, it was then. In modern terms of success, he had fallen short of the mark. Yet Moses knew God. He had seen Him use plagues for good. He had *seen* God. And he trusted that God had a plan for the ages. He spent his last days praising God with a new song, teaching it to his people, instructing them how to live after his death.

Then Moses trudged up one last mountain to see God. With 120-year-old legs, he climbed Mt. Nebo to Pisgah Peak, where he died. There would be no partial view of God this time. Moses was now Home, forever face-to-face with God.

A Final Word

Scripture showers stellar words on Moses. Deut. 34:10 says, "There has not arisen in Israel a prophet like Moses, whom the LORD knew face to face." Numbers 12 tells us that God spoke to the prophets in visions and dreams, but He spoke to Moses "face to face, even plainly, and not in dark sayings; And he sees the form of the LORD" (Num. 12:8).

The meekest man on earth rendezvoused with Almighty God on a mountaintop to bring down God's law to mankind. The man who smashed the stone tablets penned the first five books of the Bible. As a deliverer and savior of the people, he foreshadowed

Jesus Christ. As a "servant" of God (Neh. 9:14) and a shepherd of lost sheep, he was a prototype of Jesus.

Moses hitched his heart to God and never let go, even when God repeatedly grabbed the rope and pulled in the opposite direction. All the earthly riches at his fingertips could not tempt him off course. When everyone else said, "It's not worth it," Moses yearned to see more of God. He would have climbed the mountain again and again, even if he'd been the only man alive on earth. The secret of his success lies in the fact that he gathered his strength from seeing God—not from the circumstances of earth.

Evangelist Dwight L. Moody summed up Moses' life by saying, "Moses spent forty years in Pharaoh's courts thinking he was somebody, forty years in the desert learning he was nobody, and forty years showing what God could do with a somebody who found out he was a nobody."[8]

APPLIED FAITH

1. Establish your own "mountain" to pray alone with God. It can be a literal mountain, a baseball mound, a garden, or even a corner in a room—a special place where you and God meet.

2. In private, pray on your face.

3. Encourage a leader with a genuine compliment or note, knowing that he or she deals with frivolous complaints on a frequent basis.

4. Enter a supermarket asking God to grant you an opportunity to show His love to a customer or employee.

5. Ask God, "Please, show me Your glory."

CHAPTER 10

JOSHUA AND THE ISRAELITES: SEEKING GOD OFF THE BEATEN PATH

By faith the walls of Jericho fell down after they were encircled for seven days.

—Heb. 11:30

READING: JOSHUA 3-6

AFTER MOSES DIED, Joshua inherited the job of leading the Israelites into Canaan. Soon after crossing the Jordan River into Canaan, he encountered the enemy at Jericho. But before he could activate battle plans, a stranger appeared with a sword drawn in his hand. Joshua saw the "captain of the host of the LORD" (Josh. 5:14, KJV), possibly a manifestation of pre-incarnate Christ. Joshua fell on his face and worshipped.

The captain of the Lord's host gave Joshua one of the most unusual sets of battle plans ever devised. He instructed Joshua to carry the Ark of the Covenant around the outskirts of the enemy city, Jericho, once a day for six days. On the seventh day, the Israelites were to march seven times around, the priests would blow their ram's horns, the warriors would all give a mighty shout, and the city wall would fall.

The plan was preposterous. Archaeologists tell us that the Jericho wall was constructed of large stones mortared to a height of thirty feet. It was a double wall, with planks straddling the two sides. Six chariots could drive across the top, side by side. It was an impregnable fortress.

Expecting the wall to fall as the result of a shout was about as likely as expecting San Francisco's Golden Gate Bridge to collapse at the finale of a song. This unusual battle plan also elevated the risks: vulnerability to an enemy attack, loss of respect, and mutiny. Why not move forward with a more typical, time-tested plan? Why not initiate a siege, cutting off food and supplies, waiting for a less risky victory?

What convinced Joshua to move forward? Today, when God directs us to solve a problem in an unconventional way, how do we justify moving forward while more ingenious minds than ours frown at us? When He asks us to complete an unusual task, what reassurances can we carry with us? How do we justify marching off the beaten path, especially when it affects others who are dependent upon us?

Joshua's Obstacles

When Joshua and the Israelites crossed the Jordan River into the Promised Land, they were not greeted with welcome baskets or parades or smorgasbords in banquet halls. Even after forty years of arduous travel, the Israelites discovered that the land of milk and honey was not a free ride.

Moses, their great leader, had died. As his replacement, Joshua knew he was under scrutiny. Would the Israelites follow him? Or would they break off into factions, each following their own leader?

Joshua's military subordinates must have balked when he presented them with the new plan. It was illogical, weak, and it set God's people up like sitting ducks. In more modern terms, it would be like asking the Union Army to march around Atlanta seven times without firing a shot. It would be like ordering Desert Storm fighter planes to circle Baghdad repeatedly without firing a single shot.

Logistically, a plan that required seven days of passiveness invited failure. If the Israelites marched too close to the wall, miller stones could come hurling down on unprotected heads, or hot oil could stream down from windows above. Worst of all, the foolishness of the plan risked a deterioration of leadership.

As the Israelites stepped into Canaan, everything was new, everything precarious—the land, the leader, and the method of warfare. Nothing seemed comfortable or safe about the road ahead.

Five Accoutrements for Walking the Unbeaten Path

When marching into battles, soldiers usually pack along accoutrements—extra gear—to help with the journey. Who could survive a long march without a canteen, trail mix, a photo of a beloved family member, and a blanket?

When on a spiritual journey—especially of an unusual nature— what can we carry with us to keep us moving forward?

1. Stones: Remember God's hand of intervention in your past.

God does not usually slap unusual requests on a raw recruit. He often prepares the believer ahead of time. Even when He doesn't, He guides the believer with special encouragements He plants along the way. He gave David victory over the lion and the bear before David faced Goliath. He gave apostle Paul aid from fellow believers along each step of his journey.

God in His wisdom had already prepared the Israelites for Jericho. At the Jordan River, He performed a curtain call to the Red Sea miracle. As they crossed the Jordan, "the waters which came down from upstream stood still, and rose in a heap," and they all crossed safely on dry ground (Josh. 3:16). In a tangible way, Joshua and the Israelites saw the hand of God at work.

To commemorate the miracle, God instructed Joshua: "Take for yourselves twelve stones from here, out of the midst of the Jordan, from the place where the priests' feet stood firm. You shall carry them over with you and leave them in the lodging place where you lodge tonight" (Josh. 4:3). After the stones had been gathered, Joshua spoke to the Israelites: "When your children ask their fathers in time to come, saying, 'What are these stones?' then you shall let your children know, saying, 'Israel crossed over Jordan on dry land'" (Josh. 4:21-22).

Stones are invaluable souvenirs of the times when God intervenes in our lives. Whether we realize it or not, most of us have our own "stones." Perhaps our stone is a Bible verse on a plaque. Perhaps it is a diary entry or a shiny rock from the top of a mountain where God answered a prayer. Perhaps it is a picture of a doctor God used to perform a miracle in the life of a family member.

Victories—especially unconventional victories for which there are no human explanations—provide souvenirs for our pockets. The more impossible the victory, the more we surmise, God must have been in this! God weeds out the logical explanations so that we might face our next impossibility with the carcasses of a bear and a lion inside our knapsack.

2. Passports: Expect clearance for your journey.

Soon before Joshua led the Israelites across the Jordan, God assured Joshua, "This day I will begin to exalt you in the sight of all Israel, that they may know that, as I was with Moses, so I will be with you" (Josh. 3:7). After the Israelites passed over the Jordan, Scripture says: "On that day the LORD exalted Joshua in the sight of all Israel; and they feared him, as they had feared Moses, all the days of his life" (Josh. 4:14).

When God gave Joshua unusual marching orders, He didn't leave him without credentials. As with Joshua, when God gives us an out-of-the-ordinary task, He provides the means to accomplish it. He gives us the passport that opens the gate to the far country. And when we arrive feeling empty-handed, He gives us the bus ticket for transport to our hotel.

Facing the Giants. A popular 2006 Christian film, *Facing the Giants,* contains a conversation in which a wise old prayer warrior,

Mr. Bridges, says to the main character, Grant: "I heard a story about two farmers who desperately needed rain and both of them prayed for rain, but only one of them went out and prepared his fields to receive it. Which one do you think trusted God to send the rain?" Grant answered, "Well, the one who prepared his fields for it." Mr. Bridges asked, "Which one are you? God will send the rain when He's ready. You need to prepare your field to receive it."[9]

God had given Joshua a promise after Moses died. God said this: "Every place that the sole of your foot will tread upon I have given you, as I said to Moses....as I was with Moses, so I will be with you. I will not leave you nor forsake you" (Josh. 1:3, 5). Joshua stepped forward, not seeing wide-open roads, yet believing in them as wholly as if God had already cleared the way in front of him.

3. Soap: Cleanse yourself before leaving.

A strong cord of obedience runs throughout the Israelites' triumph over Jericho. It required repentance and adherence to God's ordinances. In simple terms, it required the discipline of following the rules with the same simplicity that a parent tells a child, "You have to wash your hands before you eat."

On the banks of the Jordan, Joshua "said to the people, 'Sanctify yourselves, for tomorrow the LORD will do wonders among you'"(Josh. 3:5). The next day, as soon as the feet of the priests dipped into the water, the waters pushed back into a heap and the people passed over on dry ground.

The same attitude of sanctification prevailed after the Israelites arrived in Canaan. Knowing the enemy awaited them, they obeyed God's seemingly inconvenient orders to Joshua: "Make flint knives for yourself, and circumcise the sons of Israel again the second time" (Josh. 5:2). The painful procedure would involve a vulnerable period of healing. It was not a posture in which to face an enemy, but they obeyed. After the mass circumcision, the Israelites then took time out to observe the Passover.

Matthew Henry comments:

> Circumcision was originally a seal of the promise of the land of Canaan...It was in the believing hope of that good land that the patriarchs circumcised their children....Why was this ordered to be done now?...God would hereby teach them, and us with them, in all great undertakings to begin with God, to make sure of his favour, by offering ourselves to him a living sacrifice (for that was signified by the blood of circumcision), and then we may expect to prosper in all we do....When soldiers take the field they are apt to think themselves excused from religious exercises (they have not time nor thought to attend to them), yet Joshua opens the campaign with one act of devotion after another.[10]

4. God's Word: Carry it with you.

As the Israelites traversed the Jericho wall, they carried the Ark of the Covenant snuggled in the midst of them. Inside the Ark were the tablets of the law Moses had carried down from Mt. Sinai. The Ark was the focal point of their procession, a tangible symbol of the holy presence of God. It lent them strength to walk.

The verse cards. A member of my congregation, Cammie (see foreword of this book), agreed to print fifty of her favorite verses on fifty business cards, and then exchange them with two friends, Maureen and Jill, who were doing the same. Each of the three ladies wrote out their allotment of fifty verses apiece, using verses that were special to each of them. They traded verses on an agreed-upon day, shuffled all one hundred fifty cards, and took fifty home apiece. Each day thereafter, they each read one card off the top of their respective piles.

Cammie was battling cancer. Surgeons had removed her right eye after finding a malignant tumor. For three months, she wore a pirate's patch. On the day she left town for Iowa City to get her first prosthetic eye, she took the top verse off her stack and read it. It said, "The commands of the LORD are radiant, giving light to the eyes" (Ps. 19:8, NIV).

Only God could have prepared that verse for such an unusual task. When she carried God's Word with her, it gave her strength for her unusual task.

5. Means of worship: Pack them with you.

When the Israelites walked around the wall, they risked failure, ridicule, and perhaps another risk so substantial that Christians rarely dare to admit it aloud—the risk that if God does not answer immediately, their faith would diminish. Such obedience in light of all these risks is a high act of worship.

Yet the Israelites marched regardless. Scripture says, "Then seven priests bearing seven trumpets of rams' horns before the ark of the LORD went on continually and blew with the trumpets" (Josh. 6:13). They remained silent as they marched. But on the seventh day, as God had instructed, "when the people heard the sound of the trumpet, and the people shouted with a great shout, that the wall fell down flat. Then the people went up into the city, every man straight before him, and they took the city" (Josh. 6:20).

One of the greatest values of marching around our unusual walls is the opportunity they afford us to worship. As we traverse them, we focus on God and soon find that our eyes are fixed on the Lord rather than on the mechanics or results of the task. God had assured Joshua the wall would fall, but if He hadn't told Joshua the results, I am convinced that the march would not have been a loss, even if the walls had remained intact.

The church widow. When I was pastoring in Connecticut, I marched around my own version of a wall. Our church needed land to expand. On the summit of a hill stood eleven-and-a-half acres that God laid on my heart for our church expansion. But at that time, we didn't have the funds to purchase it. I drove out to that special plot of ground, got out of my car, and prayer-walked the circumference of that eleven-and-a-half acres, asking God to give us the land. Little did I know, but God had been simultaneously preparing the heart of a widow to leave us a large sum of money to purchase land. (See the rest of the story in Chapter 5, "Sarah.")

In the interim before the answer came, I could have become disappointed. I could have questioned God. Hadn't I walked in faith? Hadn't I followed Joshua's example? God chose to answer my prayer with a resounding "yes," but I believe that He honors our exhibits of faith even when the answer is "no." I will never forget that special walk. It was an act of worship that stretched my faith and drew me closer to God. That in itself made it more priceless than the generous gift from the church widow.

Joshua's Legacy

After the wall of Jericho fell, "the LORD was with Joshua; and his fame spread throughout all the country" (Josh. 6:27). Joshua went forward to lead the Israelites to several more victories, helping to secure the land of Canaan for them.

Before Joshua died at age 110, he spoke words that have made their way onto plaques that hang on the walls of our homes today: "Choose you this day whom ye will serve... but as for me and my house, we will serve the LORD" (Josh. 24:15, KJV). In a speech that could rival any of today's presidential speeches, Joshua urged the Israelites to forsake the false gods of Canaan and to remember the Lord, who "did those great signs in our sight, and preserved us in all the way that we went and among all the people through whom we passed" (Josh. 24:17).

In true Joshua-like fashion, after he finished his speech, he set up a large stone under an oak tree as a "witness to us; for it has heard all the words of the LORD which He spoke to us. It shall therefore be a witness to you, lest you deny your God" (Josh. 24:27). Joshua, the man who could knock down a stone wall with nothing more visible than faith, built stone memorials to the end of his days.

A Final Word

Joshua and the Israelites exercised heroic faith during the demise of Jericho's walls because they applied the basics—commemorating God's past blessings, cleansing themselves, carrying God's Word, and worshipping—even in the face of an unusual challenge, precisely at the time when human minds naturally veer towards disorder and anxiety. Instead of endeavoring to experiment with new kinds of help, they went deeper.

Only when the Israelites exercised these disciplines were they privileged to see God work miracles in their midst. Only when they obediently followed God's laws were they allowed to see God overturn the natural procedures of warfare, conquering a formidable enemy with musical instruments and a glorified shout.

Applied Faith

1. Set up "stones" in your home to remind you of the times God has overcome impossibilities in your life.

2. Keep a journal of the times when God has intervened in your life. Review these blessings whenever you face a new challenge.

3. Place a bar of soap at the front door of your home or in your purse as a reminder to face your challenges with a clean, repentant heart.

4. Find two friends who will agree to write fifty favorite Bible verses on fifty business cards. Mix the business cards and trade. Each day for fifty days, read the card on top.

5. Carry the Bible (or Bible verses) with you when you face a challenge.

6. As an act of worship, walk seven times around the site of your own "wall," whether it is your home, your place of employment, your doctor's office, or any other place of spiritual battle.

CHAPTER 11

RAHAB: SEEKING GOD ACROSS A CHASM OF SHAME

By faith the harlot Rahab did not perish with those who did not believe, when she had received the spies with peace.

—Heb. 11:31

READING: JOSHUA 2, 6

RAHAB WAS A prostitute. Yet God gave Rahab a place of honor in the Hebrews 11 Hall of Fame. He set the name of a woman with a shameful past in indelible ink for the world to see for eternity.

A resident of Jericho, Rahab resided precisely in the bull's eye of God's impending destruction. God had commanded Joshua to lead the Israelites across the Jordan River into the Promised Land. In order for the Jews to move forward, they had to defeat the Canaanites at Jericho. Joshua and the Israelites would soon slaughter every human and all the livestock in Jericho with the edge of the sword—everyone except Rahab and her family.

Why spare Rahab? According to Mosaic Law, Rahab should've been dragged out to the courtyard and stoned. In the eyes of a respectable Israelite, a prostitute was of no greater worth than a street mongrel. Yet God chose to single her out, rescue her, and honor her.

What was so special about Rahab? What happened to catapult her from the pit of disgrace to the Hall of Fame of Faith? Is it possible to obtain exceeding faith when we are in need of exceeding grace? If so, how?

Behind the Veil of Shame

Rahab lived on the edge of Jericho in a house upon the town wall. Though we don't know for sure, it seems plausible that Rahab owned an inn, a logical place to entertain strangers and to exchange information. When Joshua sent out two spies prior to attacking Jericho, they lodged in Rahab's house.

The king of Jericho discovered their presence and sent word to Rahab to hand over the spies. Instead, Rahab sent word back that the men had already escaped, after which she promptly hid them on her rooftop under stalks of flax until it was safe for them to leave.

Why did God choose Rahab to host His spies? I believe God knew that Rahab already harbored an interest in Him. Her curiosity about Him was afire, despite her sins. As she confided in the spies while she hid them, note her excitement about God's miracle at the Red Sea:

> I know that the LORD has given you the land, that the terror of you has fallen on us, and that all the inhabitants of the land are fainthearted because of you. For we have heard how the LORD dried up the water of the Red Sea for you when you came out of Egypt, and what you did to the two kings of the Amorites who were on the other side of the Jordan, Sihon and Og, whom you utterly destroyed. And as soon as we heard these things, our hearts melted; neither did there remain any more courage in anyone because of you, for the LORD your God, He is God in heaven above and on earth beneath.
>
> —Josh. 2:9-11

You can almost hear the excitement in Rahab's voice: "For the LORD your God, He is God in heaven above and on earth beneath."

It was as if she was proclaiming, *God is real, and He visits us on this earth!* A spark was afire in Rahab's soul.

When Rahab asked the spies for protection from the coming attack, they replied: "Our lives for yours, if none of you tell this business of ours. And it shall be, when the LORD has given us the land, that we will deal kindly and truly with you" (Josh. 2:14).

Beneath the facades of all humans, whether their sins are concealed or worn on their coat sleeves, a heart beats and a soul lives. God peered beneath the layers of Rahab's sin, moved them aside like a swimmer displaces water, and called her up from the depths.

Stepping Out Through Grace

How did Rahab find the strength to step out from behind a veil of shame to serve God? How does a broken individual soar above the stigma of a tarnished past?

1. Look to Jesus for salvation.

In God's eyes, we are all broken people with tarnished pasts. If it were possible for mortal eyes to accurately behold the holiness of God, we would realize how far off the mark we all are. If, for example, His holiness reached to a height of a thousand miles, the condemned criminal might reach only a level of two miles, while the churchgoing Christian might have ascended all the way to mile four. Or vice versa. The point is, we all fall way short of the mark.

It's impossible to attain worthiness in our own power, no matter how spotless our past. In the eyes of God, we are all condemned criminals. Only the shed blood of God's sinless Son, Jesus Christ, makes us worthy. When Jesus erases our sin with His blood, He wipes our slate clean and catapults us to the thousand-mile marker where we reside side-by-side with all manner of saved prostitutes, saved drug addicts, saved murderers, and saved preachers—all brands of sinners who have pled His grace throughout the ages.

When the Israelites approached doomed Jericho, Rahab hung a scarlet cord outside her window, a sign for the Israelites to locate and rescue her. Author John MacArthur remarks that while the scarlet color provided a noticeable sign marking the house for protection, it also was "fitting for those whose blood was under God's pledge of safety."[11]

In the sinner's search for grace, Rahab exhibited a crucial attitude of seeking. It is interesting to note that the story revolves around windows and rooftops. Perhaps she was tired of her lot, desperate to change, seeking a new direction for her life. Often, dissatisfaction with the status quo is the first step towards grace. How rampant dissatisfaction must be in lowly places! Rahab opened her eyes and her windows, and God honored her with a visit from the spies.

Bill. In the winter of 1984, a man came to my church, hair down below his shoulders. At age thirty, his life was a mess, shattered by drugs and alcohol. He had tried church a couple of times in the '70s, but decided it wasn't for him. He spent six or seven more years under the influence of drugs and alcohol. But on the morning of January 17, 1984, Bill was back in church. I can see him now, sitting three or four rows from the back on the left side of the middle section. When I gave the invitation at the conclusion of the service, Bill walked up the aisle at a fast pace and said to me, "I am tired of my life. I need to trust Christ and be saved." That day, Bill was gloriously saved.

He began working as a custodian at our church, enjoying the camaraderie of Christians. After a few years, God called him to the pastorate, and he went to seminary. Today, he pastors his own church in his hometown. Many citizens of his small town know about Bill's past. And they know what he has gloriously become through the grace of God. Bill is able to draw on the mistakes of his past to minister firsthand to the lost and brokenhearted. Today, Bill has a heart that yearns for Jesus.

Our communities are filled with people who are reluctant to step through the door of a church because they feel they've been disqualified by past mistakes. They carry a stigma that they fear will repel others. Others stagnate in church pews, anchored by rusty sins they've never acknowledged. Yet God loves to use broken people with shattered histories. As ministers of the gospel of Jesus, they come highly qualified.

2. Understand that we're accountable to God first, man second.

The way we view life is not the way God views life. God's view is not clouded by a bad back or a bad day or by last year's sin that has already been removed from the repentant believer.

Humans are terrible judges of one another. Most of us can attest to times when we can't even understand ourselves. How can we expect to accurately judge the deepest motives of a friend or a neighbor? How can we expect them to judge us accurately?

People-pleasing seldom works. It becomes a daily game into which we sink too much time and too many emotions. Though we must carefully consider how our actions will affect others, we must focus on pleasing God first. Above all others, He is our primary audience. As difficult as it may be, we must place our fingers on life's camera and adjust the zoom until the people around us fade slightly into the background.

Focusing on God will revolutionize our outlook. When others misjudge us, the pain will no longer be so acute. Instead of basing our happiness on the approval of others, we will find it in our daily, intimate walk with God. Have we spent time with Him today? Have we studied Him in the Word and emulated His behavior? Our Lord Jesus, who walked with human feet on human pathways, is our dearest Friend. He is no less capable of smiling on a prostitute than a king. He is unchangeable, faithful, and always available.

3. Decide to make correct choices.

Rahab didn't allow her shameful past to hinder her from seeking God. When she made her decision to follow God, she refused to look back. She forged ahead through the unknown, risking ridicule, doubts, and setbacks.

Old sins, even if confessed, can immobilize us if we dwell on them. One of Satan's most effective lies goes like this: *You can't do any better. You'll soon slip back into your old ways, so why try?* We end up listening to him, and it's his lie that trips us up—not the new walk.

Here's a common trap: we tell a lie, we fail to keep a promise, or we get into an argument. Then we think, *Well, I've blown it! Now it's going to take forever to work my way up spiritually to where I was before!* Satan's got us believing that we're stuck in the woodshed until we can do something special to gain back God's trust. Until then, we break communication with God, which makes matters even worse and temptations even stronger.

If this is our thought process, we do not understand grace. None of us deserves to be forgiven, not even on days when we see ourselves as having a pretty good day. It's only through the grace of God that we can fellowship with Him on any day at all, good or bad. After confessing our sins, we must move forward with God, making correct choices as if we'd never sinned.

China. China was a woman who lived on the streets in the Bronx in New York City. She used cocaine for many years. In 2008, she died of complications from AIDS. But a few years before her death, China was led to a saving knowledge of the Lord by Bill, the former drug addict from my church who became a preacher (see his story above).

In the summer of 2008—a few months before China died—Bill's son and two members of my church went to the Bronx to see China. China invited them into her humble apartment and motioned them to an old love seat. She sat across from them on her rumpled bed, wearing a stained skirt that was so short it revealed too much. In the background, a television blared a horror movie in which a tv character was sawing off the leg of another character. She didn't seem to notice. Her attention was fixed on her visitors.

China beamed in the presence of her Christian friends. She spoke of listening to Christian tapes that Bill had sent her. She talked about the Lord and about the day she had come to know Him. She testified about how He had rescued her from a life of addiction on the streets. She couldn't have been much more joyful if her three visitors had been angels.

China, rough around the edges as she was, had risen from the depths because she had trusted in a God who was big enough to reach low enough to pull her up. In terms of cleaning up her life, she had probably accomplished more than the average churchgoer ever accomplishes. She was able to entertain "angels" in her living room despite her wretched past because she loved God more than she hated herself.

4. Be willing to take risks.

When Rahab hid the spies, she risked execution. She chose to trust in the power of the invisible Israelite God above the power of the visible king.

In his book, *Your God Is Too Safe*, author Mark Buchanan emphasizes that God is good, but God is not safe.[12] The Bible bears this out. The apostle Paul was beaten, imprisoned, and shipwrecked. Stephen was stoned to death. John the Baptist was beheaded. Job's property was destroyed and his family killed. All of these saints suffered loss specifically because they chose the way of exemplary Christianity.

When we choose to follow Jesus wholeheartedly, we step into an open battlefield between opposing forces. Satan is at war with God, and we are in the way. The stakes are high, and the ammunition is real. Jesus told His disciples, "If anyone desires to come after Me, let him deny himself, and take up his cross daily, and follow Me" (Luke 9:23). He warned, "He who loves father or mother more than Me is not worthy of Me. And he who loves son or daughter more than Me is not worthy of Me" (Matt. 10:37).

It's inevitable that we will eventually suffer as we buck the status quo of mainstream Christianity. We might feel led to surrender our savings or to befriend an ex-inmate who lives in a high crime neighborhood. Today's missionaries step out routinely, venturing into inner city drug zones, flying into the jungle on small planes, risking disease and imprisonment in foreign countries, risking disappointment and disillusionment, and even occasionally risking execution.

Why does God lead us into these situations? In Job's case, it is clear that God was interested in knowing if Job would put Him first. The question of Job's ultimate allegiance—and ours—is bound irrevocably to the first commandment. Will we continue to love Him if He takes away our property, our dearest friend, our mother or father, our spouse? Will we still trust Him if He takes our child? What if He takes a second child? The frightening truth is that when we choose to follow God wholeheartedly, we might as well name the one thing that stands between us and God, because it is no longer safe.

June Wingate. As a young preacher, I was tested with the death of my mother. My mother died of cancer when she was fifty-eight years old. I remember the day when she trusted Jesus Christ as her Savior. I remember the many times she encouraged my brother and sister and me to love the Lord. I remember how as a pastor's wife she encouraged my father. She died too young.

I have no idea why God chose to take away one of the most crucial influences in my life and ministry, but there is no question that He snatched away one of my lifelines. I could have quit. I could have given up on a God who requires too much. But I knew that even when my mother was dying of cancer, I could tumble into the arms of Jesus Christ. My mother knew it, I knew it, my family knew it, and it was enough.

Why choose Jesus if it's not safe, if indeed it invites trouble? Because you gain far more than you lose. I discovered that my love for an intangible God could withstand the loss of my tangible mother. To think it is one thing; to know it is quite another.

Would Mary and Martha choose to take back Lazarus's death if they had to give back his resurrection? Would Daniel choose to cancel his night in the lions' den? Would Paul choose to erase his years in prison? Calluses of grace are precious gifts.

Hear what Job said at the end of his great trial: "I have heard of You by the hearing of the ear, but now my eye sees You" (Job 42:5). Seeing God—knowing God better—is worth far more than the pain of the trial. Those who see God are the ultimate gainers.

God blessed Rahab for a strong faith that invited risk. After the Israelites knocked down the wall of Jericho, the spies personally returned to the window marked with the scarlet cord and rescued Rahab and her family. Everyone else in the city perished (see Josh. 6:21-23).

A Final Word

God honored Rahab's faith more than she would ever know during her lifetime. He not only recorded her name in the Hall of Fame of Faith, but He used this former prostitute in the lineage of Christ. Rahab was King David's great-great-great grandmother (see lineage in Matt. 1:1-6).

Rahab believed in a God with a long arm—a God whose arm could stretch into the depths to rescue her. She peered around the humans perched on the social ladder above her, straight up to the God of the universe who she believed was just as capable of reaching the lowest rung as He was of reaching the highest. She risked her life and the lives of her family because she trusted in a God of miracles.

God saves churchgoers and non-churchgoers, prostitutes and preachers, missionaries and murderers. He looks for seeking hearts and willing feet, and when He finds them, no earthly sin can thwart His purposes. In the end, His grace is for imperfect people, and every one of us qualifies.

APPLIED FAITH

1. The next time you confess a sin, write it down and then white it out to signify its non-existence.

2. To remind yourself of how far we fall short of God's mark for sinless perfection, use a marker on your garage ladder. Write "convicted criminal" on the bottom rung, "churchgoer" on the second-from-the-bottom rung, "grace" on every ascending rung except for the top rung, and "heaven's threshold" on the top rung.

3. Show a tangible act of kindness to an outcast of society.

$$\cdot \ \cdot$$

GIDEON: SEEKING GOD THROUGH THE EYES OF DOUBT

And what more shall I say? For the time would fail me to tell of Gideon and Barak and Samson and Jephthah, also of David and Samuel and the prophets.

—Heb. 11:32

READING: JUDGES 6-8

HAVE YOU EVER tried to blend into the crowd at your church? Have you noticed that the most comfortable pew is the one where no one approaches you for service? It's a private nook where you can worship without disturbance or conflict.

Gideon felt exactly this way. When God called upon him to vanquish the invading Midianites, he was threshing wheat down by a winepress—a stone structure built partly underground—laboring in an inconspicuous place where he could stay out of the fray. One day an angel of the Lord appeared and said: "The LORD is with you, you mighty man of valor!" (Judg. 6:12).

Me? He must have thought. *A mighty man of valor?* His reply was less than respectful: "If the LORD is with us, why then has all this happened to us? And where are all His miracles which our fathers told us about... ?" (Judg. 6:13).

"Go in this might of yours, and you shall save Israel from the hand of the Midianites. Have I not sent you?" the Lord's angel replied (Judg. 6:14).

Me? Gideon must have thought again. *Why are you choosing me? I'm not bothering anyone and I didn't ask to be bothered. I'm not your man!*

After all, Gideon's resume included no military training and no impressive credentials. He was no David with a slingshot. He was a common man who wanted to be left alone, a man who viewed the glass of life as half-empty.

How did Gideon live up to God's assessment of him? How does a doubter become a mighty man of valor? For us today, how is it possible to transform a hesitant attitude into an exuberance to serve God?

Gideon's Challenge

Gideon was similar to today's conservative Christian—a responsible, dutiful man. If he were living today, he'd probably cover himself with more-than-adequate life insurance, pay off his bills promptly, and build a nest egg. He lived and worked with an attitude of self-preservation. He was not a lazy man. He engaged in manual labor even though he owned servants.

But wheat threshing was not a job intended for the confines of a winepress. Threshing was accomplished more efficiently on the open hillside where the wind could blow the chaff from the wheat. Today, it would be like pitching hay in your basement with the door open. The hay would cling to your back, dust would stick in your throat, and grit would blind your eyes. Gideon was miserable.

When the angel approached him with a plan to vanquish the Midianites, Gideon reasoned with him much the same way that Moses argued with God about confronting Pharaoh. Gideon said: "Indeed, my clan is the weakest in Manasseh, and I am the least in my father's house" (Judg. 6:15).

You can hardly blame him. The angel's proposal was preposterous. The Midianites had invaded "as numerous as locusts; both they and their camels were without number: and they would enter the land to destroy it" (Judg. 6:5). They had swarmed over Israel like a heartless band of bullies, consuming everything edible until the impoverished Israelites fled in fear into caves and dens.

What could a mere wheat-thresher do about this? Gideon had a choice. He could either blend back into the landscape or take a chance with God. There was no middle ground.

Five Steps to Transform the Pathetic Into the Powerful

How did Gideon overcome his doubts to accomplish God's grand plans? How can we do so today?

1. Let God be the judge of your capabilities.

Spiritual heroism is not dependent upon inherent ability or strength. Rather, it is dependent upon throwing up our hands, admitting we are empty of all things useful, and asking God to fill our emptiness with His desire and strength. The irony of the matter is that those who consider themselves failures already have a head start, though they may not realize it. All they lack is full surrender and a declaration of an open invitation to God.

Our Creator knows us better than we know ourselves. While we dwell on our shortcomings and failures, He focuses on the unique features of the vessel He created. When we shake our head at the impossible climb ahead, He points us to the footholds that He has already laid out in front of us. God operates from a divine principle that we often forget: what matters is not what we are in ourselves, but rather what He can make us to be in Him.

When God looked at Gideon, He saw a warrior. While Gideon was wallowing in self-defeat, God was preparing to show him the blueprint for an epic-sized plan.

2. Seek a personal encounter with God.

In His sovereignty, God sometimes singles out men and women who aren't the least interested in seeking Him. God appeared to

Gideon out of the blue. Centuries later, He would reveal Himself to Saul, the persecutor, on the road to Damascus. He seeks weak candidates to magnify His glory. He has no qualms about tapping losers on the shoulder. He uses whomever He pleases. Jesus said: "My strength is made perfect in weakness" (2 Cor. 12:9).

Like the New Testament apostle, Thomas, Gideon required a sign before he would believe that the divine visitor was from God. The angel answered by consuming Gideon's meat and unleavened cakes with fire. It is interesting to note that Gideon would continue to require signs, for it was within his flawed nature to always need more. It is also interesting to note that God often complied.

When the full impact of a visit from God finally sunk in, Gideon said, "Alas, O Lord GOD! For I have seen the Angel of the LORD face to face" (Judg. 6:22). Gideon was stricken with such awe that God quickly reassured him: "Peace be with you; do not fear, you shall not die" (Judg. 6:23).

It is no small thing to glimpse God or one of His divine messengers. Today's believers benefit from the Bible and from the indwelling of the Holy Spirit, and thus we do not experience the frequency of direct revelations that the prophets knew. But it is a modern day mistake to think God's power has somehow dwindled from its epic Old Testament proportions. Divine encounters are not defunct. The soul in love with God begs for them.

But what about those of us who get no tap on the shoulder? I believe, respectfully so, that *we* can do the tapping. Scripture says: "He who loves Me will be loved by My Father, and I will love him, and manifest Myself to him" (John 14:21). We are also told that mankind "should seek God, in the hope that they might feel their way toward him and find him. Yet he is actually not far from each one of us" (Acts 17:27, ESV).

Once you encounter God, you cannot help but mentally sit on the edge of the church pew—not because you want to be somebody special, but because you are galvanized by the prospect of reencountering the One you love through worship and the preaching of the Word.

Gideon's encounter changed his life. He immediately built an altar to the Lord. Then he began, step by step, risk by risk, to stretch himself towards God in ways a common wheat thresher could never have imagined.

3. Surrender everything and allow God to fill you.

In the popular movie, *The Wizard of Oz*, there's a scene in which the Wicked Witch of the West appears in the sky riding her broomstick, skywriting in smoke, "Surrender Dorothy." The message incites terror in every heart that sees it.[13] This is the level of terrible sacrifice we must be willing to make if we expect to be used of God. Surrender everything. *Everything* must go. Possessions, friends, family members, the deep longings of our hearts, and *even* our desire to accomplish something great for God.

For Gideon, this meant sweeping out all the dirt from beneath his carpets. Before Gideon could undertake the glory-job of leading an army, God ordered him to destroy his father's altar of the false god, Baal. Gideon was instructed to seize his father's prize bullock, use it to pull down the altar, build a new altar to the God of Israel, and sacrifice his father's bull on it.

This stunt would cost Gideon's father financial loss and public embarrassment. In one night of vandalism, Gideon would risk losing the love and respect of his family, his reputation, and his life. For a man with a conservative nature, this was no small thing.

Yet God demands obedience. The problem with obedience, though, is that it's usually uncomfortable. We must admit and repair problems we have caused, we must mend torn relationships, and we must stake God's claim on our lives in front of friends and family who know our deepest faults. It's the inglorious beginning of a divine journey, and it weeds out all but the soul most in love with God.

I believe Gideon, still caught up in the blush of his vision of God's angel, was falling in love with God. He took ten servants and carried out God's orders under cover of night because "he feared his father's household and the men of the city too much to do it by day" (Judg. 6:27). Fearful as he was, nevertheless he carried out God's orders.

The next day, a lynch party pursued him and would have killed him if it hadn't been for his father's intervention. In the end, Gideon's father protected him, and the people began to view Gideon as a man of uncommon vision. Gideon was in the spotlight now—just the right place to start building an army.

Scripture says that after Gideon obeyed, "the Spirit of the LORD clothed Gideon" (Judg. 6:34, ESV). As soon as Gideon had poured himself out, God filled him with His Spirit. Gideon was ready for service.

4. Don't be afraid to question God.

Gideon's questions to God bordered on insubordination. When the angel appeared to him by the winepress, Gideon basically asked, "Where was God when we needed Him? Why has He forsaken us and delivered us into the hands of the Midianites?"

God's angel answered with a command: "Go in this might of yours, and you shall save Israel from the hand of the Midianites. Have I not sent you?" (Judg. 6:14).

Questions are not necessarily a sign of disobedience. Rather, they are like the grumbling of a storm cloud before it pours out its rain. The Psalms are filled with David's questions. He was constantly asking God what, why, how, when, and where. Job questioned God, though he remained loyal to Him. God created humans with the ability to think and to reason. He doesn't ask us to check our brains at the door but says, "Come now, and let us reason together" (Isa. 1:18).

Consider each of these questions. They are recognizable even without a name: How shall I father a nation if I haven't fathered a son? How can I confront Pharaoh if I have a speech impediment? How can I have a son when I am still a virgin? What do we get for forsaking all and following you? My God, my God, why have You forsaken me?

Gideon not only questioned the Lord, but he asked God to reinforce his faith with tangible signs. He asked God to dampen a fleece of wool on dry ground. By morning the fleece was so full of dew that Gideon wrung out a bowlful of water. But Gideon wasn't quite satisfied. He entreated God, "Do not be angry with me" (Judg. 6:39) and then he dared to ask God to reverse the sign by drying out the fleece on damp ground. God did so the next morning without rebuke.

God also granted special, well-timed encouragements to Gideon. He provided Gideon with a servant, Phurah, to accompany Gideon to spy on the host of encamped Midianites. God also sent a dream to an enemy soldier and positioned Gideon to overhear the interpretation: "Into his [Gideon's] hand God has delivered Midian and the whole camp" (Judg. 7:14).

Gideon was astounded at God's provision. Scripture says "he worshipped, and returned into the host of Israel, and said, Arise; for the LORD hath delivered into your hand the host of Midian" (Judg. 7:15, KJV). God knew exactly the prescription Gideon needed to boost his courage for an illogical attack.

5. When God calls, step out and trust Him against all odds.

Gideon raised an army of 32,000 part-time citizen soldiers. The Midianite army numbered 135,000—a four-to-one advantage over the Israelites. God noted the odds and said to Gideon:

"The people who are with you are too many for Me to give the Midianites into their hands" (Judg. 7:2).

What? Gideon must have thought. *You've got it backwards!*

But God did not want Israel to "claim glory for itself against Me, saying, 'My own hand has saved me'" (Judg. 7:2). Though it flew in the face of common sense, Gideon obeyed as God instructed him to send home every man who was fearful. Twenty-two thousand men departed. And then God, in effect, said, "We're going to pare it down a little bit more. Everybody that gets down on all fours to drink the water is out." Almost everyone left. Only three hundred men remained. The odds were 450 to 1.

And God was satisfied.

No sane leader would send his army into such a Waterloo. Gideon was stepping over the edge of logic, taking three hundred men with him to almost certain death. But Gideon couldn't shake the image of God's angel out of his mind.

He ordered his three hundred men to surround the enemy camp during the middle night watch. Each man carried the same weapons: a trumpet and a pottery jar containing a lantern. They spaced themselves evenly in the darkness around the sleeping camp. At Gideon's signal, they blew their trumpets, smashed their jars to reveal their lanterns, and shouted: "The sword of the LORD and of Gideon!" (Judg. 7:20).

The Midianites were terrified. They "ran and cried out and fled" (Judg. 7:21). Gideon and three hundred men watched astounded as God magnified their meager arsenal in the eyes of the enemy. In the end, the footsteps were theirs, but the miracle was God's.

The adrenaline rush of this kind of blessing cannot be measured. No man's faith could remain untouched after a night like this. I believe that Gideon and his three hundred men worshipped God with all their hearts that night.

The Aftermath

After Gideon conquered the enemy, he could have had anything he wanted. His host of admirers praised him like a massive fan club.

"Rule over us, both you and your son, and your grandson also; for you have delivered us from the hand of Midian," they urged (Judg. 8:22).

Gideon replied: "I will not rule over you, nor shall my son rule over you; the LORD shall rule over you" (Judg. 8:23). And then Gideon bowed out and "went and dwelt in his own house" (Judg. 8:29).

Gideon knew when to stop. He refused to move beyond God's will, even when tempted by peer pressure and practical invitations. He understood that anything not done for God's glory is meaningless. He gave the credit to God and then laid his service down on the altar like a retired sword.

Gideon's actions brought peace to Israel for forty years. Yet through it all, Gideon was not a model hero. He was an insecure human who needed perpetual crutches. He kept multiple wives and a concubine. He gathered jewelry from the spoils of battle and fashioned a golden ephod—a vestment commonly worn by a high priest. Scripture says "all Israel played the harlot with it there. It became a snare to Gideon and to his house" (Judg. 8:27).

Gideon "died at a good old age, and was buried in the tomb of Joash his father, in Ophrah of the Abiezrites" (Judg. 8:32).

A Final Word

Gideon was a man who needed spiritual reassurance throughout his hero's journey. He is an Old Testament version of "doubting Thomas." At several junctures, God could have dispensed with him for his hesitancy, but instead God chose to prop him up.

The story of Gideon is a step-by-step textbook study of how the Father leads a reluctant child along. It's a story of the evolving faith of an unlikely hero. As Gideon followed God's leading, this doubter vanquished a formidable army with a bare-bones troop of men and a ruse as elementary as rubber bands and duct tape.

Gideon's heroism became extraordinary as he gradually grew through God's loving promptings and reassurances. In the New Testament, when Jesus stood before Thomas and said, "Reach your hand here, and put it into My side," Thomas chose to place his hand in Jesus' side (John 20:27). So, too, Gideon, the doubter, reached out when God directed.

In Gideon, God chose a common man to do a hero's job. He chose less than the best in human eyes in the same illogical way that He reduced Gideon's army. Common men are often exactly who God calls to accomplish His work.

Gideon's unlikely triumph casts the spotlight of gratitude back on our Father, who uses His imperfect children to accomplish the tasks of heroes. He uses flawed humans to cast glory upon Himself, and then graciously offers a share of the afterglow with us.

APPLIED FAITH

1. Write out a prayer list. For your topmost request, write this: "Please grant me an encounter with You. I want to see You, Lord."

2. With utter honesty and reverence, write out your deepest, most personal question with which you would like to confront God. Pray with fervency and search the Scriptures for an answer or for a renewed sense of peace.

3. Look for an opportunity to be like Gideon's servant, Phurah. Offer to accompany a friend to a difficult place where nothing but God's intervention can conquer the impossibilities.

CHAPTER 13

BARAK: SEEKING GOD THROUGH THE WISDOM OF AN UNLIKELY VESSEL

And what more shall I say? For the time would fail me to tell of Gideon and Barak and Samson and Jephthah, also of David and Samuel and the prophets.

—Heb. 11:32

READING: JUDGES 4-5

HAVE YOU EVER been asked to work alongside someone who you thought wasn't quite up to par? If God asked you to perform the most important task of your life alongside someone you considered inferior, would you do it?

In an age of Israel's history when women were considered more property than partner, Barak found himself in a sensitive position. Deborah, a prophetess and judge, not only issued God's directives to him, but she coached him at the head of battle with such authority that she became an inspiration to him.

The Bible does not tell us much about Barak, but we do know that God brought him to the forefront through Deborah. Deborah was the only woman judge in a three-hundred-year period of judges—a time of spiritual decline in Israel. Gone were Israel's strong leaders like Moses and Joshua. Deborah's throne was a palm tree, under which she sat doling out judgments to those who stood in line. Though she seemed like an unlikely leader, she was God's chosen instrument to guide Israel through a period of judgment for their latest lapses of self-indulgence and idol-worship.

Barak could have challenged Deborah's authority, but instead he chose to seek her advice. How did Barak merit a place in the Hebrews 11 Hall of Fame of Faith by hanging onto the coattails of Deborah? Is it possible to perform a hero's or heroine's task in a situation that seems too self-deprecating to be glorious? How should we respond if God asks us to work alongside a seemingly unlikely vessel?

Barak's Challenge

When God called upon Barak, King Jabin of Canaan and his general, Sisera, threatened the Israelites with an impressive arsenal of iron chariots. In modern golf terms, Barak was in "deep weeds." Israel's army was a pitifully equipped group of weekend warriors. Most were farmers and field hands. According to ancient historians, most of Israel's soldiers didn't even own a sword. One of Israel's greatest warriors, Shamgar, used an ox goad to fight his battles (see Judg. 3:31). Whenever an enemy threatened, they improvised with the nearest weapon, much like members of a home militia.

In contrast, Sisera's highly trained soldiers made a living at warfare. Sisera's pride and confidence rested in his nine hundred iron chariots. Scythes projected out of the chariot wheels, capable of mowing down foot soldiers with horrific butchery.[14]

Barak faced a mighty war machine while leaning upon an unexpected leader—Deborah. It was not a position that would merit the respect of his peers, much less of posterity.

Three Principles for Working Alongside an Unlikely Vessel

It can fly against logic to work alongside an unlikely instrument of service, especially when the task is vitally important to us or when it jeopardizes the lives of others. How did Barak do it? How can we do it today?

1. Value godly wisdom.

It was God's idea to connect Barak and Deborah. God's call to Barak came through Deborah, His chosen vessel to relay the message. One day she summoned Barak with these words:

> Has not the LORD God of Israel commanded, "Go and deploy troops at Mount Tabor; take with you ten thousand men of the sons of Naphtali and of the sons of Zebulun; and against you I will deploy Sisera, the commander of Jabin's army, with his chariots and his multitude at the River Kishon; and I will deliver him into your hand?"
>
> —Judg. 4:6-7

As a prophetess, Deborah was God's mouthpiece. God had equipped her with the gift of ruling through His divine inspiration upon her. As a prophetess instead of a princess, and as a woman instead of a man, she wasn't perceived as a significant threat by the enemy. But God's hand was upon Deborah, and King Jabin made the mistake of disregarding her.

When Deborah relayed God's message to Barak, he replied in a way that few men would: "If you will go with me, then I will go; but if you will not go with me, I will not go!" (Judg. 4:8).

Was Barak a coward? Clearly, he was hesitant to take the initiative in battle without encouragement. He was not a natural-born leader. Coward or not, Barak was humble enough to admit that he needed help.

Could it be, too, that Barak had already been seeking God, and that he viewed Deborah as God's initial answer? Deborah's first words to Barak indicate that God had already connected them spiritually: "Has not the LORD God of Israel commanded [you]?" Barak recognized God's hand upon Deborah's life, and he latched onto her as a worthy companion who could take him closer to the face of God.

Barak's words to Deborah ring similar to the words of Moses when God threatened to withdraw His presence from the Israelites on their journey to the Promised Land. Moses cried to God: "If Your presence does not go with us, do not bring us up from here" (Exod. 33:15).

Barak risked his reputation by teaming up with Deborah. While his actions on the surface appear fainthearted, he exhibited a rare caliber of faith for a man of his time. He recognized that "he could do nothing without her head, nor she without his hands; but both together made a complete deliverer and effected a complete deliverance."[15] He embraced the unconventional for a higher purpose.

Aunt Goldie. Early in the 1920s, my great aunt Goldie and her husband moved to the hills of Kentucky to minister to the coal miners. They established a church in the backwoods where most other ministers would not venture. Aunt Goldie ministered to the women and children of the church while her husband preached.

When Aunt Goldie's husband died, she sought another preacher to take over, but nobody would come. So Aunt Goldie did something that many think is not scriptural: Aunt Goldie started to preach on Sundays. People were led to Christ, and she continued to head the church until she was too old to preach. God raised Aunt Goldie up, and though her methods may have been different, she stepped into an empty spot that needed to be filled.

Scripture outlines boundaries regarding women in church leadership, but under circumstances of His own choosing, God uses women to lead His church. Scripture is full of instances where God plugged the gap left by men who failed to act. How many times do we read of evil men stepping up to the throne of Israel when good men failed to respond? God fulfills His plan through whomever He pleases. The salvation of souls and the furtherance of the gospel are paramount above the issues of convention or protocol.

Ministry & More Inc. My church helps support Ministry & More, a food pantry in our community founded by Don and Linda Winterland. Director Alan McLaughlin and his wife, Wilma, staff the pantry primarily with church members. Throughout its history, however, this ministry has also used the help of clients, homeless individuals, and ex-inmates, all who have worked alongside one another to serve the hungry and spread the gospel. The mix is powerful. When a timid, clean-as-a-whistle church member works alongside a newly saved ex-felon, spiritual sparks fly. One learns to love people he formerly feared, and the other learns to trust again, and God gets the glory. It is God's choice whether He touches the heart of the next pantry client with the church member or with the ex-felon.

Jesus. Humanly speaking, Jesus was an unlikely vessel. He owned no home, plied no occupation, made radical statements that flew in the face of the spiritual leaders of the day, and was hunted as a rabble-rouser. To the men of His day, He was a dangerous man with whom to associate.

Jesus Christ is the author of all knowledge, but He never earned a diploma. He is King of all kings, but He never received a promotion. He created the laws of aerodynamics, but He traveled on a borrowed donkey. He owns the cattle on a thousand hills, but He never bought a house. Though He is the one true God, He never established roots in a congregation. A nomad, He attracted invalids, prostitutes, demon-possessed women, and common men. All the while, kings marveled at Him and feared Him.

God's church on earth was never intended to be a haven for conventional Christians. A million unique molds shape the church. The preacher from the country and the janitor from the inner city are both instrumental in God's plan, as are the soloist from Fifth Avenue and the guitar player from the housing project. The apostle Paul takes care to emphasize the importance of every participant, especially those members of the body "which seem to be weaker" (1 Cor. 12:22). Each part depends upon the other, well-oiled and synchronized, to achieve harmony. Each part—weaker and stronger—complements the other for the glory of God.

2. Remember that the battle is the Lord's—not yours or your partner's.

When the moment of battle arrived, Deborah cried "Up," or in Hebrew, *Charge!* She reassured Barak: "For this is the day in which the LORD has delivered Sisera into your hand. Has not the LORD gone out before you?" (Judg. 4:14). Barak responded by setting Israel's 10,000 troops in motion, and God gave him the victory.

Scripture says that "the stars from their courses fought against Sisera" (Judg. 5:20). The historian, Josephus, reported that a violent hailstorm beat against the enemy's faces.[16] Sisera's chariots were rendered useless in the mud. From a human standpoint, nature turned the tide against Sisera, but Barak knew that God had planned it all. When all the odds were stacked against Barak and nothing worked out on paper, God split the veil of heaven open, reached down, and supplied everything Barak needed at the precise time he needed it.

In *Streams in the Desert*, L. B. Cowman outlines the optimal conditions for a miracle:

> Difficulty is actually the atmosphere surrounding a miracle, or a miracle in its initial stage. Yet if it is to be a great miracle, the surrounding condition will be not simply a difficulty but an utter impossibility. And it is the clinging hand of His child that makes a desperate situation a delight to God.[17]

On this memorable day, Barak "saw" God.

3. Agree that the glory must all go to God, and be willing to give it to others before yourself.

Stepping aside so that another can stand in the spotlight should never be an issue when ultimately all the glory is meant for God. Even Jesus gave God the glory. When others tried to glorify Jesus, Jesus did not glorify Jesus. God glorified Jesus.

After his hour of uncharacteristic bravery, Barak stepped once again into the shadows. Scripture never mentions Barak's exploits in battle. Nor did God allow him to slay the prize—the Canaanite general, Sisera. Another woman, Jael, slew him by stealth before Barak could apprehend him. Deborah's earlier prophesy to Barak came true: "There will be no glory for you in the journey you are taking, for the LORD will sell Sisera into the hand of a woman" (Judg. 4:9).

Perhaps one of the most remarkable aspects of Barak's heroism is that he chose to go forward in spite of being denied a hero's recognition. Barak valued the success of God's plan more than he valued his own honor. He valued God's gaze more than the attention of men.

After the battle, Deborah and Barak sang a united song of praise to God, a ballad of the battle (see Judg. 5). Both gave all the glory to God.

A Final Word

The defining aspect of Barak's heroism seems quite unheroic in human terms. Barak humbled himself to draw wisdom and encouragement for a God-given task that came from the authority of an unlikely vessel. He believed that he could give God the glory even with someone else at the helm. In spite of his own imperfections and against all odds, Barak stepped out on God's appointed team and subdued an enemy that, by human standards, was invincible.

Barak had no way of knowing that God would one day honor him in the Hebrews 11 Hall of Fame alongside such names as Noah and Abraham and Moses. Yet centuries, generations, even eras later, God remembers the glory-giver. With Him, there is no overlooking earthly second-bests and runners-up.

APPLIED FAITH

1. Make a list of your own inferior traits and give them to God.

2. Encourage a leader with a note this week, specifically thanking this leader for his or her guidance and leadership.

3. Tell your primary encourager how much you appreciate him or her.

4. Men, strive not to be a "lone warrior," but instead, practice listening with Barak's ears to the spiritual counsel of others.

CHAPTER 14

SAMSON: SEEKING GOD
AT THE END OF FOLLY

And what more shall I say? For the time would fail me to tell of
Gideon and Barak and Samson and Jephthah, also of David and
Samuel and the prophets.

—Heb. 11:32

READING: JUDGES 13-16; NUMBERS 6:1-21

ARE YOU SKEPTICAL of people who dally away their lives
with one foolish choice after another, then run crying to
God at the last minute? Do deathbed confessions make you
roll your eyes, especially coming from someone who knew better?

Samson is perhaps best known as the man who pulled down
the pillars of the temple upon the Philistines. But this hero also
indulged in lust and immorality to the point that he betrayed God.
Even worse, he did it knowing that God had bestowed an unusual
portion of divine favor upon him. Through an angel, God had
relayed Samson's purpose in life to his mother: "For behold, you
shall conceive and bear a son... and he shall begin to deliver Israel
out of the hand of the Philistines" (Judg. 13:5).

Personally, if I were given the opportunity to choose a friend,
Samson would not be my first choice. Yet God placed Samson in
the Hall of Fame of Faith. Why? How can a man who has gambled

with heaven's plans squeak through the door into the Hall of Fame of Faith? How is it possible to reach a place of honor after having knowingly squandered God's favor repeatedly?

Samson's Blessed Beginning

As was the case with Jesus, Samson's birth was foretold by an angel. An angel appeared to the barren wife of Manoah and said, "Indeed now, you are barren and have borne no children, but you shall conceive and bear a son" (Judg. 13:3).

Samson's parents presumed at first that the angel was a human—a wise man of God, or perhaps a prophet. But when the angel stepped into the sacrificial fire and ascended into the flame above the altar, they "fell on their faces to the ground" (Judg. 13:20). Stricken, Manoah cried to his wife, "We shall surely die, because we have seen God!" (Judg. 13:22).

Samson was soon born, and his parents raised him as a Nazirite according to the angel's decree. Consecrated to God, Nazirites were pledged to separate themselves from worldly influences for the purpose of remaining holy in matters of heart and soul. Normally, the vow was taken by a Jew for a span of thirty to one hundred days. It consisted of three commands: 1) abstain from all intoxicating drink and all grape products; 2) abstain from cutting one's hair; and 3) avoid contact with dead bodies, including family members who die (see Num. 6:3-7). Scripture mentions only three individuals who took the vow of the Nazirite for a lifetime: Samson, Samuel, and John the Baptist.

As a young boy, Samson surely must have pondered the angel's plans for his life. This youth carried heaven's secrets like a general guards top-secret military plans. Rarely do mortals carry such a rich spiritual behest from their earliest years. Rarely are they raised by parents who have told them the miraculous story of their birth over and over again. As Samson grew to manhood, he began to flex his muscles in the inexplicable marvel that he was a man entrusted with a special mission from God.

Soon, "the Spirit of the LORD began to move upon him" (Judg. 13:25). Similar words would be spoken about John the Baptist: "So the child grew and became strong in spirit" (Luke 1:80). And about the boy, Jesus: "And Jesus increased in wisdom and stature, and in favor with God and men" (Luke 2:52).

Samson's course was set, his purpose to "begin to deliver Israel out of the hand of the Philistines" (Judg. 13:5). His commission had been embossed with the golden seal of an angel. Samson had been blessed with the head start of all time.

Three Ways to Avoid a Fatal Fall

A study of Samson is, in large part, a primer of how *not* to become a spiritual hero of the faith. On the surface, he seems a man supercharged with tomfoolery, unbridled anger, and brutal revenge. Commentator Matthew Henry describes him as a "riddle, a paradox of a man, [who] did that which was really great and good, by that which was seemingly weak and evil..."[18] As his muscles hardened like iron, he veered off into the most un-Nazirite life imaginable. He did everything that a hero should not do, and he followed a sure and certain recipe, step by step, for the fall of a giant.

Why did God honor Samson? How can we keep from falling as Samson did, and if we do, is there any hope?

1. Refrain from straying across the border into sin.

> Now Samson went down to Timnah, and saw a woman in Timnah of the daughters of the Philistines.
>
> —Judg. 14:1

The first sentence of Samson's adult life hits the reader in the face like a bucket of cold water. Timnah was a no-man's land, a border city populated by both Jews and Philistines. In today's terms, it was a red-light district.

Despite Samson's God-given commission by the angel, he was one hundred percent human, and the knowledge of his divine commission soon took a left turn into pride. He donned the cocky attitude of a young man who is quite sure he's invincible.

Samson soon married the woman from Timnah. He said to his father, "Get her for me; for she pleases me well" (Judg. 14:3). Yet in spite of Samson's cavalier attitude, Scripture says that his decision "was of the LORD, that He was seeking an occasion to move against the Philistines" (Judg. 14:4).

His weakness surfaced immediately during the wedding reception. Samson posed a riddle to thirty Philistines. When they couldn't answer, his wife privately ribbed him to reveal the answer to her. She played the part of a temptress, weeping in front of Samson, accusing him of not loving her until "it happened on the seventh day that he told her, because she pressed him so much" (Judg. 14:17).

It should have stopped right there. Samson should have learned his lesson, taken note of his particular weakness, and determined to curb it for the rest of his life. But Samson seemed to consider temporary indulgence acceptable as long as he did not stray too far from the main thoroughfare of his mission for God. A man of great strength had great appetites, didn't he? He needed nourishment, diversion, and even a little fun, didn't he? He'd killed a lion with his bare hands before the wedding and dined on the honey of bees from its carcass. He was not a man of obscurities or dull living.

Samson believed the same lie that Satan told Eve, basically that "This one little thing won't matter." He believed the same lie Ananias and Sapphira swallowed: "It won't hurt to keep one little thing back." Samson's *one little thing* was beautiful women. This one thing he would not give up.

Instead of seeking God's guidance, Samson poured his shame into personal vengeance against the Philistines. From the very beginning, there was too much pride and anger in the blade of his slaughter. It is interesting, but fact, that the "Spirit of the LORD came upon him mightily" to enable him to kill thirty Philistines in another city, using their spoil to pay a debt (Judg. 14:19). In spite of Samson's imperfections, God used him.

Hollywood's thrillers could not produce any more gruesome barbarism than Samson's ongoing battle with the Philistines. He waded in blood and corpses. When he discovered that his father-in-law had given his bride away to another man, he tied the tails of three hundred foxes together, set them on fire, and sent them fleeing through the Philistines' corn. When the Philistines retaliated by killing his bride and father-in-law, he "attacked them hip and thigh with a great slaughter" (Judg. 15:8). The Philistines hunted him in the land of Judah until three thousand men of Judah betrayed him and delivered him to the enemy. But he escaped and the "Spirit of the Lord came mightily upon him," (Judg. 15:14) strengthening him to slay one thousand Philistines with the jawbone of an ass.

Exhausted, Samson called upon God: "I die of thirst" (Judg. 15:18). His words are much like the words of Jesus on the cross: "I thirst!" (John 19:28). So God "split the hollow place" in the jawbone, and filled it with water to revive Samson (Judg. 15:19). There is little question that God's divine favor rested on Samson. Once revived, Samson judged the nation of Israel for twenty years.

2. Refuse to cater to your weakness.

> Now Samson went to Gaza and saw a harlot there, and went in to her.
>
> —Judg. 16:1

Whoa! What was Samson thinking?

Despite Samson's extraordinary physical strength, he crumbled in front of women. This "hero" of Hebrews 11 was a paradox of terrible strength and terrible weakness.

Samson became paralyzed with the sin of lust just like a character in a video game that repeatedly steps on a stun spot. He counted himself powerless to fix it, his conscience became dulled to it, and eventually he excused it. Why, after all, try to fight it when it's so difficult to overcome? It became like a safe base to him, exempted from God's law unlike any of the other areas of his life.

Weak as Samson seems, he was really not so different than today's Christians. Most of us suffer from at least one particular weakness. Often, it is so noticeable that friends and family can pinpoint it—laziness, jealousy, pride, excessive appetite for food or drink, self-pity. Our weakness defines a portion of our character and hosts the potential of spreading beyond our control. It plagues us until we throw up our hands and cease asking God to help us as if it's as unfixable as an extra finger or toe. Satan is a master at pricking us in the same spot again and again. But every time it recurs, we have a choice: succumb to it and sin, or fight it and draw closer to the Lord. Samson succumbed.

The Philistines capitalized on Samson's weakness. When they learned he was visiting the harlot, they surrounded the house to pounce on him. But Samson arose at midnight, and "took hold of the doors of the gate of the city and the two gateposts, pulled them up, bar and all, put them on his shoulders, and carried them to the top of the hill that faces Hebron" (Judg. 16:3). Truly, God was longsuffering with Samson.

3. Guard against spiritual hibernation.

> Afterward it happened that he loved a woman in the Valley of Sorek, whose name was Delilah.
>
> —Judg. 16:4

All we can do is shake our heads. How long would Samson continue to play with fire? He'd already been burned. How long before the flames would ignite the sacred commission God had entrusted to him?

Delilah mesmerized Samson. He was a helpless babe in her arms. Meanwhile, the Philistines awaited him behind the scenes. They bribed Delilah with 1,100 pieces of silver to uncover the secret of Samson's strength, after which she immediately began probing, coaxing him to reveal his secret.

A red flag should have waved in Samson's mind. But instead, he played the game with her, giving her more and more rope each time she asked. She "pestered him daily" until "his soul was vexed to death" (Judg. 16:16). "You don't love me," she accused him, just as his wife had accused him at the wedding reception twenty years earlier. But Delilah was a new love, and he plunged headfirst into the pleasure of her. Finally, he revealed the secret: "If I am shaven, then my strength will leave me, and I shall become weak, and be like any other man" (Judg. 16:17). Delilah collected her silver and called in her cohorts to cut his hair.

The moment he revealed the secret, Samson's strength left him. I don't believe there was anything magic about his long hair. Had Samson's hair been ripped off by a passing storm, his strength would not have left him. His long hair was merely an outward symbol of his lifelong Nazirite covenant to God, such as a man's wedding ring is a symbol of his promise to his wife. But in breaking the covenant, he chose Delilah's love above his love for God. He gambled his life's mission and he gave something to Delilah that belonged to God. When he handed his sacred secret away, he handed his allegiance away, and the scissors sealed the deal.

Scripture says that Samson "awoke from his sleep, and said, 'I will go out as before, at other times, and shake myself free!'" But Samson "did not know that the LORD had departed from him" (Judg. 16:20). This is perhaps one of the saddest statements in the Bible. Samson had gambled on God always being there. After all, Samson was God's special emissary, wasn't he? But he had coasted for so long that he never noticed God leave. He had gradually numbed himself into spiritual hibernation and God was no longer at his elbow. At the hour of Samson's greatest need, God was gone.

The Philistines showed no mercy. Death was too good for him. They gouged out his eyes, then threw him into prison to sit blind at a grindstone, one of the most pitiable slaves in the cellblock.

Victory at the End of Folly

Samson was at the end of his rope. The eyes that had lingered too long on feminine flesh were sightless holes. He possessed no strength with which to impress beautiful women. There were no first aid kits in prison, no wigs, no fancy prosthetic eyes. Samson was ruined in the very areas of his life that had meant the most to him.

It is difficult to muster much sympathy for Samson. Sin is sin, and God owed this fool no mercy. But Jesus tells us that "there is joy in the presence of the angels of God over one sinner who repents" (Luke 15:10).

Unless you've done time at the bottom of a spiritual gutter, there's no way to understand the depth of Samson's misery. It's one thing to recover from tragic circumstances, but quite another to recover when you are responsible for the calamity. A man or woman who has been wronged still has legs to stand upon, but one who knows he's committed the deed is stripped of all limbs. He has no legs upon which to rise.

Scripture doesn't spell it out, but something marvelous happened to Samson between the barbershop and the temple. I believe that as he was working the grindstone, he was seeing his life in clearer focus than he had ever seen it when he had sight.

As a shipwrecked man on a raft dreams about food, Samson was no doubt thinking about the things he would choose to see if he were granted vision again. I believe that instead of conjuring up more women, Samson searched further back in his memory to the days of his childhood. I believe he recalled his mother's story about the angel, and he yearned for the hope she had nurtured in him. After many years of wanton living, Samson awakened and came to himself.

If Samson wanted God, he had no choice but to grab hold of God. At exactly the point in his life when it was physically impossible, I believe that Samson yearned to see God.

Scripture says that as Samson worked at the grindstone, "the hair of his head began to grow again after it had been shaven" (Judg. 16:22). This was a beginning, a trace of hair, God's favor upon Samson, and an indication to us of Samson's renewal of faith.

One day, the Philistines summoned Samson out of prison. "Call for Samson," they said, "that he may perform for us" (Judg. 16:25). Samson walked out in front of three thousand spectators, many who were the elite lords and ladies of the Philistines. His world was blank, but he could hear the taunts of the crowd, feel the spit land upon his face and arms. For decades, the Philistines had waited to humiliate this child of miracles who had outwitted and overpowered them repeatedly.

Samson was not only their prize prisoner, but he was their sacrifice to Dagon. Scripture says that "when the people saw him, they praised their god; for they said: 'Our god has delivered into our hands our enemy, the destroyer of our land, and the one who multiplied our dead'" (Judg. 16:24). Samson's defeat would mean Dagon's victory. This battle was not merely between Samson and the Philistines; it was between God and Dagon.

God looked down from heaven and used a little boy to guide Samson's hands to the two main supports of the building. Samson called upon God and said, "O Lord GOD, remember me, I pray! Strengthen me, I pray, just this once, O God, that I may with one blow take vengeance on the Philistines for my two eyes!" (Judg. 16:28).

Admittedly, I would prefer that Samson's prayer had added, "that Your name might be glorified." But everything Samson did regarding the Philistines was tinged with vengeance, so it is no surprise that vengeance was part of his final prayer. Samson's submission to God is evident in his humble words, "just this once." He realized that he didn't deserve a speck of strength.

As Samson braced himself between the pillars, he called upon the One whom he had betrayed. He dared to believe that God's grace was bigger than his sin. And then, he went a step further. He asked God to restore his gift—without the benefit of a head of full-length hair. In his asking, he admitted that God's strength had been the real strength all along. He believed that God would restore his gift even after he'd sold it to Satan. In spiritual terms, Samson walked out on thin air.

In the last seconds of his life, as the building began to crumble, I can imagine Samson looking up at the ceiling, seeking God blind. He lifted his head, devoid of eyes, seeking God as the walls cracked and the ceiling crashed down, killing him and all the Philistine lords and ladies.

Samson's death was a victory, the fulfillment of the angel's revelation to his mother and father. With the destruction of the Philistine leadership, Samson began to "deliver Israel out of the hand of the Philistines" (Judg. 13:5). He chose to cash in his life for God's glory. He accomplished his Father's plan with the last triumphant breath of his life.

A Final Word

In some ways, it seems unfair that such a flagrant sinner should merit a place in the Hebrews 11 Hall of Fame. He is like the vineyard laborers who came at the eleventh hour and received the same wages as the laborers who worked all day (see Matt. 20:1-16).

But for all his foolishness, Samson did not enjoy a free ride. Sin's consequences tailgated him everywhere he went. No one liked him. We read of no long-lasting friendship, no devoted wife or children. For all his strength, Samson was a lonely, miserable man.

God uses whomever He pleases. As He told His parable of the eleventh hour laborer, Jesus voiced this truth through the words of a landowner paying his laborers: "'Is it not lawful for me to do what I wish with my own things?'" (Matt. 20:15). His plans are more vital than an unworthy man's sin. God honors His word, even when His servants don't.

Author C. S. Lewis said this about his own conversion to Christianity:

> The Prodigal Son at least walked home on his own feet. But who can duly adore that Love which will open the high gates to a prodigal who is brought in kicking, struggling, resentful, and darting his eyes in every direction for a chance of escape?[19]

Samson kicked and screamed until his eyes were gouged out. But when he came to the point where he had nothing, he asked for everything. He dared to believe that God would restore a divine gift that he had already gambled away and that God would do so without Samson having legs to stand on or eyes to see it. Samson stepped out onto a spiritual tight rope and balanced on grace alone.

Like every other imperfect hero in the Hebrews 11 lineup, Samson cast the spotlight back on God. With heroes, the praise always returns to God, for there is no other way to account for the blessing of heroism.

APPLIED FAITH

1. Ask a repentant sinner to dine with you, and serve your best "fatted calf."

2. Visit a prisoner, knowing that you might be visiting a broken Samson.

3. Assist a blind person.

4. If you are hopelessly mired in sin, dare to take your first step towards forgiveness and healing. Go to a private place, get alone with the Lord, and discover His abounding grace.

CHAPTER 15

JEPHTHAH: SEEKING GOD AFTER RECKLESS RUIN

And what more shall I say? For the time would fail me to tell of Gideon and Barak and Samson and Jephthah, also of David and Samuel and the prophets.

—Heb. 11:32

READING: JUDGES 11-12

HAVE YOU EVER told God, "I'll give you *anything* if You do this one thing for me"? Jephthah, one of the judges during the four-hundred-year period of judges in Israel, bargained with God without considering the consequences. He vowed that he would sacrifice the first thing that walked out his door if God would grant him victory in battle. His story is perhaps the most controversial in all of Scripture. Godly people differ in their interpretations and applications.

God gave Jephthah a tremendous victory over the Ammonites. But the first thing that walked out Jephthah's door was his beloved daughter. Like the pagans, Jephthah sacrificed his daughter as a burnt offering to satisfy his God. The deed broke his heart, but there is no mention of subsequent repentance. Nor is there anything obviously glorious about the remainder of his life.

Why did God memorialize a man who had committed a heinous act of worship? And how is it possible to go on living after destroying someone you love? How do you walk with God after that?

Jephthah's Infamous Beginning

Jephthah was a loser from the beginning. He was the son of his father's lust, a child born of a harlot in Gilead of Israel. Jewish society regarded illegitimate offspring as human garbage. In the eyes of his family, he was unworthy to eat at their table, unworthy to share in their inheritance, unworthy to be called brother, an embarrassment to the family. Eventually, Jephthah's half-brothers booted him out on the street.

Jephthah fled to the land of Tob and sought companionship in the company of a band of outcasts. Josephus, the first century historian, refers to him as a "potent man" who maintained his own army at his own expense.[20] Whether he was a type of Robin Hood or whether he was the captain of an ancient band of elite forces, no one knows. Regardless, he made a reputation for himself in the art of guerilla warfare.

One day, his half-brothers came to Tob to ask for his help. The Ammonites had attacked Israel. Masters at intimidation, the Ammonites could subdue entire cities without having to fit a single arrow into the bowstring. During the time of Saul, their barbaric terms of surrender were these: submit to having your right eye plucked out, or be annihilated! Because a warrior's shield covered his left eye, the removal of the right eye would permanently incapacitate a warrior.[21]

It is no wonder that Jephthah's half-brothers sought a man of unconventional warfare. They asked him to captain the Gileadite army. Baffled, Jephthah replied, "Did not you hate me, and expel me from my father's house?" (Judg. 11:7). They repeated their request without a shred of remorse. They needed his help.

Jephthah could have declined out of spite, but instead he asked, "If you take me back home to fight against the people of Ammon, and the LORD delivers them to me, shall I be your head?" (Judg. 11:9).

Jephthah wasn't asking for leadership. His half-brothers had already offered it to him. He was bringing God into the equation.

God had become sovereign in Jephthah's life. Possibly, Jephthah had turned to God in Tob. Great men of faith have encountered God in times of banishment—in wildernesses, in caves, and on windswept mountaintops. A desolate position is often a promising place to meet God.

I believe that Jephthah grabbed hold of God like a man who seizes a rope on his way over a cliff. All of a sudden, the loser of Gilead had become a four-star general with God as his commander in chief.

Ruin

When Jephthah returned to Gilead to defeat the Ammonites, all the pistons were firing. He was a comeback kid chosen for a hero's role.

Jephthah immediately sent emissaries to the king of Ammon with the intention of eliminating the threat peacefully. Though unsuccessful, the attempt reveals Jephthah's character. This "mighty man of valor" (Judg. 11:1) was *not* first and foremost a man of blood. Nor was he bent on revenge. He could have sent his half-brothers into the heat of the front lines, as David sent Uriah (see 2 Sam. 11:15), but there is no mention of any retribution.

He also sought God in his decisions. He "spoke all his words before the LORD in Mizpah" (Judg. 11:11). As he prepared for battle, the "Spirit of the LORD came upon Jephthah" (Judg. 11:29).

The eyes of the entire nation were upon Jephthah. In a moment of passion, he flung out a vow to the God of the universe:

> If You will indeed deliver the people of Ammon into my hands, then it will be that whatever comes out of the doors of my house to meet me, when I return in peace from the people of Ammon, shall surely be the LORD's, and I will offer it up as a burnt offering.
> —Judg. 11:30-31

God answered by delivering the Ammonites into Jephthah's hand with a decisive victory. When Jephthah returned home, his daughter came out to meet him with "timbrels and dancing" (Judg. 11:34). Horrified, he "tore his clothes, and said, 'Alas, my daughter! You have brought me very low! You are among those who trouble me! For I have given my word to the LORD, and I cannot go back on it'" (Judg. 11:35).

Jephthah's daughter was his only child. She was intensely loyal to him, and he loved her. Scripture does not mention his wife. Possibly, she had died. His daughter was, perhaps, the only human alive who loved him.

Two months after the battle, after Jephthah's daughter returned from a prayerful retreat, Jephthah slaughtered her. Was Jephthah a cold-blooded murderer? There's no question that the deed was premeditated. It also violated one of the Ten Commandments: "Thou shalt not kill" (Exod. 20:13, KJV). But on the other hand, Jephthah must have known about God's command in Deuteronomy: "When you make a vow to the LORD your God, you shall not delay to pay it; for the LORD your God will surely require it of you, and it would be sin to you" (Deut. 23:21; also see Num. 30:2). Jephthah was caught between two Old Testament laws.

Some Bible scholars interpret Scripture to mean that Jephthah did not actually kill his daughter, but rather gave her up to a sequestered life of devotion, much like a nun. She would never marry, nor would she bear children to continue Jephthah's line. Commentator Matthew Henry disagrees, pointing out that Old Testament law and customs set no precedents that confer greater holiness upon women who purposely devoted themselves to single life. Even the prophetesses married. [22]

We can be sure that the idea of child sacrifice was not foreign to Jephthah. In the neighboring pagan lands, child sacrifice was commonplace. God had made it clear to the Israelites that He abhorred human sacrifice (see Deut. 12:31). Considering Jephthah's background in Tob, it's not unlikely that he'd already played the role of cutthroat. Jephthah was no stranger to bloodshed.

Scripture is silent about Jephthah's thoughts during the two-month interim between the vow and the execution. Perhaps he beseeched God to send an angel to stay his hand of execution upon his daughter, just as God had done for Abraham. One thing is certain—his communion with God cemented a vow that most Christians would consider revocable, and it propelled his steps to the misty borderline where craziness and faith sometimes meet.

Nearly every modern reader would strike down Jephthah's decision. Why didn't Jephthah stand up and say, "Hey, the deal is off because I didn't count on my daughter walking through the door!" Why didn't he attempt to circumvent the vow by redeeming her according to the provisos of Mosaic Law (see Lev. 27)? Why didn't he choose to suffer the consequences of breaking the vow rather than making his daughter pay the price for it?

After all, God never once asked Jephthah to sacrifice his daughter. God *did* ask Abraham to sacrifice Isaac. The historian, Josephus, states that Jephthah offered his daughter as a literal burnt offering and claims it was an "an oblation as was neither conformable to the law nor acceptable to God…"[23]

But which of the two choices—*Do not kill,* or *Do not break a vow to the Lord*—lies closer to the heart of the first commandment: "You shall have no other gods before me" (Exod. 20:3)? And which choice lies closest to its counterpart spoken by Jesus in the New Testament: "'Hear, O Israel, the LORD our God, the LORD is one. And you shall love the LORD your God with all your heart, with all your soul, with all your mind, and with all your strength.' This is the first commandment" (Mark 12:29-30)?

Jephthah decided that it was more important to honor his vow to God than to stay his hand of execution upon his daughter. He refused to allow circumstances or feelings to circumvent his commitment. He chose his invisible God above his visible child. Because Jephthah had grown to know God intimately, he was able to offer back the one human who had come along in life to love him. *God* was Jephthah's first love.

Stepping Out Beyond Ruin

One of the worst kinds of human pain comes as a result of inflicting injury or death upon someone you love. Life can seem pointless after that.

How did Jephthah go on living after his terrible deed? How and *why* did he ever walk with God again? Today, how do we go on living for God after destroying someone we love?

1. Realize that rescue is not a measure of God's love.

Imagine how many times Jephthah must have second-guessed himself and questioned God. Why didn't You stay my hand upon my daughter as You did on Abraham's son? A young child today might ask his father the same sort of question. Why didn't you stop my bicycle from falling over?

God's choice to withhold His hand of rescue is not a measure of His love for us. In the New Testament, John the Baptist sent an anguished word to Jesus from prison, asking, "Are You the Coming One, or do we look for another?" (Matt. 11:3) In other words, if You are the Son of God, why have You forgotten me in prison? Don't You love me? John and Jesus were kindred spirits from the outset. John leapt in his mother's womb when he sensed Jesus in the womb of Mary (Luke 1:41). John baptized Jesus (Matt. 3:13-16). Scripture calls John "the friend of the bridegroom" (John 3:29). But Jesus' reply to His imprisoned friend was cold fact: "The blind see and the lame walk; the lepers are cleansed and the deaf hear; the dead are raised up and the poor have the gospel preached to them" (Matt. 11:5). He offered no promise of eventual rescue, nor even a word of sympathy. Not only did John remain in prison, but Herod beheaded him.

Did Jesus love John the Baptist? Did He value him? Hear what He said about His friend to the multitudes: "Among those born of women there has not risen one greater than John the Baptist" (Matt. 11:11). When Jesus learned of John's death, He withdrew to a desolate place by Himself (Matt. 14:13), possibly to grieve and pray.

Very simply, God's sovereign plans for John the Baptist trumped temporal circumstances. They trumped human anguish—even the anguish of Jesus. But John the Baptist's honor was never lost though his head rolled. A man or woman of faith knows that God can be trusted even when He chooses not to rescue. The real treasure lies in our ever-deepening relationship with God—not in the safe resolution of our temporal circumstances.

2. Understand that God judges the heart, not the deed.

By His very character, God must demand justice. Jephthah paid dearly for his sin. He lost the only human who loved him. And with the death of his only child, he lost all descendants. While modern day courts would execute or imprison Jephthah, God imparted honor upon him for eternity.

God's measure of justice is infinitely more accurate than ours. He can read minds, He can plumb the depths of motives, and He can blot out sin with extraordinary grace. Had New Testament characters been included in the Hebrews 11 Hall of Fame, imagine the lineup. Possibly Paul, the persecutor; Mary Magdalene, the demon-possessed; and Peter, the disciple who denied Jesus three times. Who loved Jesus more than these?

God Himself said: "'For the LORD does not see as man sees; for man looks at the outward appearance, but the LORD looks at the heart'" (1 Sam. 16:7). God knows the deepest thoughts of kings and of murderers, of priests and of prisoners. The trophies in heaven's Hall of Fame will represent the gamut of life's experiences. Like a flea market, every size and shape of plaque will adorn God's wall.

3. Reject the world's accusation of "Hypocrite!"

I know of very few men who could slay a child after two months of premeditation and still have the audacity to worship God. The whole earth would shout "Hypocrite!" Gossip would fly: "What else would you expect from the son of a harlot?" Condemnation would suck the sinner down a spiritual drain.

Jephthah could have committed suicide, withdrawn from life, drowned himself in liquor, or allied himself with his old cronies in Tob. But he chose to continue ruling Israel, leading them in battle against their enemies (see Judg. 12).

Though Jephthah had initiated his own tragedy, after the deed was done, he donned an attitude like Job's: "Though He slay me, yet will I trust Him" (Job 13:15). Jephthah chose to stick with a God who had established harsh rules that had trapped his only child in a deadly vise.

In the halls of human heroism, there comes a point—from a godless standpoint—when the creature should muster a rebellious brand of fortitude, stand up and say "Enough!" or "I curse God and die!" to the Creator before bowing his back for the final blow. To the man on the street, Jephthah seemed either a hypocrite or a pathetic coward. He chose to discard all human dignity and to believe in the face of horrific circumstances that God is good. Jephthah walked out of the storm naked and pointed to the rainbow.

4. Know that God's faithfulness is not depleted by our worst mistakes.

We err grievously if we judge God's capacity to forgive us by our own capacity to forgive ourselves. If we limit God's forgiveness, we in effect equate His ability to create planets to our ability to build houses. And if we refuse to forgive ourselves when God has already forgiven us, we clothe ourselves with the arrogance of a tyrant.

God is not bound by mortal revulsion to sin. While the outraged world shouts "Sinner!," the Father runs to the sinner, falls on his neck, and kisses him (see Luke 15:20). The one deemed worthless finds the best robe on his shoulders, a ring on his finger, shoes on his feet, and a fatted calf roasting on the spit (see Luke 15:20-23).

Who was the greatest sinner of all time? When Jesus carried the sins of the entire human race upon His back, He became the chief sinner. God accepted the sacrifice for the tallest garbage heap of sin on earth and gave the sacrificial Lamb a seat at His right hand forevermore. Sin has a bottom, but God's love is depthless.

5. **Understand that we worship God *not* because of who we are, but because of who He is.**

If God had chosen to rescue Jephthah's daughter, His decision would have been first and foremost about Himself—not about Jephthah and his daughter.

Everything God orchestrates revolves around who God is. Just as earth is not the center of the solar system, we are not the center of God's purpose. Had we been born a worm, we should worship God. Had we been born a star ten thousand times bigger than our own sun, we should worship God. Who we are is immaterial. We must trust that God knows our position and that, in His goodness, He will draw us to His own glorious self where the love we seek so desperately abides forever.

When we fall more deeply in love with God, we begin to realize that we can trust Him *even* with the lives of those we love more than we love ourselves. Because the love of God is so great for us, we can let go of the handlebars of our lives and say: *Take me where You please. You are enough for me.*

6. **Realize that God's love is more enduring than our pain.**

Jephthah knew that his own love for his daughter was bigger than his act of murder. Could the Father's love for him be any less?

Jephthah also understood that God's plans are not confined to the interim between our date of birth and our date of death. He trusted that the Creator would guard his enduring love and purify it in heaven. All the holes would be mended there and all the tears filtered into the beautiful receptacle that love was intended to be from the onset of time. While still earthbound, Jephthah strode forward through sorrow, day by day, as if God had already whispered to him the verse, "For I am persuaded that neither death nor life, nor angels nor principalities nor powers, nor things present nor things to come, nor height nor depth, nor any other created thing, shall be able to separate us from the love of God which is in Christ Jesus our Lord" (Rom. 8:38-39).

177

Anyone who has sought God after a tragedy knows that He imparts grace at the most unexpected moments. I believe that God dabbed lavish salve on Jephthah's heart before he ever departed earth. Psalm 34:18 tells us that "The LORD is near to those who have a broken heart, and saves such as have a contrite spirit." Sometimes He comforts us through a wildflower in exactly the right spot, or a knock on the door from an unlikely visitor. But to the broken heart, it is a telegraph straight from God emblazoned with the words, "I am here."

The six remaining years of Jephthah's life, while they were cloaked with shame, demonstrate a steadfast walk with God. He embodied the spirit of Hebrews 12:1, which invites us to "lay aside every weight, and sin which so easily ensnares us, and let us run with endurance the race that is set before us." Like a pilgrim with his eyes on the Promised Land ahead, Jephthah existed to see his daughter again, to embrace her in his arms, and to meet the God of unbendable laws and unfathomable grace face-to-face.

A Final Word

Spiritual victory sometimes comes packaged in peculiar wounds. Jephthah was a hero not because of his actions, but because of his godly reactions to his unorthodox self-actions.

Jephthah's actions are not meant to be emulated. His case was extraordinary. But the tenor of his vow reverberated an all-out love and trust for God.

If there is anything honorable about Jephthah, it is that he continued seeking God after ruin. A man who casts the lives of his beloved ones and himself into ruin and still seeks God after the ashes have fallen is either a very small man or he is a man who is a companion to a big, big God. Jephthah knew God beyond murder, beyond shame, beyond self-hatred. Because Jephthah's unrelenting faith was in a God who cannot be boxed in, God honored this premeditated murderer in the most prestigious Hall of Fame in history.

APPLIED FAITH

1. Write down each of the vows you have made to God. If Jephthah's vow to sacrifice his daughter was so important to him, how important is your marriage vow to you? Or other vows?

2. The next time you give a gift, concentrate on the card. Realize that your words might be more important than your gift.

3. Think twice the next time you are tempted to label anyone a hypocrite.

4. If you are surrounded by self-ruin today, continue to walk with God even if all the world sees you through condescending eyes, bolstered by the realization that God sees your heart.

. . . .

CHAPTER 16

DAVID: SEEKING GOD WITH UNBRIDLED PASSION

And what more shall I say? For the time would fail me to tell of Gideon and Barak and Samson and Jephthah, also of David and Samuel and the prophets.

—Heb. 11:32

READING: 1 SAMUEL 16-31; 2 SAMUEL 1-24; 1 KINGS 1-2; 1 CHRONICLES 11-29

DAVID IS UNDOUBTEDLY one of the largest characters in the Bible. Any attempt to contain his life within a single chapter is like trying to contain the ocean in a fishpond. He is large in terms of his range of experiences, his reign over Israel, and the multitude of Bible verses written by and about him. He was a shepherd, a giant-killer, a musician, a king, a fugitive, a cave-dweller, a warrior, a husband of many wives, a father, an adulterer, a murderer, a dancer, an administrator, and a poet.

David's range of experiences is vast, but I am even more amazed by the range of his heart. God refers to him in Scripture as "a man after My own heart" (Acts 13:22; 1 Sam. 13:14). According to Bible scholars, his name means "beloved." The diversity of his experiences expanded his heart like an accordion that extends until it blares off key.

181

There was nothing half-measure about David. He killed all-out, he battled all-out, he grieved all-out, he committed adultery all-out, he murdered all-out, he repented all-out, he befriended all-out, he extended mercy all-out, and he worshipped all-out. No one could ever accuse him of being lukewarm. David was about stretching forward, even if it meant doing so in an abnormal way, even if it meant increasing the likelihood of straying onto sinful ground.

Why would God refer to a murderer and adulterer as a man after His own heart? Why did God include such a blatant sinner in the Hall of Fame of Faith?

And how can today's Christian attain David's level of passion? Was his unusual stretching a trait of his God-given personality? What then, can we do if we're born with a passive personality? And if we do manage to open the gate to unbridled passion, how do we avoid the pitfalls of sin?

David's Hurdles

King David's life began as commonplace as the everyday life of today's everyday man. The youngest of eight brothers, he was the overlooked sibling stuck with the chores in the sheep field. When the prophet, Samuel, arrived at David's father's house to anoint a new king, David was laboring in the field amid the weather and the manure. Like Cinderella, he was left next to the servant's hearth while his siblings lined up in the parlor waiting to see if the glass slipper of favor would fit. Yet, God in His sovereignty pointed Samuel to David and paved a unique road to the throne. "I took you from the sheepfold," God said, "from following the sheep, to be ruler over My people Israel" (1 Chron. 17:7).

As Samuel sought God's chosen ruler that day, God advised Samuel to refrain from judging David by his outward appearance because "the LORD does not see as man sees." Rather, "the LORD looks at the heart" (1 Sam. 16:7). From the outset, David's legacy zeroed in on the heart.

If we think it unfair for God to have lavished unmerited favor upon a nobody, we need only take one look at the obstacles in David's pathway—enough to frighten anyone away from coveting

David's position. His brothers envied him, the former king attempted repeatedly to murder him, his best friend died in battle, his newborn son died as a result of David's sin, his son Absalom led an army against him, a plague ravaged his country as a result of his own pride, and God rejected his dream to build a temple.

David also confronted inner battles, especially his own guilt. This man after God's own heart stumbled into blatant sin of the caliber that would require no additional Hollywood embellishment. Through a series of circumstances that he no doubt never expected to occur, he caved in to his passions to the point that he committed adultery and premeditated murder.

How could a man guilty of adultery and murder continue to govern God's people? A Bible scholar might endeavor to seek an extracurricular explanation or a previously unexplored answer tucked backstage behind the curtain, but it doesn't exist. The answer lies in depth, not in scope. It lies deep, deep within David's abounding passion for God and within God's depthless mercy.

Seven Ways to Unbridle Our Passion for God

How did David practice unbridled passion in the midst of his many challenges? What aspects of his faith prompted God to list him as a hero of the faith despite his blatant sins?

Today, how do we consistently reignite our passion for God amidst life's overwhelming responsibilities and stark realities? If we do ignite our passion, how do we run in God's direction without tripping over sin?

1. Get to know your Master.

On the surface, unbridled passion is dangerous. It risks straying from the boundaries of truth, careening down the pathways of emotion without engaging the guidelines of knowledge and discernment. We've all heard about well-intentioned people who became victims of cult leaders who took advantage of their loneliness. Unbridled passion can have ill-fated results.

183

Equestrians know that if you ride your horse without a bridle, you need to have an exceptional relationship with the horse if you hope to control the direction the horse will run. With David, it was a "given" that he would run in the direction of obedience—not because he longed to follow all the rules, but because he loved the Rule Maker. Yet, we must never think God's laws were unimportant to David. Before his death, he called his successor and son, Solomon, to his side and instructed him to "keep the charge of the LORD your God: to walk in His ways, to keep His statutes, His commandments, His judgments, and His testimonies, as it is written in the Law of Moses, that you may prosper in all that you do and wherever you turn" (1 Kings 2:3). God said of David: "I have found David the son of Jesse, a man after My own heart, who will do all My will" (Acts 13:22).

In Psalm 19, David expressed his desire to follow the rules:

> The statutes of the LORD are right, rejoicing the heart: the commandment of the LORD is pure, enlightening the eyes. The fear of the LORD is clean, enduring for ever: the judgments of the LORD are true and righteous altogether. More to be desired are they than gold, yea, than much fine gold: sweeter also than honey and the honeycomb. Moreover by them is thy servant warned: and in keeping of them there is great reward.
>
> —Ps. 19:8-11, KJV

The steering factor for David was his intimate relationship with God. But how did he form it? First Samuel 16:13 says, "Then Samuel took the horn of oil and anointed him in the midst of his brothers; and the Spirit of the LORD came upon David from that day forward." A good portion of it was a gift. But I'd like to think there was more.

As a young shepherd, David spent time in solitude in the fields tending the sheep. Possibly he played the harp to calm them; possibly he practiced writing early drafts of the psalms. In addition to God's sovereign hand upon David's life, the solitude of those early fields may have been the most formative component of David's faith.

Even as king, David continued to spend significant periods of time in solitude. He hid from Saul in the wilderness, woods, and caves. He sought refuge and encouragement from the prophet, Samuel, in the quietude of Naioth, a retreat for prophets. In these places, David schooled himself to seek, trust, and praise God.

David is like a master writer who knows grammar rules from the inside out. Not until after he mastered the rules did he dare to move beyond the restrictions of colons and commas to create the cadences and lyricism that make words sing. David yearned to know God so fervently that a bridle would have restrained his creativity in reaching Him. David longed to run beyond the boundaries in uncommon ways that bridles do not accommodate. He was like a child who runs off the front porch, despite his mother's disapproval, for the express purpose of falling into the arms of his returning father.

At its best, passion for God and for others bears within its embrace the prerequisite of obedience. While it may momentarily veer off course as a result of its ardor, it outruns the feet past the common threshold to untilled ground where untold delights await the seeker. When passion is directed at God, the side roads become less of a concern. All eyes are focused ahead on the Beloved.

The more intimately we know God, the less we'll have a problem igniting a passion for Him. Like a horse, we may become sick or lazy at times, but with the bridle off, when we spot the Master at the finish line, there will be no stopping us from running hard and fast, even though it may mean tripping a time or two.

2. Take risks for God.

Within the camps of conservative Christianity, risk-taking is often considered unwise. We are taught to save for a rainy day, update our insurance policies, and place the personal safety of our family at a priority. This was not the lifestyle of Christ's apostles. While God does require us to be responsible and to obey His commandments, conservatism in spiritual matters is paralyzing. Often, it is nothing more than disobedience disguised in fashionable prudence.

How can God guide our future if we've already mapped out and paid for every cobblestone in our pathway? While we may indeed find security and comfort by pre-planning our route, the miracles and awe of God's provision will find sparse room for a foothold.

By the time David met Goliath on the battlefield, he had already learned about risk-taking in the sheep field. One day, a bear came to attack the sheep. Another day, a lion came. God enabled David to defeat the bear and the lion with his bare hands. These victories would become landmarks that would shape David's perception of God for a lifetime.

The story of David and Goliath is the proverbial story of the underdog. One day, David came from the shepherd's field to the soldiers' camp with food for his brothers. There he observed Goliath taunting the Israelites. To David, Goliath was a bear among the sheep, a lion among the lambs. Fortified by his own consistent communion with God, David volunteered to fight Goliath. Even when his jealous older brother ridiculed him, he continued forward.

As with the bear and the lion, he required no fancy accoutrements of war—only his shepherd's bag, his sling, and five smooth stones from a brook. He loaded his slingshot and flung a stone at Goliath. It hit him in the forehead, Goliath collapsed, and David borrowed Goliath's sword to cut off his head.

In some ways, Goliath was not as formidable to David as he seemed to the others. David focused on God's past provisions, remembering with each step how God had aided him in the past. That memory shrunk Goliath down to a conquerable size. Similarly, David's victory against Goliath would give him a fresh memory to go forward towards the next formidable foe.

Risk-taking for God builds momentum on itself. Each experience of God's presence adds a new memory block. Block on block, faith on faith, the risk-taker finds himself above common ground in a position where others look up and say, "Get down! Aren't you afraid?" But it's too late. The risk-taker has already become addicted to meeting God at the rendezvous point, and he is consumed by the impending arrival of his Beloved. Until he looks down, he may never even realize he's standing above ground.

David's decision to fight Goliath was also driven by his belief in God's long-range plans. David cried out, "For who is this un-circumcised Philistine, that he should defy the armies of the living God?" (1 Sam. 17:26). He recognized that Goliath was not only defying Israel, but also Israel's God. He looked beyond the surface information, beyond the battle of the day, beyond the boundaries of his life. Like Moses, who peered ahead for the Promised Land, David desired to sustain and carry forward God's Kingdom into a future where his mortal body would not go.

To David, success in battle was not about King David; it was about God's plan. David's railings against the enemy were not a personal affront motivated by pride or personal gain. Rather, his fervency in battle was motivated by the knowledge that Almighty God, for one reason or another, had anointed a shepherd boy to oversee His people at this hour in His plan. God had handed David the staff, whether he deserved to hold it or not. Like Frodo carrying the ring in J.R.R. Tolkien's popular novel, *The Lord of the Rings*, David wielded the slingshot for the ultimate good of his kingdom and the future generations who would enjoy it without him.

Amazing things transpire when we cease allowing personal success to control our steps. We end up moving further than our ambitions had planned because we cease fearing failure. We don't view failure as failure any longer. We view it as part of God's multigenerational plan. When we cancel self from the equation, we also cancel self from the fallout of failure. We are freed to take the next step of faith, and we run unfettered, racing forward with the childlike anticipation of encountering God.

3. Love lavishly.

One could effectively argue that advances in technology and transportation have squelched modern day expressions of love. All we need do is take a trip to a historical library and read letters from nineteenth century Americans to observe the openness of their affection—husband for wife, father for daughter, brother for brother, sister for sister, friend for friend. During the 1800s, a lifespan of seventy years wasn't normal. Epidemics ran rampant. Antibiotics were nonexistent. A daughter who moved to California might never see her East Coast parents again. A letter from a loved one was an item to be cherished and read aloud again and again.

While this may seem overly sentimental to us today, the same outcome holds true: when a loved one dies today, he is just as unreachable whether he subscribed to e-mail before his death or not. The gulf between life and death is just as impassable as it ever was.

David was the caliber of man who wouldn't *just* have a friend; he'd have a friend whose soul was knit to his (Jonathan). He wasn't *just* kind; he'd take a lame man and give him a lifetime seat at the king's table (Mephibosheth). He didn't *just* forgive; he repeatedly spared the life of a man who was attempting to murder him (Saul). He didn't *just* marry; he married multiple wives (Michal, Bathsheba, and six others). He didn't *just* grieve; he wept and fasted outdoors in the dirt (for his newborn son conceived with Bathsheba).

One of the supreme "stretchings" in David's life came in response to jealous Saul, who clung to the kingship of Israel even after God had transferred the kingship to David. David's deference to Saul was not due to a lack of backbone, but rather due to respect for God's formerly anointed one. He was fully aware that Saul was plagued by evil spirits. For a time, he played the harp to chase away Saul's evil spirits, serving as Saul's advocate against evil. He also married Saul's daughter, Michal. He called Saul "Father" and Saul called him "Son." Shifting Saul to the enemy category ripped David's heart asunder. He wrote of his distress in Psalm 55:

> My heart is in anguish within me; the terrors of death have fallen upon me. Fear and trembling come upon me, and horror overwhelms me....For it is not an enemy who taunts me—then I could bear it; it is not an adversary who deals insolently with me—then I could hide from him. But it is you, a man, my equal, my companion, my familiar friend. We used to take sweet counsel together; within God's house we walked in the throng.
>
> —Ps. 55:4-5; 12-14, ESV

The eventual deaths of Saul and Jonathan in battle sent David into throes of grief, as if Saul and Jonathan were his blood father and blood brother. The cost of David's unbridled passion, taken several lengths beyond sensible boundaries, was extreme.

Today, well-meaning friends and family admonish us to guard our heart. But David did not guard his heart. His love drained all-out with no provision for a plug. If his heart broke, he begged God to mend it, and then he stood in line again. "Wait on the LORD," David said, "Be of good courage, and He shall strengthen your heart: wait, I say, on the LORD!" (Ps. 27:14).

David understood that a heart sanctioned with free will is not containable. Love always reaches outside the gate, like a horse that seeks the proverbial green grass. It is the nature of love to outstretch itself. David said, "As the deer pants for flowing streams, so pants my soul for you, O God" (Ps. 42:1, ESV).

If David seems overboard in his love for man, it was because he had already discovered depthless love in his relationship with God. While the typical churchgoer today may sojourn in the antechamber outside God's throne room, content to enjoy a morning and evening appointment with Him, David was pacing the hallway and knocking on His door impetuously, begging for frequent entrance.

David was enthralled with God because he watched Him answer again and again, and he stoked those answers in his heart like a campfire on a frozen frontier. David said, "I love the LORD because He has heard my voice *and* my supplications. Because He has inclined His ear to me, therefore I will call upon Him as long as I live" (Ps. 116:1-2).

In our society, a tendency exists to love with conservatism, as if we need to preserve a dough-starter with which to begin again in the event a relationship goes stale. But God never taught us this. When Jesus said, "You shall love the LORD your God with all your heart, with all your soul, with all your mind, and with all your strength" (Mark 12:30), He did not include a complimentary fire escape. And when He said, "You shall love your neighbor as yourself," He did not include a trap door (Mark 12:31). David understood this. He gave God and his neighbor his whole heart.

4. Allow yourself to publicly repent.

After Saul died, David's reign as king flourished. He fought and overcame numerous formidable enemies. The Biblical accounts of his victories are bloody enough to taint the image of David, the gentle shepherd boy. Even God would later exempt David from building a temple because he had shed too much blood. God said: "You have shed much blood and have made great wars; you shall not build a house for My name, because you have shed much blood on the earth in My sight" (1 Chron. 22:8).

Just at a time when David's popularity as king was running at an all-time high, he decided to coast. Scripture says, "It happened in the spring of the year, at the time when kings go out to battle, that David sent Joab and his servants with him, and all Israel; and they destroyed the people of Ammon and besieged Rabbah. But David remained at Jerusalem" (2 Sam. 11:1).

David's downfall began with an innocent day off. As king, David knew that his rightful place was at the head of battle. But he loitered, giving pause for temptation to enter the void. While strolling on the roof of his house, he spotted Bathsheba, beautiful wife of Uriah, bathing. He sent messengers to fetch her, committed adultery with her, connived to pin her resulting pregnancy upon Uriah, plotted to send Uriah into the thick of battle, sent the orders for Uriah's demise in Uriah's own pocket, and then married the widow, Bathsheba.

God's consequences fell hard—even on David, the man after His own heart. Scripture says that "the thing that David had done displeased the LORD" (2 Sam. 11:27). God admonished David through Nathan, the prophet:

> Now therefore, the sword shall never depart from your house, because you have despised Me, and have taken the wife of Uriah the Hittite to be your wife. Thus says the LORD: "Behold, I will raise up adversity against you from your own house; and I will take your wives before your eyes and give them to your neighbor, and he shall lie with your wives in the sight of this sun. For you

did it secretly, but I will do this thing before all Israel, before the sun."

—2 Sam. 12:10-12

As if a light had been switched on in the cellar of his mind, David finally understood the seriousness of his hiatus from God. He said to Nathan, "I have sinned against the LORD" (2 Sam. 12:13). Despite David's pleas for mercy, Bathsheba's baby died. In the years that followed, God's judgment continued to manifest itself. The house of David shuddered with violence. David's son, Amnon, raped his half-sister, Tamar. Enraged, David's son, Absalom, arranged to have his servants murder Amnon. Absalom rebelled against David, entered Jerusalem with his own army, and defiled David's concubines in public on a rooftop. David's general, Joab, speared Absalom through the heart. Another son, Adonijah, was executed after he tried to usurp David's chosen heir, Solomon, to the throne.

God did not excuse David, his chosen leader, with a light tap on the hand. Yet we must be cautious when judging David's sins. Sin is sin, but the slippery slopes of sin are not necessarily the same length from culture to culture and generation to generation. Sleeping with Bathsheba and sending her husband to the most dangerous position in the battlefield were only two steps forward over a blurry line of the bigamy and slaughter David had been practicing all along. Satan subtly moved the bar slightly forward during a lapse in David's communion with God, and David took the bait. Amazing as it may seem, David's plotting and deception were perhaps the most drastic deviances from the faithfulness he had been practicing all along.

But if anyone ever repented, David repented. After Nathan, the prophet, exposed David's sin and said, "You are the man!" (2 Sam. 12:7), David acknowledged his guilt, even though he could have ordered Nathan's execution. As his baby son lay dying, David fasted on the ground and refused to rise even when the elders of his house attempted to lift him up. His Psalm 51 is a heart-wrenching plea to God:

Have mercy upon me, O God, according to thy lovingkindness: according unto the multitude of thy tender mercies blot out my transgressions. Wash me thoroughly from mine iniquity, and cleanse me from my sin. For I acknowledge my transgressions: and my sin is ever before me. Against thee, thee only, have I sinned... Purge me with hyssop, and I shall be clean: wash me, and I shall be whiter than snow....Create in me a clean heart, O God; and renew a right spirit within me. Cast me not away from thy presence; and take not thy holy spirit from me. Restore unto me the joy of thy salvation; and uphold me with thy free spirit.... The sacrifices of God are a broken spirit: a broken and a contrite heart, O God, thou wilt not despise.

—Ps. 51:1-4, 7, 10-12, 17, KJV

David realized that he had not only sinned against Bathsheba and Uriah, but most importantly, he had offended God. He longed for the baby to live, but he also longed to be restored to God. He not only repented, but he put it in writing. There is nothing private about his psalm.

Our modern day American society commonly sidelines repentance as a messy necessity that should be handled in private. It is too uncomfortably close to humility, which involves bowing oneself to a lower position where one's authority becomes vulnerable.

But the greatest men I know are the first to say, "I was wrong." Apostle Paul admitted he was the "chief" of sinners (1 Tim. 1:15). Job, who was guilty of nothing worse than complaining about his plight, repented in "dust and ashes" (Job 42:6). I have been more affected by godly, humble men who apologized than by godly men who are consistently correct in everything public. The repentant man takes an extra step towards restoring himself to God and his fellow man.

While repentance should never be staged as a show for the sake of pride or gain, neither should it be cloaked with such privacy that it fails to cleanse the guilty soul or soothe the injured party. Perhaps it would not be such a bad idea for today's Christian bookstores to stock a healthy supply of sackcloth and ashes next to the communion candles and baptismal gowns.

5. Get up and run after each fall.

After David and Bathsheba's baby died, David rose out of his grief, worshipped God, and ate. Scripture says: "So David arose from the ground, washed and anointed himself, and changed his clothes; and he went into the house of the LORD and worshiped. Then he went to his own house; and when he requested, they set food before him, and he ate" (2 Sam. 12:20). When they inquired about his grief, David simply said "But now he is dead, why should I fast? Can I bring him back again? I shall go to him, but he shall not return to me" (2 Sam. 12:23).

After David's rebellious son Absalom was killed—a son whose defiance arguably was a by-product of David's permissiveness—David mourned him long and hard. But when David's general, the man who had slain Absalom, urged him to pull himself together, David shook off his grief. He "arose and sat in the gate," resuming his post at his seat of authority (2 Sam. 19:8).

When David sinned by conducting a census of Israel—a sin that seems trivial at first glance, though many Bible scholars attribute it to his pride of leadership—God punished Israel with a plague that killed 70,000 men. David cried, "Surely I have sinned, and I have done wickedly" (2 Sam. 24:17). Instead of blaming God or immobilizing himself with self-pity, he consulted with the prophet, Gad, and followed Gad's instructions to build an altar, where David sacrificed burnt offerings to God.

After each of these tragedies, largely resulting from his own sins, David picked himself up off the ground because he continued to believe God was good and because he desired a restored relationship. In the ranks of God's anointed, David realized that self-pity was not a long-term option. Like beleaguered Job, he seemed to hear God say, "Now prepare yourself like a man" (Job 38:3).

In Psalm 51:7, David said, "Wash me, and I shall be whiter than snow." I don't believe that today's average Christian fully believes God will wash him whiter than snow after repentance. Not really, not deeply. While he may acknowledge that he's been forgiven, he privately thinks that somehow he's come out slightly grayer than before, like a new garment that has been washed for the first time.

Many sinful men and women are derailed not so much by the sin, but by the guilt they wear after having asked for forgiveness. Sometimes, particularly when public shame is involved, the weight of the guilt can become heavier than the sin. The sinner begins to see himself as unworthy of anything good. He sees his self-pity as an admirable trait suggestive of his remorse, while in reality it is an albatross that becomes sin itself, choking off the good he might have done and the praise he might have offered had he not been bound by his own ropes in a spiritual basement.

Perhaps part of the difficulty is in our perception of sin. Author Martyn Lloyd-Jones hones in on the genesis of sin:

> We tend to think of sin as we see it in its rags and in the gutters of life. We look at a drunkard, poor fellow, and we say: There is sin; that is sin. But that is not the essence of sin. To have a real picture and a true understanding of it, you must look at some great saint, some unusually devout and devoted man. Look at him there upon his knees in the very presence of God. Even there self is intruding itself, and the temptation is for him to think about himself, to think pleasantly and pleasurably about himself and really to be worshiping himself rather than God. That, not the other, is the true picture of sin. The other is sin, of course, but there you do not see it at its acme; you do not see it in its essence. Or, to put it in another form, if you really want to understand something about the nature of Satan and his activities, the thing to do is not to go to the dregs or the gutters of life; if you really want to know something about Satan, go away to that wilderness where our Lord spent forty days and forty nights. That is the true picture of Satan where you see him tempting the very Son of God.[24]

While clothed in human flesh, we have no hope of ever erasing sin completely from our lives. Even if we were to lie face down on the ground all day long, our minds would be contemplating sin. The moment we arise, choices would confront us. Do we take the best sandwich in the refrigerator or do we leave it for a brother? If we decide to leave it for a brother, do we pat ourselves on the back for having been so unselfish? The mercy of God, extended to us through the sacrifice of Jesus on the cross, is the only answer to this dilemma. Like David, the adulterer and murderer, we must appeal to the mercy of God even after having entertained two seconds of pride for having left the best sandwich for our brother.

We may tend to think that David sported a cavalier attitude in asking God to forgive his murder and adultery while yet retaining his kingship. Instead, I think David knew a God who is big enough to forgive a plot of murder just as completely as a prick of pride.

6. Worship with abandon.

One day, while bringing the Ark of the Covenant from the house of Obededom to Zion, the "City of David," David "danced before the LORD with all his might" (2 Sam. 6:12, 14) while girded in a linen ephod (a ceremonial loincloth or apron). He accompanied a large parade of worshippers as they followed the Ark in a holiday-like celebration. They shouted, sang, blew trumpets, crashed cymbals, and played psalteries and harps. The Ark was coming home to the City of David! David's heart cried out in a song of joy:

> Oh, give thanks to the LORD! Call upon His name; Make known His deeds among the peoples! Sing to Him, sing psalms to Him; Talk of all His wondrous works! Glory in His holy name; Let the hearts of those rejoice who seek the LORD! Seek the LORD and His strength; Seek His face evermore!
>
> —1 Chron. 16:8-11

His wife, Michal, watched. Embarrassed by his public display, she "despised him in her heart" (1 Chron. 15:29). The pepper in her voice when she confronted him is almost audible: "How the king of Israel honored himself today, uncovering himself today before the eyes of his servants' female servants, as one of the vulgar fellows shamelessly uncovers himself!" (2 Sam. 6:20, ESV).

David replied, "It was before the LORD, who chose me above your father and above all his house, to appoint me as prince over

Israel, the people of the LORD—and I will make merry before the LORD" (2 Sam. 6:21, ESV).

Why was David's wife so hateful? I believe she was more interested in appearances than in worship, more concerned about the opinions of onlookers rather than the favor of God, and possibly jealous. She was unwilling to let David express his love for God in his own, natural way.

When we fall deeply in love with God, our praise increases in frequency and volume. There's no stopping the songs, the praises, and the private meaningful acts of prayer. Our prayer time is never long enough, and it spills into our everyday activities.

Yet each of us expresses our passion for God in a different way. Just as some worshippers raise their arms and sway back and forth in church, the businessman in the next pew is beating his little finger on the edge of the pew with a fervency that hurts his finger. The lady beside him is closing her eyes and bowing her head to envision Jesus. Each of these worshippers is engaging the heart, selecting their own preference for outlets. All are worshipping.

You will know you are truly worshipping when you find yourself straining to hold yourself back. You will know you are worshipping when you are more pleased by the other guy's exuberance than you are suspicious of it.

Cheryl. Cheryl is a mentally handicapped lady with a talent for expressing her praise in dance. When Cheryl attended a local performance by a Christian jazz musician, she became so excited that she leapt from her seat during a song, ran to the stage, and danced in an all-out beautiful expression of her heart. She was so drained at the end of the song that she fell into the arms of a friend. Her object was not attention; it was praise. The audience was not an enticement; the audience was a hindrance. But Cheryl's love overcame her inhibitions. Cheryl was worshipping in the purest sense of the word.

While we may be uncomfortable with exhibiting our praise in public, there's nothing to prevent us from doing so in private. The

Old Testament abounds with worshippers who sprawled on their faces to pray, blew on instruments, fasted, repented in dust and ashes, and danced. Have you ever pulled up to a stoplight beside someone who is singing aloud in her car? Suddenly she notices you and abruptly stops singing, embarrassed to find you watching. It wouldn't have crossed David's mind to be embarrassed. David stretched beyond the limits of the customary because he yearned to bust through the veil of the mortal to see the immortal. If he was oblivious to his unconventional behavior, it wasn't because he was flippant about offending others. It was because he was careening headlong into the nebula of God's presence.

7. Pour excess emotional energy into positive efforts.

David was not only a poet and psalmist, but also a prophet. Near the end of his life, he said: "The Spirit of the LORD spoke by me, and his word was on my tongue" (2 Sam. 23:2).

His psalms were a positive outlet for his passion and talent. His pain, his shame, his frustration, his fear, his love, his exuberance, and his joy poured out into some of the finest poetry ever penned. Though his psalms were intended primarily for the eyes of One, God distributed them across the oceans and the ages. If there was any untamed passion loitering in David's blood, he channeled it through his pen as an offering to God, which funneled down through the ages to benefit us today.

In yet another effort to channel his energy into positive efforts, David decided to build a temple for the Ark of God. But because David had spilled so much blood in battle, God said "no" and gave the privilege to David's son, Solomon. Yet God did not leave David empty-handed. He gave David a solemn promise that satisfied his soul:

> And it shall be, when your days are fulfilled, when you must go to be with your fathers, that I will set up your seed after you, who will be of your sons; and I will establish his kingdom. He shall build Me a house, and I will establish his throne forever. I will be his Father, and he shall be My son; and I will not take

My mercy away from him, as I took it from him who was before you. And I will establish him in My house and in My kingdom forever; and his throne shall be established forever.
—1 Chron. 17:11-14

David could've moped about his thwarted construction plans, but instead he busied himself with the next-best task: he created a blueprint for the temple, assembled the craftsmen, and gathered the building materials to equip the temple. He busied himself with positive outlets to enhance God's plans, even though the preparatory work wasn't his first choice. David recognized the value of continuity in God's plan, just as a grandfather recognizes the value of planting an acorn for a grandchild. He knows he won't see the full-grown oak in his lifetime, but he is more interested in the grand plan than he is in his enjoyment of it.

David's Death

David served as king of Israel for forty years. He died at about age seventy (see 2 Sam. 5:4) "in a good old age, full of days and riches and honor" (1 Chron. 29:28) and was buried on a site that Bible scholars believe to be on Mt. Zion near the old city of Jerusalem.

Before he died, he prayed for Solomon: "O LORD God of Abraham, Isaac, and Israel… give my son Solomon a loyal heart to keep Your commandments and Your testimonies and Your statutes, to do all these things, and to build the temple for which I have made provision" (1 Chron. 29:18-19). To the very end of his mortal life, David focused on God's overarching plan. David knew that if faith is nothing else, it is a selfless commitment to the continuity of all portions of the divine plan, seen and unseen.

A Final Word

As a young man, David perceived God as One who rescues the lamb from the lion and the ewe from the bear. His perception of God never changed, even when Goliaths of many kinds invaded every chamber of his life.

Except for weak (and unfortunately devastating) lapses in his life, it could be said that David desired two things: to please God, and for God to be pleased with him. Because this was his motive, the danger of running erratically was minimized.

The apostle Peter, testifying to the Israelites about Jesus, casts light on David's outlook.

> For David says concerning Him [Jesus]: "I foresaw the LORD always before my face, for He is at my right hand, that I may not be shaken. Therefore my heart rejoiced, and my tongue was glad; Moreover my flesh also will rest in hope. For You will not leave my soul in Hades, nor will You allow Your Holy One to see corruption. You have made known to me the ways of life; You will make me full of joy in Your presence."
>
> —Acts 2:25-28

David foresaw the coming of Christ. And when Jesus came centuries later, the parallels between David and Jesus were unmistakable. Both were called shepherds, both were born in Bethlehem, and both led and fled from multitudes of men. Though not divine in nature, David exemplified the far-ranging poles of justice and mercy that characterize God and great men of God. He slaughtered and he pardoned; he led and he served; he addressed multitudes and he sought God in holy solitude.

David lived life to its top. He was all about stretching forward, about yearning after God on the farthest frontier. He reserved none of his passion for a rainy day. He spent it all and then gathered more. If life were a sponge, he squeezed everything out of it and poured it over himself in an exhilarating song to God. He did everything in Olympic proportions and he did it as an open book before God and man. He set every footstep on overdrive, but because his passion was foremost for God, his overdrive of obedience saved and revived the nation of Israel.

Today, when we read David's psalms, the concentrated oil of his heart, we can be refreshed in knowing that David still chose to love God after exploring Him beyond the gates of conventional boundaries. Like an astronaut who has trod on the moon, he charted new frontiers of worship for us, came excitedly back to his desk, and sang these words:

> Where can I go from Your Spirit? Or where can I flee from Your presence? If I ascend into heaven, You are there; if I make my bed in hell, behold, You are there. If I take the wings of the morning, and dwell in the uttermost parts of the sea, even there Your hand shall lead me, and Your right hand shall hold me.
>
> —Ps. 139:7-10

May we, too, stir a passion to be unbridled so that we might see and know God beyond the boundaries of conventions and customs where faith encounters the holy wake of the glory of God.

APPLIED FAITH

1. Begin a journal in which you record incidents when you encountered God on unsafe ground.

2. Go to a relative or friend you've neglected and express your love to him or her.

3. Write and sing your own psalm to God.

4. Plant an acorn as a gesture of faith in the maturation of a majestic oak tree you will never see.

. . . .

CHAPTER 17

SAMUEL: SEEKING GOD IN THE MIDST OF FAILURE

And what more shall I say? For the time would fail me to tell of Gideon and Barak and Samson and Jephthah, also of David and Samuel and the prophets.

—Heb. 11:32

READING: 1 SAMUEL 1-4, 7-10, 11-13, 15-16, 19, 25, 28

THE FOLLOWING OLD Testament verse stands out for Christians who wonder if their meager offerings will amount to anything in God's eyes. The verse speaks about Hannah, Samuel's mother: "Moreover his mother used to make him a little robe, and bring it to him year by year when she came up with her husband to offer the yearly sacrifice" (1 Sam. 2:19).

This detail is perhaps one of the most memorable details referring to the character, Samuel, the recipient of the little robe (the Hebrew indicates an upper, outer garment—a cloak, coat, or robe). Before Samuel's birth, Hannah was barren. Distraught, she prayed for a son, vowing she would "give him to the LORD all the days of his life" (1 Sam. 1:11). True to her word, after Samuel was weaned, she brought him to the temple in Shiloh and left him in the care of the high priest, Eli, who became his mentor and caregiver.

After such a great sacrifice, one would expect that Samuel would become a spiritual paragon of success, such as Abraham or Moses. But his life was fraught with failure, even though he became Israel's primary judge and prophet. His two sons pursued money instead of God. His two appointees as king, King Saul and King David, seemed like bad ideas—at least initially. God eventually rejected King Saul because he didn't live up to God's standards of obedience. Saul's successor, King David, spent his days fleeing from jealous Saul. The leadership of Israel was in disarray. Samuel was an old man, and his efforts seemed like a long trail of failures.

Why would God refer to a failure as a hero? What did God admire about Samuel?

Today, how do we continue seeking God when our efforts have resulted in one failure after another? Why keep moving forward at the risk of creating more failure?

The Gathering Clouds of Failure

If Samuel's profession had been baseball, his "spring training" would have prepared him for a shot in the National Baseball Hall of Fame. As a soon-to-be prophet of God and judge over Israel, everything was working in his favor. His mother and father, Hannah and Elkanah, had brought him as a toddler to the finest "training camp" for a career in spiritual leadership. At the temple in Shiloh, numerous priests gathered, sacrifices were offered, and the Ark of the Covenant was held in reverence. Samuel resided at a hub of spirituality and government where he was saturated with the things of faith and of leadership. The Israelite judge and high priest, Eli, became his teacher, mentor, and surrogate father.

In this environment, Samuel grew "in favor both with the LORD and men" (1 Sam. 2:26). But all was not well in Eli's household. His sons mishandled the sacrificial offerings for their own gain and took sexual advantage of the women who came to the tabernacle to worship. God sent a messenger to warn Eli about his sons, to no avail.

One day as Samuel was sleeping, he heard a voice calling his name. Three times, he presumed the voice was Eli's. The fourth time, he realized God was calling him. Yet God's first message must have seemed like a disappointment to a young man who had striven to respect his teacher, Eli. God told Samuel: "I will judge his [Eli's] house forever for the iniquity which he knows, because his sons made themselves vile, and he did not restrain them" (1 Sam. 3:13).

Later, though Scripture is not specific how much time had passed except to say that "Samuel grew" and was "established as a prophet of the LORD" (1 Sam. 3:19-20), Eli's sons, Hophni and Phineas, were slain in the same battle. Thirty thousand Israelites were slaughtered and the Ark of the Covenant was taken. When ninety-eight-year-old Eli heard that his sons had died and that the Philistines had taken the Ark, he fell backwards, sustained a broken neck, and died.

Four Ways to Seek God in the Midst of Failure

Samuel would live to become an old man with very few marks in the "win column" of his life, despite being one of the most consistently obedient heroes of the faith. What kept Samuel seeking God in spite of the failures? How did he refuel his strength?

Today, how can we make spiritual progress in the absence of earthly success? How can we continue taking positive steps forward?

1. **Obey God's leading, even when He seems to be contradicting Himself.**

One could effectively argue that Samuel's life was generally a success, but that it was overshadowed by the type of failures that grab the spotlight. First Samuel, Chapter 7, covers a long period in Samuel's mid-life when he faithfully judged Israel on his circuit to Bethel, Gilgal, Mizpah, and Ramah.

Samuel's close connection with God is evident when he besought God to save the Israelites from the Philistines. As the

Philistines gathered to attack, Samuel led his frightened country-men in a sacrificial offering while the enemy forces approached. "Samuel cried out to the LORD for Israel; and the LORD answered him" (1 Sam. 7:9). God thundered a "great thunder" that confused the Philistines so effectively that they became an easy target for the pursuing Israelites. Thankful for the victory, Samuel set up a memorial stone and called it *Ebenezer*, saying "Thus far the LORD has helped us" (1 Sam. 7:12). From that day forward, the Philistines ceased to trouble the Israelites during Samuel's rule.

But Samuel's life was far from perfect. His two sons, Joel and Abiah, became judges in the city of Beersheba. However, they "did not walk in his ways; they turned aside after dishonest gain, took bribes, and perverted justice" (1 Sam. 8:3). Scripture is silent about Samuel's responsibility for his sons' sinful behavior. Whether he was at fault or not, certainly his sons must have disappointed him.

The major tests of Samuel's spiritual strength came near the latter part of his life. His sons, though corrupt, sat as judges in Beersheba. All seemed quiet until, one day, the elders of Israel converged at his door.

"We want a king to rule over us," they said, in essence.

Until now, during this era of judges, God had been the "understood king" of Israel. To ask for a human king displayed a deplorable lack of faith. It placed Israel on par with the heathen nations. Humanly, Samuel must have felt insulted that his own long-standing role as judge and prophet was suddenly being deemed inadequate. The Israelites wanted another flesh-and-blood man to rule above him. Samuel called upon God for direction. God essentially replied:

"Listen to them, Samuel. But warn them of the dangers."

Listen? Samuel must have thought. *Why would God even consider a human king when God Himself was king? Would God allow a man to reign in His place?*

But Samuel obeyed God's instructions. His attitude exemplifies Proverbs 3:5-6: "Trust in the LORD with all your heart, and lean not on your own understanding; in all your ways acknowledge Him, and He shall direct your paths."

According to God's instructions, Samuel warned the elders about the dangers of a human king, but they insisted:

"We want a king to judge us and to fight our battles!"

So Samuel went to God again.

God said: "Give them a king."

God's command seemed contradictory to His character. But Samuel obeyed God and anointed Saul as king. Samuel gave Saul, a man of exceptionally tall stature from the tribe of Benjamin, the best seat at his table, fed him, anointed him king, and then presented him to a large gathering of the tribes of Israel. *Here is the king you asked for*, his actions proclaimed. Against his own human understanding, he trusted God's voice just as he'd done from the first day God called him. "Speak; for Your servant hears" was ever his reply (1 Sam. 3:10).

2. Fill your horn with oil and go.

Like any human in the face of disappointments, Samuel reached a day when he became weary, sat down, and wept. One of the lowest times in his life came when God rejected Saul as king.

In his own mind, Samuel had already "gone the extra mile" by anointing a king against his own wishes. He'd obeyed God, and he'd vouched for the new king in front of the people. Once Saul was in place, he advised Saul as a father passes wisdom to a child or as a coach passes instructions to a player. But Saul cut corners when it came to obeying God. When Samuel instructed Saul to kill *all* the humans and livestock in a battle with the Amalekites, Saul captured the king and spared the finest head of livestock for sacrificial offerings.

Saul's offenses didn't seem serious, at least on paper. By man's logic, they seemed prudent. But Saul had usurped God's authority as it was channeled to him through God's prophet, Samuel. His disobedience revealed a quiet defiance and a heart attitude that was not God-honoring. Saul elevated his own opinion above the opinion of an omniscient God. Finally, years into Saul's reign, God told Samuel: "I greatly regret that I have set up Saul as king, for he has turned back from following Me, and has not performed My commandments" (1 Sam. 15:11).

Samuel grieved all night. It was as if God had said, "Too bad! It didn't work out after all." But who among men would dare say to God, "I told you so!" Samuel was weary. He mourned for Saul as if for a death.

But God didn't coddle Samuel. Instead He prodded him: "How long will you mourn for Saul, seeing I have rejected him from reigning over Israel? Fill your horn with oil, and go" (1 Sam. 16:1). The horn, or flask, was the receptacle that held the oil for anointing. Immediately, God gave Samuel an assignment to anoint the next king.

Sometimes there is no more profound remedy to disappointment than to say, "Just get up out of bed and go!" It's the same bottom-line reasoning children hear from parents: "Because I said so!" Who can argue with the fact that if we don't move, there won't be momentum for anything new? God's question, "How long will you mourn for Saul?" implies that He understood a little grief but didn't honor prolonged, debilitating sorrow. Such sorrow does not advance God's kingdom.

Samuel had to force himself to set aside his self-centeredness, and go. Perhaps he recalled his mother's sacrifice when she took the final step to place him into Eli's arms. Just like his mother, he had to remind himself, "My life is not about me. It's all about God and His plan. I must trust Him."

Samuel filled his horn with oil and went.

3. Think outside the box.

Thinking outside the box is a popular analogy for keeping an open mind beyond the periphery of standard protocol, choices, or results. When I was a boy, some of my friends participated in a popular prank. They would call a grocery store and say, "Do you have Prince Albert [pipe tobacco] in a can?" When the voice on the other end of the line would answer yes, they would say, "You better let him out before he suffocates."

Many believers spiritually suffocate because they limit God. If He does not answer in the way they think He should answer, they conclude that He's either nonexistent, not present, or uncaring. Since none of those answers are acceptable, their church attendance begins to wane, they break ties with fellow believers, and sometimes they even abandon their faith. There are a variety of ways we can think outside the box:

- **Think outside the Ark (or church building).** Thinking outside the box expands our comprehension to accommodate a God whose thoughts are beyond human understanding. We cannot fit infinity inside a box. The more we discover about God, the more we realize how little we know. Yet even still, the rewards of faith lie in the attempt to broaden our thinking. Those who fail to engage in this quest suffer from a deplorable lack of awe.

    In Samuel's day, the Ark of the Covenant was just such a box. It was a sacred container, adorned with cherubim, containing the stone tablets inscribed with the Ten Commandments, pieces of manna from the Israelites' wilderness journey with Moses, and the budding rod of Aaron. It was symbolic of God's historic leading in the nation of Israel, deemed so holy and powerful that it elicited reverence in those who honored God and fear in those who did not.

    Whenever the Israelites carried the Ark into battle, they expected victory. "Bring God in the box and we will get victory!" was their mantra. But Samuel's contemporaries discovered, to their surprise, that the box didn't always bring victory. The Israelites were sometimes defeated even when they carried the Ark into battle.

    Though well-intentioned, the Israelites were using the Ark the same way many modern day Christians use the church building: "If I touch base in church on Sunday morning, I'm safe the rest of the week." But the Israelites were tinkering with false gods, just as Christians today tinker with materialism and personal ambition. They were more interested in their own preservation than they were in knowing God. They wanted a safe haven—not a relationship.

A relationship with God, if nurtured, will always take us beyond the periphery of conventional behavior and boundaries. It demands more than the norm because God cannot be contained. If we are chasing an uncontainable God, we cannot expect to be contained, either. When we stretch ourselves to apprehend God, we will inevitably wear out the padlocks on our comfort zones, again and again, for the purpose of finding *more* of God. Christianity is never about finding a safe haven from the rest of the world. It is, rather, a love relationship that makes a beeline into the chaos of the world.

- **Think outside the obvious choice.** Samuel sought relationships to the point that he obeyed God by choosing leaders who appeared less-than-heroic. After God rejected Saul, He directed Samuel to Bethlehem. God gave Samuel one detail: the new king was among the sons of Jesse, the Bethlehemite. When Samuel spotted Eliab, Jesse's firstborn son, he presumed Eliab was God's choice. Scripture implies that Eliab was tall in stature, just as Saul had been. But God told Samuel, "Do not look at his appearance or at his physical stature, because I have refused him. For the LORD does not see as man sees; for man looks at the outward appearance, but the LORD looks at the heart" (1 Sam. 16:7).

  Samuel looked at the next eldest, Abinadab, then the next eldest, Shammah. He looked at all of Jesse's eight sons, except for the youngest who was out tending sheep. When God chose none of them, Samuel asked for the youngest. Young David walked in, "ruddy, with bright eyes and good-looking." God told Samuel, "Arise, anoint him; for this is the one!" (1 Sam. 16:12). Samuel anointed David king and "the Spirit of the LORD came upon David from that day forward" (1 Sam. 16:13).

How difficult it must have been for Samuel to trust God in this matter! It was as if God had told him, "I want you to begin all over again, and this time with a youth." An old man and full of wisdom, Samuel must have seen David as a grandfather sees his youngest grandchild—inexperienced in almost every way, wet behind the ears, the whelp of the litter. Like a batboy on a baseball team, David ran back and forth from the sheep herd to Saul's army, where his brothers had joined the ranks. He played the harp and wrote poetry. Samuel must've thought, "You've got to be kidding! You want this boy to be king of Israel? You want him to fight the Philistines?"

Little did Samuel know that this youth had already begun apprenticing for the job. David had singlehandedly slain a lion and a bear while protecting his father's flock of sheep, which he tended with diligence and care, as if caring for sheep was just as important as slaying Philistines. Who would expect that a keeper of lambs, the "little lamb" of his own family, could lead God's nation of Israel? Samuel must have suffered many doubts, but he obeyed God.

- **Think outside common worship.** Samuel sojourned in quiet places where he could be refreshed by spiritual retreats with the Lord. Nearby his home in Ramah was Naioth, a hub where prophets gathered to worship, a virtual college for prophets. The Spirit of God was so evident at Naioth that one wonders if Samuel glowed as Moses did when he came down from Mount Sinai.

  Yet it was not the *place* that blessed Samuel. The vital aspect of Samuel's worship was his pursuit of God, driven by his desire to be within God's will and presence, just as a toddler follows his mother because he feels "at home" in his mother's arms.

  Is it even possible for us today to fully imagine the privilege of being God's personal prophet? Samuel was called "the seer" by the people, a term interchangeable with "prophet" (1 Sam. 9:9). Whenever God spoke a message to Samuel, he was invited into the inner sanctuary of God's presence. Samuel heard God's voice. He was so awed that the content of the message wasn't even the primary thing.

We can imagine how shocked we would feel if the president of the United States would phone us and ask us to personally deliver a message for him. He would grant us clearance to the White House, clearance past the Secret Service guards, and clearance to the Oval Office, after which he would shut the door and personally speak the message to us. The aura of the encounter, whether the president was of our political persuasion or not, would overshadow the message. Possibly, we wouldn't even understand the message. Samuel must have felt this way every time God called.

One day, King David came to Samuel at Ramah and "told him all that Saul had done to him" (1 Sam. 19:18). Samuel took him aside to Naioth. There David lodged with Samuel, basking in the Spirit-filled presence of his old mentor.

When Saul learned of David's hideout, he sent messengers to take him so that he could slay him, but the messengers were so overcome by God's Spirit that they began prophesying. When his messengers failed to bring David back, Saul went himself. His evil intentions disintegrated, and he "stripped off his clothes and prophesied before Samuel in like manner, and lay down naked all that day and all that night" (1 Sam. 19:24). He worshipped God in the presence of David, his intended victim. When others heard about it, they said, "Is Saul also among the prophets?" (1 Sam. 19:24).

This worship, which is more unconventional than anything we would practice in our churches today, demonstrated God's absolute power over impossible circumstances. David watched God transform a lion into a lamb. Samuel watched God bring his old anointed student, Saul, back and transform his soul once again, if only temporarily. What a blessing these moments must have been to Samuel, who had earlier grieved over Saul's dethroning! The experience gave him a tangible foretaste of what God *can* do, and thus *might* do someday within the limitless scope of eternity. I believe God gave Samuel this moment as a gift.

Samuel gravitated consistently to the place where he could bask in the awe of God. His heroism was not about what he accomplished, but rather about who he became because of the saturation of God in his life.

- **Think outside visible results.** What must Samuel have thought when the rejected king, Saul, set out on a quest to kill the new king, David? What must he have thought when young David fled, escaping out windows, hiding in caves, then sparing the life of his would-be murderer? Is it possible he doubted God's sovereignty regarding the leadership of Israel? After all, God had commanded Samuel to anoint these two specific, imperfect men.

  One of the most amazing things about Samuel's relationship with God was that it was sealed with such trust that Samuel *consistently* accepted the bad with the good. Though he could not see the full outcome, he trusted God. Little did he know that the rivalry between David and Saul was already producing far-reaching results, birthed with tears on scrolls inside remote caves. The Psalms were being penned as a result of Saul's murderous pursuit of David.

  Because Samuel's faith in God was grounded upon relationship rather than results, he acceded that God's plans were more important than his own plans. He understood that God's agenda began before Samuel's date-of-birth and would be completed after his date-of-death. If the prime of Samuel's career happened to intersect with a dark chapter in God's plan, Samuel persisted in obedience even when it made no sense. Even though he was a prophet, Samuel knew he wasn't omniscient enough to assess his own success or want of it. He trusted God to do the tabulating.

4. Serve God with your heart.

Would Samuel's mother have been disappointed in Samuel's outcome?

I think not. Unnatural as it feels, both Hannah and Samuel set the compass of their faith towards the inward honing of their hearts rather than towards the outward products of their hands. The robe Hannah made for Samuel every year was not the main issue: the main issue was the love that made the robe.

After Hannah gave young Samuel to the Lord, she prayed with jubilant thanksgiving, straight from her heart: "My heart exults in the LORD; my strength is exalted in the LORD. My mouth derides my enemies, because I rejoice in your salvation" (1 Sam. 2:1, ESV).

Samuel emulated his mother's heart attitude. When he admonished the Israelites, he frequently referred to the heart. When the Israelites worshipped false gods, he said, "Return to the LORD with all your hearts" and "prepare your hearts for the LORD" (1 Sam. 7:3). After they demanded a king, he said, "Do not fear. You have done all this wickedness; yet do not turn aside from following the LORD, but serve the LORD with all your heart" (1 Sam. 12:20).

Samuel's emphasis upon the heart would later echo with the shepherd boy, David. Samuel was an early influence upon the man whose heart was renowned to be patterned after God's own heart (see Acts 13:22). The love woven into Hannah's little robes may very well have carried down through Samuel to David into the very fabric of the Psalms.

Samuel's Death

Samuel died an old man and was buried in his house in Ramah. The Israelites gathered together and mourned him. Unlike his mentor, Eli, and many other heroes of the Bible who stumbled after a life of spiritual strength, Samuel finished strong.

A bizarre occurrence is recorded in 1 Samuel 28, in which Saul speaks with deceased Samuel through the powers of a witch in Endor. The Philistines were preparing to attack, and Saul was desperate for advice. When he received no timely answer from God or the prophets, he disguised himself and snuck out at night to the witch's residence, asking her to rouse Samuel from the dead. Many Bible scholars claim that Samuel's instructions to Saul that night were not actually Samuel's, but came instead from a satanic spirit impersonating Samuel, an interpretation with which I am inclined to agree. The incident does, however, show Saul's continued respect for a teacher he still revered. Saul "stooped with his face to the ground and bowed down" (1 Sam. 28:14).

A Final Word

Samuel "saw" God through God's spoken word. Even when he disliked the content of God's message, he never abandoned his assignments. As long as he could hear God's voice, he could move forward. God's voice was his fuel. In it, he found acceptance, purpose, and direction not only for himself, but with enough surplus to lead God's people.

When Samuel anointed Saul, he gave Saul advice that stands as a representation of his own walk of faith: "Now when these signs meet you, do what your hand finds to do, for God is with you" (1 Sam. 10:7, ESV). Samuel followed God's signs, carried out God's directions in spite of disappointing results, and gathered his strength from the presence of God. If God was with him, Samuel was well.

Samuel's life revolved around his relationship with God. In that sense—the highest sense of all—Samuel was a tremendous success.

APPLIED FAITH

1. Make a list of times when you followed an order with which you disagreed, only to discover later that it worked out for your own good.

2. Make a list of spiritual leaders who persisted in spite of overwhelming hurdles before and/or during their careers.

3. Make a list of men and women you know who seem like failures on paper, but whose godly character you admire.

CHAPTER 18

THE PROPHETS: SEEKING GOD WHEN THERE'S NO DELIVERANCE

And what more shall I say? For the time would fail me to tell of Gideon and Barak and Samson and Jephthah, also of David and Samuel and the prophets: who through faith subdued kingdoms, worked righteousness, obtained promises, stopped the mouths of lions, quenched the violence of fire, escaped the edge of the sword, out of weakness were made strong, became valiant in battle, turned to flight the armies of the aliens. Women received their dead raised to life again. Others were tortured, not accepting deliverance, that they might obtain a better resurrection. Still others had trial of mockings and scourgings, yes, and of chains and imprisonment. They were stoned, they were sawn in two, were tempted, were slain with the sword. They wandered about in sheepskins and goatskins, being destitute, afflicted, tormented—of whom the world was not worthy. They wandered in deserts and mountains, in dens and caves of the earth. And all these, having obtained a good testimony through faith, did not receive the promise, God having provided something better for us, that they should not be made perfect apart from us.

—Heb. 11:32-40

READING: JOB 13:13-16; DANIEL 3:13-30; MATTHEW 11:1-11;
MATTHEW 14:1-14; ACTS 7:54-60; LUKE 23:32-43

THE ACCOUNT OF the Hebrews 11 heroes and heroines
takes a sharp turn when it comes to the prophets. The list
of victories and miracles shifts to nightmares and doom. We
read of mockings and beatings, stonings, stabbings, imprisonment,
destitution, and torment. Not only this, but despite their sacrifices,
many of these heroes and heroines are nameless. Unlike sailors who
drown at sea and are honored on brass plaques, these martyrs seem
forgotten, as if they died in vain.

Even today, the vast majority of Christian martyrs die without
public honor. Is their faith any less important to God than the faith
of Noah? Of Abraham? Of Moses? If the results of sacrificial faith
are so unpredictable, why pursue it?

Rarely is the average American Christian called to die a martyr's
death, but most of us have known faithful Christians who weren't
delivered from a tragic ending despite fervent prayer. How do we
continue to love a God who won't rescue? How do we adore a God
who won't deliver a loved one from cancer, from drowning, from a
fire? How do we pursue God when this same dearth of deliverance
knocks on our own door?

But If Not...

One of the most amazing things to me about the Hebrews 11
heroes and heroines is that some of them saved entire nations from
destruction, while others equally as faithful perished in isolation.
Scripture is clear that the same caliber of faith that leads to victory
can also lead to execution. It can cast a mother into the ecstasy
of witnessing her child rise from the dead, or it can send a father
into exile. It can turn a small boy's basket of loaves into enough to
feed thousands, or it can send a friend of Jesus to his beheading.
Scripture tells us that no matter the end result, all of the Hebrews
11 heroes and heroines "obtained a good testimony through faith"
(Heb. 11:39).

It is clear to me that victorious faith is not necessarily synonymous with long life. Nor is it synonymous with comfortable circumstances. Linking prayer with deliverance is about as accurate as linking good seed with a good crop. Good seed may help, but God has a more elaborate plan in mind.

In the Old Testament book of Job, Job's three friends equated his misfortune to his sins. But Job knew God's eternal plans were bigger than the pocket-watch-sized logic of his friends' minds. Even though he was not privy to the debate between God and Satan, Job trusted God. For all he knew, he would soon die, and yet he was able to say, "though He slay me, yet will I trust in Him" (Job 13:15). Today, the written record of Job's tribulations has served as a testimony to billions.

Shadrach, Meshach, and Abed-Nego chose death in a fiery furnace in lieu of bowing to King Nebuchadnezzar's false gods. As they faced their demise, they told the king, "Our God whom we serve is able to deliver us from the burning fiery furnace... But if not, let it be known to you, O king, that we do not serve your gods, nor will we worship the gold image which you have set up" (Dan. 3:17-18). They held fast to their faith, even in the face of silence from heaven.

Victory and death are both acceptable to a hero of the faith, yet they are not *equally* acceptable. Listen to Hebrews 11:35: "Others were tortured, not accepting deliverance, that they might obtain a better resurrection" (Heb. 11:35). Despite all our natural inclinations to the contrary, the best deliverance is heavenly resurrection. When all earthly rescue plans have been exhausted, lack of deliverance—often resulting in death—is the higher prize.

Four Ways to Face a "Better Resurrection"

How did the heroes and heroines of the faith continue to seek God when their efforts led straight towards death, with no last-minute rescue plan? How do we rewire our minds from a natural inclination to stay alive longer to an eager expectation to cross over to the abode of a "better resurrection"?

217

1. **Change your goals.**

Medical science has progressed with such remarkable success that we tend to forget our own mortality. We live as if it's our constitutional right to remain alive. Even when the outlook is grim, our natural human response is to change the circumstances. We send up fervent prayers. We consult top-notch doctors. We try experimental drugs.

But God never taught us that exemplary faith guarantees long life. When John the Baptist sent Jesus a message from prison asking if Jesus was really the Messiah, Jesus chose not to rescue him even though He knew John would be beheaded. Yet Jesus said of him: "Among those born of women there has not risen one greater than John the Baptist" (Matt. 11:11).

When Jesus was dying on the cross, He did not summon angels to come to His rescue. He chose the "better resurrection." When Stephen was interrogated about his faith prior to being stoned, God did not create a way for him to escape. Instead, He allowed Stephen to see Jesus standing at the right hand of God (see Acts 7:55).

Tom DeVilbiss. In 2004, while I was recovering from my heart attack, I received word that Tom DeVilbiss, a fellow pastor and missionary supported by our church, died at a younger age than I. Why did he die, and not I?

I don't know. But one thing I *do* know. There is a greater miracle than healing. It is called "resurrection." It is somewhat ironic that Christians spend such an inordinate amount of time praying their family and friends out of heaven. From God's standpoint, I lost out—at least temporarily. Today, Tom is in the presence of God. Yet, both Tom and I are still getting to do what we long to do. We are both glorifying God. The difference is that I'm glorifying God on earth, and Tom is glorifying God "on location."

The reward of a God-seeker like Tom is *not* extended longevity on this earth (though it can be). The reward is to see God. If we, like the average human, make longevity our goal, we are mistaken.

218

The good news is this: if our goal is to see God, bad circumstances cannot hinder us. Whether we live or die, tragedy transports us to God. Author John Piper wrote:

> The common feature of the faith that escapes suffering and the faith that endures suffering is this: both of them involve believing that God himself is better than what life can give to you now, and better than what death can take from you later. When you can have it all, faith says that God is better; and when you lose it all, faith says God is better....Faith believes that there is a resurrection for believers which is better than the miracle of escape....Faith says, "Whether God handles me tenderly or gives me over to torture, I love him."....The great challenge of the book of Hebrews... is to cultivate and spread a death-defying passion for God....Our aim is to cultivate and spread the unshakable confidence that God is better than what life can give us and what death can take from us.[25]

When it comes to facing death or serious circumstances, the end of the matter is this: we must reach the point of believing that God's presence and glory is superior to our mortal life. We must believe that He is our home just as completely as a mother's arms is home for an infant, as our garage is home for our car, as our bed is home for our sleep. The prospect of our eternal presence with God should evoke the same happy exhalation of relief we experience the second we pull into our driveway after a long journey. For indeed, God is the center of our existence, our beginning and our end, the warm lodge of our heart and soul, our all in all, our abode of rest.

But how do we reach this pinnacle of faith? There is no better answer than to pray the first commandment: *Lord, help me to love the Lord my God with all my heart, and with all my soul, and with all my mind, and with all my strength* (see Mark 12:30). You must pray it again and again throughout the day, day after day, unceasingly, until you love God more than you love your next breath. No one can give you that caliber of love but God himself. And when He does, you will never be the same again.

2. Look for alternate miracles.

When a beloved relative or friend is dying, is the only miracle deliverance? The "but if" of Shadrach, Meshach, and Abed-Nego's prayer presupposes that God has other plans that can be promoted through death.

In his book, *The Misery of Job and the Mercy of God*, John Piper states: "The great purpose of life is not to stay alive, but to magnify—whether by life or by death—the One who created us and died for us and lives as Lord of all forever, Jesus Christ."[26] If we can magnify God through death, why not do so? Isn't that what Jesus did? Why not you? Why not me? It is entirely possible that losing our life might become the capstone of our ministry.

Heidi White. On March 10, 2004, a healthy, talented member of my church died in childbirth after the sudden onset of toxemia. At age twenty-seven, Heidi was a music teacher, vocalist, and a lover of the underprivileged. She dedicated her free time to sharing Jesus with children in a low-cost housing project.

A few months before her death, on October 26, 2003, Heidi directed a college choir at our church in a song about heaven, "I Can Only Imagine." Before the choir sang, she turned and addressed our large congregation in a voice that trembled with awe. Heidi didn't normally speak in front of our congregation, so it wasn't easy for her. She stretched past any nervousness she might have felt, and she spoke from her heart. Her words were routinely recorded as part of the Sunday evening service:

> Isn't it wonderful sometimes just to sit and think simply about heaven and nothing else, what heaven is going to be like? I don't know about you, but I don't do that as much as I should. I think that we get so caught up in living our life here on earth that we don't just sit and daydream and *wonder* how awesome it's going to be.
>
> And I love this song that this choir's going to sing tonight because it doesn't talk about the streets of gold and that there'll be no more sickness and no more pain and some of the things that

we automatically think about. We think about how wonderful heaven is going to be for *us*, how perfect it's going to be for *us*, how much we're going to enjoy it, but the song focuses on *God* because that is the true, true awesome part about going to heaven is that forever we'll be in His presence and we'll be worshipping Him and nothing else. We'll just be glorifying His name and just singing praises to Him continually. And it's all about God and it's all about Jesus and this song is just a powerful testimony and I hope that tonight as this special choir sings for you that it brings you closer to the presence of God, and I hope that it makes you excited and *long* for your home and long for heaven.[27]

Months later, Heidi's words were replayed at her funeral in front of more than 1,400 mourners. She was the chief comforter to those who needed comfort—to her husband Andy, to her parents Alan and Wilma, to her sister Summer and husband Matt, to her friends, to our congregation, and to her newborn son, Drew. Her words have been recorded on a CD that has sold thousands of copies. Heidi's Holy-Spirit-led words gave evidence that Heidi, in some way, had glimpsed God.

Hebrews 12:1 speaks about being "surrounded by so great a cloud of witnesses," referring to the heroes and heroines of the faith in Hebrews 11. I believe that Heidi, along with Moses and Noah and Abraham and others, "surrounded" the mourners at her own funeral in testimony of God's awesome presence. Through her death, Heidi became a modern day witness, a modern day heroine of the faith.

3. Help the other guy in your boat.

When Jesus was dying, suspended on the cross, He was busy ministering to the thief on the cross. Though in agony of body, heart, and soul, He spoke words of comfort to the dying man beside Him (see Luke 23:39-43). No matter His personal dilemma, His mind was always on God or others.

The terminal cancer counselee. I heard a story about a woman who sought counseling because she couldn't handle the emotional trauma of terminal cancer. The counselor searched the Scriptures, but he couldn't settle upon a particular verse to help her. Then an idea struck him, and he related it to the lady in the form of a question. "Who," he asked her, "knew he would die in three years, yet turned the world upside down during those three years?" The answer, of course, was Jesus. The woman began to view her cancer as an opportunity and commenced visiting the cancer ward in her local hospital to encourage the patients. Her mortal body eventually perished from the cancer, but not before she had comforted two years' worth of patients. [28]

Mel Barth. One of my assistant pastors, Mel Barth, returned for additional cancer treatments after his cancer recurred a second time. Mel lives within walking distance of our local cancer center. (Mel is the son of Mrs. Mona Barth and Rev. Ken Barth, a dear friend and a much-beloved music minister at my church. Ken passed into heaven in 2006 after his own battle with cancer.) Rather than avoiding that intimidating building, Mel took daily walks on the cancer center property and sat on a bench near a window to pray for the patients.

Strange as it may seem, there's a remarkable freedom in knowing how you are going to die. All your life you've looked both ways at intersections, rushed to the doctor for antibiotics, eaten heart-healthy foods, and locked your front door. But once the method of death has been identified (unless another unexpected method intervenes), the mystery is solved. You experience moments of intense relief. Now that the end of the journey has been mapped out, you are free to drop your baggage and live life with abandon. There is no clearer breathing air for ministering to others.

4. Trust in God's long-range plan.

Hebrews 11:39-40 is a prescription for teamwork: "And all these, having obtained a good testimony through faith, did not receive the promise, God having provided something better for us, that they should not be made perfect apart from us."

Just for a fresh vantage point, let's condense God's plan for mankind down to a basketball game. God and His disciples are the "home" team and Satan and his demons are the opposing team. The game is fierce, the stakes higher than any game ever played. Every player has a specific ability and role. Some excel at shooting, some at dribbling, some at rebounding, and some at outrunning their opponents. But most of the players, no matter how talented, will not remain in the game for the duration. Some will be injured, some will foul out, and others will be pulled out of the game without any explanation at all. In each of these cases, those players are asked to sit out so another teammate can play. Yet even while on the bench, they know they are part of the team. When the game is finished, they will all participate in the celebration. None will be excluded, no matter whether they started at the opening tip-off, commenced playing at the third-quarter jump ball, or subbed at the end. They are all winners, all part of God's team. Every shot mattered, every rebound mattered, and every pass mattered. No player failed due to fouling out, wearing out, or being replaced without explanation.

Our Christian lives are much like that basketball game. Our efforts are not primarily about us, nor are the results confined between the boundaries of our life and death. We are not privy to the game plan, though we have been told that in the end, God's team wins. In the meantime, whether we make the three-pointers or not, our service is about God and who He is. It extends all the way from everlasting to everlasting. Like the 1986 "Hands Across America" human chain, our lives touch one another in a long line, from generation to generation, carrying (or *not* carrying) God's love forward. The stakes are far higher than you or me.

The heroes and heroines of the faith saw their faith in terms of a genealogical chart. At the top was Adam. At the bottom were the promised Messiah and the children of Israel. In between lie thousands of years, generation after generation. If God chose not to bestow a desired result within the boundaries of a faith hero's lifetime, the hero still trusted God. He simply trusted Him to bestow the desired results on the chart beneath his name.

Faith heroes and heroines care more about God's plan than they care about their own lives. Their goals are God-centered rather than me-centered. They do not measure success by their accumulated trophies upon the day of their death. Instead, they pass the torch to the next person down the line and trust that they will one day join all the torchbearers at the grand victory banquet in the halls of heaven.

A Final Word

One of my favorite phrases in all of Scripture is, "of whom the world was not worthy" (Heb. 11:38). God spoke those words about the nameless, faceless heroes and heroines of the faith who died obscure deaths. Though they may seem like victims and failures in the world's eyes, God stated that the world did not deserve them.

One hallmark characteristic about the heroes and heroines of the faith was their selflessness. Instead of looking for miracles that would save their skin, they sought miracles that would glorify God. While in torment, they helped someone else in torment. Despite unfinished business and seeming failure, they gladly handed off the torch to someone else who would advance God's master plan.

There was nothing normal about their faith. To the world, they were and are strange. They believed more in the unseen than in the seen, more in the promise than in the on-hand results. Today, through their sacrificial lives, we can glimpse the "substance of things hoped for" and "the evidence of things not seen" (Heb. 11:1). While they stood alone on the thin air of their faith, we have been made more perfect by the solid examples of their faith.

Applied Faith

1. Pray daily that God will help you to "love the LORD your God with all your heart, with all your soul, with all your mind, and with all your strength" (Mark 12:30).

2. Make a list of alternate miracles that resulted from the death of a relative, friend, or acquaintance.

3. When you are afflicted with a disease or injury, seek to help your neighbor with the same disease or injury.

4. Support persecuted Christians. Pray for them daily. One active organization is The Voice of the Martyrs (www. persecution.com), where you can find names and prayer requests.

EPILOGUE: A FINAL WORD

WHAT IS HEROIC faith? Is it possible to become a hero or heroine of the faith in today's world?

The common perception of heroism combines a potent mixture of unusual abilities with extraordinary events. While this brand of heroism is admirable, this is not God's definition of a faith hero. God doesn't require us to be super-smart, super-strong, super-talented, super-wealthy, super-attractive, or even super-saintly. Nor does He require that we be relocated to a war zone, a disaster scene, or a new frontier.

In the New Testament, Jesus places emphasis on the faith of children, as if adults have somehow managed to lose sight of the basics. Jesus said, "Truly, I say to you, unless you turn and become like children, you will never enter the kingdom of heaven" (Matt. 18:3, ESV). When an infant or young child is separated from his or her parent, that child yearns for that parent to the point of crying. When the parent comes into view, the child leaps into the arms of his parent, returning home to the love to which he knows he belongs.

Our faith in God is remarkably similar. Having been separated from our Father by sin and by our sojourn on earth, we yearn for our Father. As we seek Him across the span of a lifetime, our yearning ideally increases to such a degree that we take risks to encounter Him on earth as we stretch forward to fall into His loving arms, where we will once again be home safe.

To the world, this seems dependent—almost humiliatingly so. But the monumental difference between the world's view and our view is the identity of the One upon whom we are dependent. The character and position of God are fundamentally at issue.

Faith in God, by its very definition, presupposes that our certainty in God is unproven or incomplete. Why base our lives on an unproven God? Why make the sacrifices? Why take the risks?

One reason for seeking God is to verify the truth of God's existence and sovereignty, particularly during the initial part of the process, before the intoxication of God has consumed the believer. Hebrews 11:6 tells us that God "is a rewarder of those who diligently seek Him." The usual idea of a reward speaks of tangible treasures. For more selfless Christians, rewards might mean great accomplishments for the glory of God, possibly including the conversion of a multitude of souls. But if we are after accomplishments or souls, we have stopped short in the front row of the auditorium. It is God-on-the-stage that we want. Very simply, the reward of a God-seeker is to see God.

But is that enough? What makes God so sufficient and worthwhile? God answers:

> Thus says the LORD: "Let not the wise man glory in his wisdom, let not the mighty man glory in his might, nor let the rich man glory in his riches; But let him who glories glory in this, that he understands and knows Me, that I am the LORD, exercising lovingkindness, judgment, and righteousness in the earth. For in these I delight," says the LORD.
>
> —Jer. 9:23-24

God is the nucleus of all existence, the purpose of all existence, the beginning, and the end. He loves perfectly, judges perfectly, and restores all people and things to their proper places and conditions. All reasons, all explanations, all answers merge and park in God. He is the only entity whose egotism is not selfish. All glory belongs to Him just as naturally as the halo belongs around the moon. And when God draws us into the center of His glory, we become as satisfied as a child in the arms of his parent. There we are home. Home safe.

How then, can an obviously marred sinner become a hero of the faith? There's no question that the Hall of Fame of Faith is stained with sin. Abraham committed adultery with Hagar, Jacob stole his brother's blessing, Samson lusted after women, Jephthah slaughtered his daughter, and David murdered Uriah. The list goes on. It is so polluted that we might wonder if the extremities of sin are a prerequisite for the extremities of grace. Is it necessary to have been an outrageous sinner to become a hero of the faith? If so, we all qualify. God punishes sin, but He doesn't fixate on it; He focuses on His relationship with the sinner.

So what exactly is heroic faith? I believe it is nothing more complicated than a child stretching out his arms across a gap to his father, trusting that his father will embrace him. It's the caliber of seeking God that risks stretching our arms across the chasm of the unseen. It's the heart's posture of outstretched arms towards God and His promises. Whether long-term or short-term, each of the heroes and heroines exhibited this caliber of yearning, despite the cost.

Picture Abraham raising his knife to slay his son, Noah reaching up to pound another nail into the ark, Rahab climbing onto the roof to hide Joshua's spies, and Samson reaching up blind to bring down the Philistine house. Picture Moses raising his rod to divide the Red Sea, David slinging a stone at Goliath, Isaac reaching out to bestow the blessing a second time on Jacob, Samuel pouring oil over the heads of Saul and David, and Gideon holding high a lamp to defeat a formidable enemy.

In the New Testament, Simeon held out his arms to receive the promised Christ child. Zacchaeus climbed into a sycamore tree to see Jesus. A woman suffering from hemorrhages reached through the crowd to grasp the hem of Jesus' garment. And a Canaanite woman prolonged her entreaties even after Jesus implied she was a dog.

The stretching of a faith hero is an act of love. Stretching, or yearning forward, is the fuel that empowers faith. Without the fuel of love, faith is a car without an engine. Without love, a baby's arms would remain limp at the appearance of his mother. The verb of heroic faith is love.

No wonder Jesus frequently steered His inquirers to the first commandment, or to a particular plan to enact it. When Jesus said "And you shall love the LORD your God with all your heart, with all your soul, with all your mind, and with all your strength" (Mark 12:30), He gave us the key to heroic faith. There's no conservatism in this commandment. It calls for all-out stretching.

The key to seeking God on earth today is no different than it was in Moses' day or Jesus' day. Very simply, we must pray the first commandment, digest it, and live it every day of our lives. It must become our primary prayer, lengths above "take my cancer away" and "help my mother survive heart surgery." A hero of the faith cannot be self-centered or even others-centered. Nor can he be lazy. Yearning takes effort.

But how do we seek God? The methods of seeking God are as varied as the talents and personalities of God's children. Abel sought God through obedient sacrifice. Enoch sought God by walking with Him. Jacob sought God during a wrestling match. Joseph sought God through his gift of interpreting dreams. David sought God through music, dance, and poetry. Barak sought God through an unlikely vessel. Sarah sought God through the authority of an imperfect husband. Isaac sought God by digging wells.

Admittedly, a lifetime of seeking and stretching can become wearisome, especially when the knocks and disappointments of life chafe at us like sea waves buffeting a coastline. God is not unaware of the challenge. Scripture seems to sense our weariness, advising us to "run with endurance the race that is set before us, looking unto Jesus, the author and finisher of our faith" (Heb. 12:1-2). Scripture also tells us to "strengthen the hands which hang down, and the feeble knees, and make straight paths for your feet" (Heb. 12:12-13).

Contrary to the world's perception, there are more heroes of the faith walking unnoticed in common clothing on the sidewalks of our cities than can be found in our history textbooks. I believe that it requires greater strength to persevere on a journey of faith than it takes to enter a forest for a day to slay a dragon. While earthly accolades go to the dragon slayers, the bulk of God's accolades go to the carpenters and the secretaries of this world who will never manage to find their way into the history books.

Still, we may experience moments of glory, especially as we take uncommon risks to pursue God. In some respects, our Christian journey is like that of an aspiring astronaut. Astronauts spend years preparing, only to experience a few "glory" days in outer space. For them and for us, heroism is not so much in soaring above the earth as it is in staying faithful during the dry years when it seems as if God has forgotten that you applied for soaring. The marathon is won on the dull, uneventful days.

Arduous as our journey may seem, we can take heart. Our journey of faith is not one-sided. In this lifetime marathon, God appears at the ten-mile marker with a cup of cold water. He sends a stranger with a bandage when we fall on mile fifteen. Even more incredible, He fills every Christian with His Holy Spirit—God living inside us. Even a blind man who has little hope of literally "seeing God" can attest to God's presence inside himself. To explain it is fruitless; he simply *knows* it. And knowing it, all is well, as if he has sat in his Father's lap for a good talk.

The crux of boredom in Christianity today is that we fail to take into account the nearness of the One we are worshipping. When the Christian awakes to the realization that the power of the Holy Spirit indwells him, then he will become like a Clark Kent. His perception of himself will no longer be a mere image of an ordinary fellow walking to work in a gray suit. Instead, he will be looking at the sky, waiting for his chance to dash into the telephone booth to don the cloak of Superman, pulsing with the knowledge that God uses common businessmen for His glory.

After you have encountered God once, it is not such a hardship to continue looking. A schoolgirl effervescence fizzes in the soul as if your encounter is the best-kept secret in the school. The word *witness* takes on a more personal meaning than the duty-oriented, one-dimensional admonition to "tell others about Christ." Gathering souls becomes as natural as an autumn wind whipping up scattered leaves in the resolute pursuit of its destination. The leaves are welcomed into the swirl of the pursuit, but they are as secondary to the journey as the train of a bride's wedding gown is to the groom at the altar.

A passionate love for God stirs up the same momentum experienced by the men and women healed by Jesus' touch—excited, tripping over their words, running to town even after Jesus instructed them to keep their miracles silent. This love carries the same urgency that Mary Magdalene felt after seeing the risen Christ, when she ran with joy to tell the disciples that their crucified friend and Lord had risen from the dead. In Bible times and in modern times, every witness of God carries a unique story that he or she is trying to communicate to us. "This is why it was okay for me to be beheaded," they are telling us. "This is what I saw the moment the stones came at me." And "this is the Love that gave me legs to walk into the lion's den. Oh, let me tell you. Let me tell you!"

When we truly endeavor to pinpoint the profound essence of faith, everything falls prostrate to the simplicity of the gospels—to the quickened legs of a man healed of blindness, to the night-and-day prayers of an eighty-four-year-old widow in the temple, to the lunch of a young boy by the seaside, to the mite of the widow, to the publican who smote his breast, and to the baby lying in a manger in Bethlehem. God has made His truth so profoundly simple that the scholars are in danger of bypassing it.

I once heard a story about the developmentally disabled residents of Shepherd's Home and School in Union Grove, Wisconsin. The janitors couldn't keep the windows clean. Again and again, they returned to the same windows to wipe nose prints off the panes. The residents had been taught to expect Jesus' eminent return. Daily they pressed their faces to the windows, seeking Him.[29]

These residents practiced "charity," or love, in a heroic way. I believe their nose prints on window glass are no less precious to God than Noah's ark. Scripture tells us: "And now abide faith, hope, love, these three; but the greatest of these is love" (1 Cor. 13:13). Love is the only one of the trio that is everlasting. In heaven, faith and hope will drop off like spent rockets. Love will endure forever.

After my heart attack in 2004, my doctors warned that my heart problems may eventually recur. Occasionally, I experience brief spells of breathlessness, as if God is purposely reminding me of my mortality. Nothing has changed about my date of death—it remains the same as it was before I was born—and as my friend and colleague, Jerry McCorkle, is fond of saying, I believe I'm invincible until God calls me Home. Yet my heart attack has awakened me to a new sense of living on borrowed time.

As I ponder the fleeting days of my service, I am conscious that now is my "time at bat." Now is my golden opportunity to show my love for the Lord. After all, how hard will it be for me to prove my love for Him when we are standing face-to-face in heaven? Now is my time—now when it costs me something.

There is one special moment I will never forget. On the night of my surgery after family and friends had gone home, the nurse injected morphine into my IV line and I knew I'd be fast asleep in a few moments. I lay after midnight alone in the dimly lit hospital room amidst sterile sheets and plastic basins and tiled floors, acutely conscious of every fluttering heartbeat beneath my hospital gown.

As the muted conversations of nurses drifted in from the hallway, the knowledge of having narrowly passed death's door flooded over me in a sweet thanksgiving too great for me to hold. With all the strength I could muster, I lifted my arms, feeble as they were, and I thanked God for my family, my friends, and my church. And then I thanked Him for His character, especially for the love that had guided me through the biggest storm of my life.

As I lay trembling, arms raised, I knew, as only the Holy Spirit can convey, that God was visiting me. His quiet presence astounded me. His love overwhelmed me. Joy filled me, spilling over. He was there, even there. At that moment, He accepted my meager offering of praise and transformed it into one of the most heroic acts of my life.

I knew then and I know now that He is worth it all, He is all in all, and His character surpasses every atom of existence. I desire to live each day in breathless awe. I desire each day to know Him better and love Him more. Every sermon, every prayer, every opportunity to serve others is a gift. But if I could do nothing more than breathe these few simple words of praise, I would require no other satisfaction:

I love You, Lord.

THREE POEMS

I WROTE THE words to *"Even There"* in the summer of 2004 after my heart attack and surgery. I plucked out a melody and asked Isaac Judd, a talented member of our church, to arrange it into a song for me. When he came back from college in May of 2005, he had finished it.

My son, Jason, and two other members of our church, Jennifer Collins and Tia Bursack, performed its debut in our church on June 26, 2005 in the Sunday morning service, with Isaac Judd accompanying them on the piano. This debut version is special to me because the emotion in Jason's voice is evident in the latter half of the song.

To hear the song and read the story behind the song, go to the "Even There" page on www. calvarybaptistnormal.org.

The song and story are also available on a CD entitled, "Even There," Calvary Baptist Ministries, 2006. To inquire about obtaining a copy, write to: amy@cbcnormal.org.

Even There

Lyrics by Ralph Wingate, Jr.

Lord, You know my thoughts and my fears,
You know each step I take when darkness nears;
No matter what the road ahead may be,
I know You'll hold my hand continually.

Even there, even there, I learned of You,
Even there, even there, You're by my side;
And when fear surrounds my soul,
I know You're in control,
Even there, even there, You're by my side.

In dark moments I see Your face,
It's then I know of Your amazing grace;
Your joy and comfort overwhelm my soul,
It is then I know that You are in control.

Even there, even there, I learned of You,
Even there, even there, You're by my side;
And when fear surrounds my soul,
I know You're in control,
Even there, even there, You're by my side.

The trial is still present with me,
Its pain is not so hard that I can't see;
Your presence with me is always so real,
And in the pain Your joy I still can feel.

Even there, even there, I learned of You,
Even there, even there, You're by my side;
And when fear surrounds my soul,
I know You're in control,
Even there, even there, You're by my side.

Touched by the Master's Hand

Ralph Wingate, Jr., July 15, 2004

The road was blocked by things I didn't see;
A life-changing experience God had waiting for me.
Not the way I intended to take,
But in my journey I realized much was at stake.

Not my life, but surrender to His plan,
To allow God's way when struggles first began.
I found in my relationship with the God of the Universe
My walk with Him was more than chapter and verse.

Attitude and surrender to the Great "I Am"
Involves the knowledge that it's not about me, it's all about Him.
I realize wherever that road may lead,
My comfort is in Jesus, He is all I need.

Then joy filled my heart; security flooded my soul,
I learned it was about Him, He was in control.
I seek the Glory of God by placing all in His hand.
It doesn't matter what happens, it's part of His plan.

To reveal Jesus in a world lost in sin
My purpose for now, not "what might have been."
To be a tool God uses in this land,
Gives my walk meaning and I'm touched by the Master's hand.

The Climber's Prayer

Cammie Quinn (1985)

O God,
Keep before my eyes a vision of Your supreme greatness.
In my weakness, remind me that with You anything is possible.
Grant me one heavenly task to accomplish on Earth for Your glory.
Set me in a large, mountainous place
That I might not hide in a secluded cove.

As I begin climbing,
Captivate me when the cares of the world entice me down.
Keep me on the path when friends discourage and beckon me home.
When I stumble and fall,
Lift me and turn me upward again.
And when I have reached the steepest wall of the mountain,
And I am cowering in the heights,
Breathe beneath my frail body a mighty updraft.
Renew my strength that I may mount up with wings as an eagle.
Cause me to soar higher and higher
Until You gently but triumphantly set me upon
The summit of the mountain.

And Lord,
If this ascent costs me a lifetime of effort and pain,
May I know that if Your task is achieved,
My life will have been most richly blessed.
For I will have seen Your face more brilliantly
From the top of the mountain.

ENDNOTES

1. William Temple, *Readings in St. John's Gospel* (London: Macmillan and Co., Limited, 1930), 68.
2. Henry David Thoreau, *Walden* (Boston: Ticknor and Fields, 1854). Quote taken from www.quotationspage.com, 2010.
3. Neil Armstrong, spoken upon landing on the Moon, July 20, 1969. Quote taken from www.quotationspage.com, 2010.
4. Helen Keller. Quote taken from www.wisdomquotes.com, 2010.
5. L. B. Cowman, *Streams in the Desert* (Grand Rapids, MI: Zondervan, 1997), 157-158.
6. *The Wizard of Oz*. Film directed by Victor Fleming, Metro-Goldwyn-Mayer, 1939.
7. Matthew Henry, *Matthew Henry Commentary on the Whole Bible*, Hosea, Chapter 12, http://bible.wiktel.com/mhc/, accessed 2010.
8. Quoted in Philip Graham Ryken, *Exodus: Saved for God's Glory* (Wheaton, IL: Crossway Books, 2005), 197.
9. *Facing the Giants*. Film directed by Alex Kendrick. Sherwood Baptist Church of Albany, Georgia. Sherwood Pictures, 2006.
10. Matthew Henry, *Matthew Henry Commentary on the Whole Bible*: Joshua, Chapter 5, http://bible.wiktel.com/mhc/, accessed 2010.

11. John MacArthur, *The MacArthur Study Bible* (Nashville, TN: Word Publishing, 1997), 307.

12. Mark Buchanan, *Your God Is Too Safe* (Sisters, OR: Multnomah Publishers, 2001), 132.

13. *The Wizard of Oz*. Film directed by Victor Fleming, Metro-Goldwyn-Mayer, 1939.

14. Matthew Henry, *Matthew Henry Commentary on the Whole Bible*, Judges, Chapter 4, http://bible.wiktel.com/mhc/, accessed 2010.

15. Ibid.

16. Ibid.

17. L. B. Cowman, *Streams in the Desert* (Grand Rapids, MI: Zondervan, 1997), 388.

18. Matthew Henry, *Matthew Henry Commentary on the Whole Bible*, Judges, Chapter 14, http://bible.wiktel.com/mhc/, accessed 2010.

19. C. S. Lewis, *Yours, Jack* (New York: HarperCollins, 2008), 9.

20. Flavius Josephus, *Antiquities of the Jews*, Book 5, Chap. 7, Section 8, www.sacred-texts.com/jud/josephus, accessed 2010.

21. Flavius Josephus, Book 6, Chapter 5, Section 1.

22. Matthew Henry, *Matthew Henry Commentary on the Whole Bible*, Judges, Chapter 11, http://bible.wiktel.com/mhc/, accessed 2010.

23. Flavius Josephus, Book 5, Chapter 7, Section 10.

24. David Martyn Lloyd-Jones, *Studies in the Sermon on the Mount*, Vol. 2 (Grand Rapids, MI: Wm. B. Eerdmans Publishing Company, 1959-1960), 301.

25. John Piper, "Faith to Be Strong and Faith to Be Weak," sermon, 10 August 1997, www.desiringgod.org, accessed 2010.

26. John Piper, *The Misery of Job and the Mercy of God* (Wheaton, IL. Crossway Books, 2002), 9.

27. Heidi White. Audiotape recorded 26 October 2003 at Calvary Baptist Church, Normal, IL.

28. Foundations of Biblical Counseling seminar, Biblical Counseling Center, Shaumburg, IL. Seminar held Sept.-Dec. 2006, Liberty Bible Church, Eureka, IL.

29. "Dirty Windows," devotional from "Daily Strength with Joe Stowell," 22 December, 2008, www.rbc.org/bible-study/strength-for-the-journey/all-messages.aspx, 2010.

WinePressPublishing
Great Books, Defined.

To order additional copies of this book call:
1-877-421-READ (7323)
or please visit our website at
www.WinePressbooks.com

If you enjoyed this quality custom-published book,
drop by our website for more books and information.

www.winepresspublishing.com
"Your partner in custom publishing."

9 781414 117980